Experiential Learning in
Foreign Language Education

D1610221

APPLIED LINGUISTICS AND LANGUAGE STUDY

GENERAL EDITOR

CHRISTOPHER N. CANDLIN

Chair Professor of Applied Linguistics
Centre for English Language Education &
Communication Research Department of English
City University of Hong Kong, Hong Kong

For a complete list of books in this series see pages v–vi

Experiential Learning in Foreign Language Education

VILJO KOHONEN
RIITTA JAATINEN
PAULI KAIKKONEN
JORMA LEHTOVAARA

Longman

An imprint of **Pearson Education**

Harlow, England · London · New York · Reading, Massachusetts · San Francisco
Toronto · Don Mills, Ontario · Sydney · Tokyo · Singapore · Hong Kong · Seoul
Taipei · Cape Town · Madrid · Mexico City · Amsterdam · Munich · Paris · Milan

Pearson Education Limited
Edinburgh Gate
Harlow
Essex CM20 2JE
England

and Associated Companies throughout the world

Visit us on the World Wide Web at:
www.pearsoneduc.com

First published 2001

ISBN 0–582–31570–0 PPR

British Library Cataloguing-in-Publication Data

A catalogue record for this book is available from the British Library

Library of Congress Cataloging-in-Publication Data

A catalog record for this book is available from the Library of Congress

Set in 10/12pt Baskerville by 35
Printed in Malaysia ,LSP

APPLIED LINGUISTICS AND LANGUAGE STUDY

GENERAL EDITOR

CHRISTOPHER N. CANDLIN

Chair Professor of Applied Linguistics
Centre for English Language Education &
Communication Research Department of English
City University of Hong Kong, Hong Kong

Contents

General Editor's Preface

For many readers, I suspect, distinctions in language education among the constructs of *learner-centeredness, cooperative learning* and *experiential learning* have not been especially clearly drawn. In papers and presentations one hears them interchangeably drawn upon and used, as well as separately and individually, and with often confusingly similar attributes. This is probably so because it seems each term defines itself by a concentration on learners as key participants in the process of learning and emphasises the development and enhancement of their social, cognitive and linguistic abilities, facilitated by teachers within a reflective and supportive group environment. Stress is laid in all three terms on the importance of processes of task-based problem-posing and problem-solving, and teachers are cast in a range of similar roles, instructional, facilitative and mentoring, as they co-participate in the execution as well as the design of such tasks. Indeed, this emphasis on problems has itself given rise to a further educational construct, that of *problem-based learning* (PBL) which highlights that dimension as its characteristic, and has attracted widespread attention in many disciplinary fields, especially in higher education, but also more widely outside the academy or the school, as in, say, corporate management training, or in the military.

A rich array of metaphors for learning circulates among all these terms, with considerable emphasis in *cooperative learning*, as an example, on positive *interdependence* and individual and group *accountability*. It is, perhaps, these metaphors which provide one way of distinguishing the constructs to afford them some individuality. While *learner-centeredness* is more banner-like and self-evident in its connotation (how could one not sign up under it?) and appears to cover a vast range of possible stances from focusing teachers' attention on the learners' accomplishing of pre-set tasks, to some full-blown negotiation of curricula by learners and teachers together, *cooperative learning* has a certain overlay of contractual learning, the establishing of commitments among learners and among teachers and learners in the achievement of certain (ideally, but not always in practice, co-constructed) goals, and where in the service of such accomplishment considerable emphasis is laid on the notion of the *team*, its membership and its associated rules and responsibilities. Indeed, there is at least a sense of moral suasion lurking in the term, a hint of group-induced individual sanction on the backslider. At the same time in its directiveness towards nominated goals and their accomplishment, it leans closely towards *action research* in its reflective potential. Certainly, while there is little opportunity for the overarching vagueness of *learner-centeredness* as a topic to engender carefully targeted and controlled research, *cooperative learning*, on the other hand, has been the topic of a wide range of well-conducted research, at various levels of education, especially at secondary and tertiary, and in the latter across a range of disciplines. For a comprehensive discussion of the principles of cooperative learning, and case studies of supportive research in relation to language learning, see Crandall's excellent account (1999)[1].

What then of *experiential learning*, the theme of this latest contribution to the *Applied Linguistics and Language Study Series*? A glance at the contents list of this exceptionally coherent and well-edited collection of commissioned papers by Viljo Kohonen and his Finnish colleagues will immediately serve to distinguish it as a construct *sui generis*, related in certain parts, of course, to those others above, but given here its own original and characteristic definition. What their papers, and their construction of the term, make clear is that *experiential learning* involves nothing less than a comprehensive reconstruction of language education and one which goes far beyond a reorientation of the relationship between language learning and language teaching, or the organisation and enactment of learning within the individual class. It achieves this comprehensiveness by asserting from the start a commitment to the social, not just to the internal social order of the classroom and its participants, but to the location and positioning of the school as institution within the wider social formation which gives rise to it, and which so closely and strongly governs its practices.

Experiential learning, or perhaps more appropriately as Viljo Kohonen's own major contributing chapter entitles it, experiential *education*, arises therefore as a response to particular historical, social and cultural conditions of learning and teaching and has the transformation of the institutional sites of schooling, and their educational processes, as a characteristic objective. This critical commitment to *transformation* lies at the heart of its stance towards the school as a key institution within the social formation, and in the emphasis, within the construct of *experiential education*, it lays on the *languaging* of schooling as a key means, especially reforming and reconstructing the nature of the interactions and their discourses between teachers and pupils. For Kohonen and his colleagues, however, the restructuring of classroom discourses towards a more participatory, and individual experience-based interaction order is not motivated so much by how they view this as a necessary condition for successful second language acquisition, as has been the case with many SLA theorists, though it is and they do, but by their philosophical commitment to the humanising of learning and to the signalling of such discursive restructuring as a prime agent in the development of a critically aware citizenry in the context of social interaction outside the school.

What then of the focus on foreign language education? Why is *this* so central? Chiefly, I think, because foreign language education is centered on language, or more correctly, centered on *discourses*, and as such has the potential, along with the study of the mother tongue, to orient its themes and processes towards an exploration of how the institutional practices of other communities are articulated by its participant members, and how these discoursed practices reflect conformity with and support for, or display opposition to, those ideological forces within such communities which in part construct and reinforce the beliefs and practices of their members. In so doing, of course, foreign language education has also a self-reflective and critical potential for those who engage in it at school. How might this be so? Does not foreign language education focus on the foreign? In an obvious sense, of course, it does, but in Kohonen's and his colleagues' construction of the discipline, the *foreignness* of foreign language education is not merely a means by which exotica can be paraded, external to the lived experience and consciousness of teachers and pupils seen as *voyeurs*, but as a means and method through which, *inter*culturally, learners as selves and persons may experience through their engagement with the Other, now *intra*culturally, the nature of their membership of their own society, and may be enabled to hold its practices and beliefs up to critical observation and evaluation. Foreign language education, in this sense, is as much about *own* language education, and own *social* education, as it is about the *foreign*. At the same time, in an increasingly globalised, web-wired, multilingual and multicultural world, foreign language education is nonetheless the prime promoter of the foreign perspective, playing a key role in enabling learners to accommodate to the social and cultural diversity of that world and to derive advantage from it.

Important to the encouragement of this sense of diversity and Otherness in foreign language education is the stance and role of teachers and learners within the school, more especially, the multiplicity of such stances and such roles. For teachers, it is clear that alongside the by now customary array of roles of instructor, mentor, facilitator, evaluator, we have an expanded professional identity being called for, one which is as much concerned with the wider social community outside the school, and the school's relationship to it, as it is with the social goings-on of the classroom. The teacher as community developer, as a main contributor to the gradual broadening of society's image of itself through changing the perception by its participants of themselves and their roles, is more novel. Such a role, for the authors, is deeply educational, aimed at helping learners to meet the challenges of adapting their personal growth to enable them to meet the uncertain demands of life in the changing world of Giddens' 'high modernity'[2]. For the learner, this suggests new roles which are no less varied, but which do extend their typical scenes of enactment. Such a community orientation would seem to imply, for example, that those roles common to learners outside the school ought not to be sealed off from their roles within the school, especially, as is often

the case, where these external-to-school roles involve pupils in just that engagement in participatory problem-posing and problem-solving, in just that
collective addressing and dialoguing of issues, that is sought after, but rather
rarely achieved, *within* the school. In one sense, of course, such externally-
enacted roles are as much carried on by pupils in a 'foreign' language to that
sanctioned within schooling as the more traditionally construed foreign languages of foreign language education within the school. Code-switching and
heteroglossia are, after all, within-language as well as cross-language phenomena. Such a blurring of roles and practices has its curriculum implication,
that of accommodating greater *interdiscursivity* between the discourses of the
street and playground and the discourses of the class. In sum, experiential
education, and the discourses of experience, have the potential to direct
themselves to the creative enhancement and fulfilment of learners' identities
through the practices of schooling, mediated through a range of discourses;
those of the school and its curricula, those of the local Other, personal and
social, and those of the 'foreign'.

   The debate in Kohonen's own extensive and deeply thought-through chapter on what it means to be an *intercultural learner* and what it means to be an
intercultural educator sets down the principles and practices associated with
this new agenda. In practical terms within the school it suggests that the
curriculum, in its content and processes, needs to achieve a balance between
factors which are external to the learner and his or her life outside the
school, and those factors internal to learners which govern, among others,
their commitment and motivation. The richness of that external and internal
experience, and how the learners' personal voices articulate responses to it,
becomes a crucial means by which this contextualisation process within the
individual and in relation to the social can be understood. From this we may
say that the curriculum needs to be contextualised and interpreted in relation to the socio-political conditions, values, and practices outside the school,
characterised through particular ratified discursive practices of society at
large, but it also has to be contextualised within the lived experiences of the
participants within the school, and equally characterised by the frequently
unratified discursive practices of the learners. It is this double contextualisation, and the tension between them and their discourses, that drives the
focus on *experience* in experiential education.

   It is in this sense that foreign language education can play a central and
mediating role, not only in the school-external sense of forging links with
communities outside the school, between the content and precepts of the
school-internal foreign language curriculum and that which is held to be
foreign by the communities outside the school, but also in terms of its role in
building bridges across what is held to be distinctive and 'foreign' in terms of
particular disciplines *within* the school, in particular the blending of the
content of their curricula. What are history and geography, or sociology, or
the contemporary intercultural teaching of science and mathematics after
all, if not essentially matters relevant to, and in part mediated by, the content

and themes of foreign language education? Moreover, given the increasing interculturality of the wider society, as this very modern book suggests, as migration and population movements create increasingly cosmopolitan communities, then foreign language education is an obvious candidate to engender the personal reorientation of citizen's perspectives to enable the conditions for such migration to be successfully and harmoniously accommodated. It would be paradoxical wouldn't it, if our learners became so familiar with the mores, histories, social practices and cultural artefacts and processes of those safely-distanced exotic societies that they ignored the immediate substance and potential for their foreign language education in their neighbourhoods and next-door streets? Not that such an enterprise will be easily achieved, though it has been with success in some communities, for example in Australia through the work of Michael Clyne and his teacher colleagues in schools in Melbourne.

Nonetheless, in a world increasingly constructed for its citizens, as Ulrich Beck[3] points out, as one of personal calculation of, and response to, risk, of personal uncertainty, insecurity and anxiety, it would be foolish to proclaim foreign language education as a some kind of transforming personal and social panacea. At most what it can do is to reduce the isolationism usually contingent on those personal states of being, and vicariously, virtually, or ideally through actual lived contact to increase the collective experience of such individuals towards an understanding of the nature of their common condition. Through that cathartic process they may not only obtain some pause and solace through discovering mutualities of interpretation of experience, but also explore new and as yet unimagined pathways towards a greater sense of personal balance and security. This, I take it is at the heart of the authors' construction of learning: as a means of creating knowledge and understanding through a continuous process of accommodating and harmonising differentially grounded experience. Enhancing transaction and interaction in the classroom is necessary for learning, especially in contrast to the proven unproductiveness of transmission, but in itself it is not sufficient for the engendering of that transformative *reculturing* of the curriculum and the school. For that to happen, schooling must re-emphasise the personal experiences of learners and teachers as a basis for curricula which will develop a new humanity of learning, where the Other is a challenge to the self, in terms of experiences, actions, constructs of time, place and identity, and participants' understanding of learning and teaching.

Achieving this reculturing is the prime motive for the paradigm shift that Kohonen talks of. But such a shift cannot remain at the level of the conceptual, however well-argued and constructed. It has to be actualised in practice. The papers in this collection by Kaikkonen and Jaatinen offer clear directions and illuminating examples as to the ways in which teachers can engage in this reculturing of the curriculum. Pauli Kaikkonen's emphasis is on the development of the theory of intercultural competence as a prime objective of the foreign language curriculum, but intercultural learning not seen as a mere accumulation of objectified and reductionist 'facts' or 'experiences' but as a continual process of discovery arising from a process of dialogue between the self and the Other. In emphasising this sensitivity to diversity, this tolerance of ambiguity, the chapter nonetheless does not remain at the level of experience, but is committed to action and is intent on confronting discriminatory and disruptive social attitudes and actions, racism, xenophobia and personal exclusion.

Riitta Jaatinen's emphasis on rich and detailed 'memory-work' among social care and nursing students and their teacher, drawing on lived experiences as a means of articulating the learners' own learning growth and personal development, not only re-emphasises the *experiential*, central to the argument of this book, but draws on it to provide a means for learners to define for themselves the language and discourse goals of their own specialised curriculum. Understanding themselves holistically as professionals in their field provides the means by which the nursing students can create for themselves the components of the curriculum. Such a process, distinct from that typical, external, and increasingly barren and routinised situational needs analysis so beloved of special purpose language instruction, imbues the program with both professionalism and humanity and avoids that reductionist modelling of others so often encountered in such courses. In a recent professional development course in Hong Kong for students from a range of related special purpose fields to those of Jaatinen's students, exploring with my colleague V K Bhatia with adult professional learners the nature of their acquisition of expertise, not only did our learners articulate in rich detail their own experiences of such acquisition, but came to see discourse as a key means by which this expertise could be defined, and as the chief means by which these experiences could be articulated and transferred to others. Central to this articulation, of course, as to experiential education in general, is the process of dialogue, whether face-to-face or mediated.

Throughout this Preface, and throughout this admirable and innovative book, runs a constant and pervasive message; that foreign language education does not begin from technique and technology. It begins from the cultivation of a capacity to discourse on the human experience of encounters. In Jorma Lehtovaara's final, more philosophically-attuned chapter, we confront the argument why foreign language education is to be seen, in his view, as a central element in the school's development and enhancement of its pupils' awareness of their own humanity. Achieving that goal will be made possible by what he refers to as 'open dialogue', about (foreign) language and discourse, about experience, about the contact of self with Other, about the impact on individuals of institutional and social governances in an increasingly wired and globalised community. In a pervasively nominalising, reifying and objectifying world, he argues for verbalising, conditionalising and relativising lived experience. That, we may say, is what foreign language education as experiential education is centrally about, and that is why, amid the welter of wall-to-wall predigested bite-sized manuals for language learning, this deeply thoughtful and thought-provoking book needs reading. To achieve that among teachers would be, in Kohonen's phrase, another and quite momentous paradigm shift.

Christopher N Candlin
General Editor
Centre for English Language Education & Communication Research
City University of Hong Kong

NOTES

1. Crandall J (1999) Cooperative learning and affective factors. In J Arnold (ed) *Affect in Language Learning.* Cambridge. Cambridge University Press.
2. See Giddens A (1991) *Modernity and Self-Identity: Self and Society in the Late Modern Age.* Cambridge. Polity Press.
3. Beck U (1992) *Risk Society.* London. Sage.

Chapter 1

Introduction

Viljo Kohonen, Pauli Kaikkonen,
Riitta Jaatinen and Jorma Lehtovaara

Current shifts in foreign language teaching. As noted by Diane Larsen-Freeman at the 1996 AILA Congress in Jyväskylä, Finland, there is a certain turmoil in the field of applied linguistics. The boundaries between the different disciplines are getting permeable and blurred. In order to broaden our professional knowledge base and understanding, we need to *look into different disciplines that are relevant to foreign language education in the changing world.*

We need to put together the developments in a number of related fields of research, such as philosophy, epistemology, linguistics, applied linguistics, learning psychology, intercultural learning, evaluation, the teacher's professional growth, society restructuring and the culture of schools and other teaching institutions. We also need to consider what kind of a new research orientation might emerge for promoting foreign language education and what possibilities it could open for language educators and learners.

In this book we attempt to explore and integrate some elements that we believe are important for such an expanded knowledge base. We wish to support language educators in developing their sense of direction in the seemingly turbulent context of being a language teacher in the middle of a professional paradigm shift at the time of major social changes in a number of national settings. Foreign language education does not take place in a social vacuum – if this has ever been the case. The ongoing developments suggest a *need for a deep reorientation in the language teaching profession.*

We give some brief snapshots of the processes as experienced by the participants, to serve as an introduction to the topics to be discussed further in the book.

As a language teacher I feel like being on a scenic point when working with young students. We get along well together. Previously I used to make detailed lesson plans and wanted to carry them through as well as possible. Now I have the courage to be in touch with my students and listen to them. I have become a keen experimenter. Currently I am inspired by cooperative learning . . . Very often I feel I am an educator more than a language teacher . . . I feel like a social educator, a psychologist, a family therapist, a listener, a comforter, a referee . . . At times I find it difficult to distinguish between my personal growth and being a language teacher . . . what I am as a person impinges on what I am as a teacher . . . The school of life has made me humble. I can do the kind of work I like.

On my lessons we also talk about other things than the language . . . I have tried to help my students to see their learning and personal growth as a broad cross-curricular goal on which they can influence themselves if they wish to . . . I see this as my duty. The teacher cannot any longer be confined to the language curricula alone, but I find it difficult to communicate this view to my students, the parents and the colleagues in school . . . School is still like an island detached from the rest of society . . . There should be more cooperation with the parents . . . The staff should have a strong feeling of belonging together before any radical changes can be brought about . . . but the lack of time is a persistent problem.

The quotes by two Finnish foreign language teachers show that language teaching has a broader goal than promoting linguistic and communicative skills only. It contributes to the wider task of *fostering the students' personal growth and thus educates them for life in a changing society.* The foreign language teaching profession is becoming increasingly aware of the broad educational values in language learning. The emerging values emphasise the need to support socially responsible learner education and affective learning. Developing learner autonomy in language learning entails holistic goals for language learning as learner education. Accordingly, *language learning involves a broad range of complex thinking and learning skills and emphasises the importance of such qualities as self-direction, self-control, self-reflection and a capacity for responsible social interaction.*

To enhance their learners' social and learning skills in their classes, language teachers need to cooperate not just within the foreign languages department but also across the curriculum. This means developing a new culture of teacher collaboration in school. *Language teachers need to give up their traditional isolation and assume an increasing responsibility for developing their school as a collegial work place.* This new orientation invites them to expand their professional identity towards becoming a language educator and a community developer.

The developments pose a number of challenging questions for foreign language educators:

- How might foreign language education prepare students to face the complexities of living as responsible citizens in the changing world?
- In what ways could teaching arrangements foster the learner's capacity for self-directed, autonomous learning?
- How could foreign language learning be designed so that it promotes the development of the learner's holistic personal and intercultural competence?
- How do the changes affect the teacher's professional knowledge base, identity and role in the class and in the work place? What kind of new institutional cultures might schools develop in different cultural settings?

Obviously such questions are interpreted differently in different cultural environments, leading to diverse strategies and practices of developing language learning. So *there is no one (and even less any 'right') way of tackling the pedagogical problems.* Rather, the solutions need to be *worked out with regard to the values, traditions and resources in the given national, regional or local context.* In any case, the developments suggest the need for a clear shift towards more learner-centred ways of organising language learning, however these are conceptualised and carried out in the different national contexts.

> The concept 'foreign language' is a peculiar one. All over the world people speak in a foreign language except here at home. We no matter who we are speak a language; everybody else speaks a foreign language. The bartender in New York knows not only about our cows, our mountains and our watches, but also that in Switzerland we have four languages no, not three but four, he is duly impressed by that and he asks the name of the fourth.
>
> This is always awkward for me. To be modest for once, I have to admit that I cannot speak Romansch. And I do not live in a quadrilingual Switzerland, but rather in a country where my own language is a foreign language. Those who share my fate, my compatriot Swiss tourists, have spun my bartender a yarn. They have explained that Switzerland is quadrilingual; and yet it is monolingual just like other regions of the world. French is a foreign language even in Switzerland, and so is German. There's a good measure of arrogance in the myth of quadrilingualism that we spread among bartenders all over the world. Since Switzerland is quadrilingual, then so are we Swiss. Moreover we are convinced that we are the only ones who are good at foreign languages – the Germans certainly aren't, and nor are the English. We believe, so to speak, that quadrilingualism is something we collectively own. I, an individual Swiss, might not speak the four languages, but we Swiss do.
>
> There are people who speak a language and people who speak a foreign language. Those who speak a foreign language are the ones who are different. They are indeed quite different, they have a lot more temperament, are more superficial or more profound, have the soulfulness of the Slav or the dourness of the Portuguese. In any case, the middle ground is occupied by us and by me. Anyone who is sad is sadder than me, anyone who is jolly is jollier than me. Foreign (the foreign language) can be better or worse. It cannot be the same. It is only us who are the same, only me.
>
> (Peter Bichsel: *Only One Language*)

The quote by Bichsel suggests that the processes of learning the native language and the foreign language are qualitatively different at the emotional level. While the first language is acquired more as an affective process of developing a belonging to the native culture in early childhood, the foreign language remains inevitably foreign, no matter how well we learn to master it. Therefore, *foreign language instruction needs to be enhanced by the emerging goals of intercultural learning.* Important in this goal orientation is to see foreign language learning as developing a capacity to encounter foreignness and otherness in intercultural communication. It is not enough to know the language primarily as a formal linguistic system. Language use is always contextualised, purposeful and interactive communication which involves negotiation between the participants, the tolerance of ambiguity and respect for diversity. These views pose new challenges for developing affective, experiential language learning processes. Literary and cultural texts are also used increasingly as an important means of promoting authenticity in the language classroom. The *construction of the learning tasks is a crucial question of pedagogical design and implementation*, aiming at both communicatively and personally meaningful processes and contents.

> I'm very interested in English even though my threshold for speaking is quite high. When begin to speak or translate texts into English and notice that I cannot do it I get immensely tense and anxious, I feel kind of back-locked. I hope the course will strengthen my self-esteem and unlock my vocabulary and language skills . . . [pre-course expectations by 'Tiina'].
>
> I have experienced the course as meaningful learning . . . The best experience on the course has been the feedback from the teacher and the class mates. I had thought that I cannot do anything. Being able to understand and talk after all has been a good experience for me. I am now enthusiastic about learning more English. Even though I haven't been able to understand everything word by word, I've been able to understand the essential meanings, and that has been a strong experience for me [after-course reflections by 'Tiina'].

The quote shows the *importance of attending to learner beliefs, assumptions and expectations about her own learning.* The learner's role is changing from a relatively passive recipient of language knowledge and skills towards an active and creative role in constructing the foreign language system for herself. Prior knowledge gives a valuable bridge for new learnings and needs to be utilised with care. The learner is also a responsible member of the social group and is actively involved in co-managing the learning process. This underscores the importance of the emotions and attitudes as part of foreign language education. More emphasis is thus placed on the *affective component in language learning: the impact of learner beliefs about language, herself and her own role as a student.*

As part of the changes, *assessment is not merely a matter of measuring the learning outcomes, but also an important means of enhancing the learning processes.* Reflective self-assessment develops learners' awareness of their thinking and learning skills as well as of their social skills and intercultural attitudes. In addition to the traditionally important verbal-linguistic skills, learners are taught to develop their interpersonal and intrapersonal skills that are necessary for responsible social interaction. They learn to take an increasing amount of responsibility for their learning and thus socialise their own learning.

Essential in the new orientation is the *shift towards a more balanced emphasis between factors external to the learner and the properties that are inside the mind of the learner.* While the former include class size, time on task and the teacher effectiveness variables, the latter properties include the learner's prior knowledge, beliefs and assumptions of language and learning; his or her information-processing capacity, emotional intelligence, anxiety and ambiguity tolerance, and motivation and ownership.

Outline of the book. In his chapter *Towards experiential foreign language education* **Viljo Kohonen** considers foreign language education in the context of the current changes and ongoing developments in society, teaching, learning and communication. The developments suggest the need to redefine the traditional roles of teachers, learners and curricula and work towards a new institutional culture based on an active collaboration of all participants. Experiential learning provides new perspectives for such a fundamental process of redesigning foreign language education. Kohonen discusses the basic concepts and some foundations in experiential learning and examines current directions in experiential learning.

Kohonen then proposes a theoretical framework of experiential foreign language education which includes the following elements: (1) language teaching as learner education, with reference to the essential concepts of awareness, autonomy and authenticity; (2) evaluation as a shift towards authentic assessment; (3) coherence through the teacher's professional growth; and (4) coherence through the development of a collegial institutional culture and the relationships between the school and society at large. These developments are interdependent, and together they constitute the powerful concept of coherence in experiential foreign language education. This goal orientation entails redesigning the language teaching profession and reculturing the schools.

Pauli Kaikkonen provides a chapter on *Intercultural learning through foreign language education* in which he discusses the needs and foundations for intercultural learning in the increasingly multicultural world. He suggests the notion of intercultural action competence as the new goal of foreign language education. The chapter considers foreign language learning and teaching both in relation to the learner's native language and culture and to the foreign language and culture. The author then discusses the important concepts of foreignness and diversity and the culture-based conceptions of nature, space and time. He examines some usual terms (like racism, ethnocentrism, prejudice, stereotype) which are connected with how individuals shape foreignness. He moves on to discuss some central concepts in the culture-based foreign language education.

Kaikkonen also considers the connections between language and culture and presents his model of culture which he used as the basis for his teaching experiments on the foreign language education. The chapter concludes with a presentation of the findings and experiences from the work with some student groups in senior secondary school and describes an action research teaching experiment to advance intercultural learning in the school context. In addition to this experiment, Kaikkonen offers perspectives to foreign language learning based on the individually and culturally orientated experiences of the learners. Finally he gives some examples of the tasks which were developed in the teaching experiment.

Riitta Jaatinen has written the chapter *Autobiographical knowledge in foreign language education and teacher development.* She outlines some important goals of teaching and learning a foreign language. She discusses the nature, content and advantages of using an autobiographic approach in foreign language learning. The language learning environment is seen as a valuable resource for human growth, as an opportunity to learn encountering other people in a dialogue and to broaden one's views through understanding different patterns of thought, societies, cultures, systems and traditions.

She suggests an extensive use of students' experiential autobiographical knowledge in language learning classes: the opportunity to reminisce about, narrate and explore oneself and one's life, and to be a subject in the classroom. She explores the use of autobiographical knowledge in foreign language teaching and relates it to a teaching experiment conducted as a dialogical process. She discusses some guiding principles and the role of the autobiographical content in a language course for specific purposes. She gives examples of the language learning tasks and activities utilised in one of her English courses.

Jaatinen claims that the teacher's autobiographical knowledge functions as the basis for how the teacher understands his or her experiences, the uniqueness of human learning, and foreign language learning. She discusses some important aspects of autobiographical knowledge in teacher development. As a subjective interpretation of the teacher's life, autobiographical knowledge offers a down-to-earth and valuable starting-point for teacher education. By inquiring into and interpreting their autobiographical knowledge – lived experiences – teachers learn to disclose their implicit pedagogical theories. Jaatinen concludes by suggesting that reminiscing about, interpreting and reinterpreting our lives is a way to assemble ourselves when reaching towards a better personal integration in life. Such a process helps us to see ourselves anew in constantly changing times and environments.

In his chapter *What is it – (FL) teaching?* **Jorma Lehtovaara** seeks to clarify the essence of (FL) teaching and learning. He intends to provide (FL) teachers with a conceptual framework which helps them to investigate questions concerning all aspects of (FL) teaching for themselves. He first outlines the current *Zeitgeist* immersed in which (FL) teaching takes place nowadays. He highlights the importance of seriously considering the effects which the basic mode of approaching reality inherent in modern science and technology exerts on (FL) teaching and our ways of understanding in general. Although appreciative of the merits of modern science and technology, Lehtovaara claims that we should see the alliance of modern science and technology only as *a* possible rational(istic) theory of reality. The essence of modern technology is that it frames or prearranges everything so that things can manifest themselves only as objects to be used for some external purpose, not as what they are in themselves. The stance or attitude of technology is accompanied by reckoning or calculative thinking. The tendency to see man, too, in this frame seems to gain ever greater popularity nowadays. Lehtovaara contends that, if we really believe that man has an intrinsic value and a capacity for ethical conduct, we must search for a new view of the nature of man that can compensate for the one-dimensionality of the picture of man prevailing in the current *Zeitgeist*.

As one possible alternative view of man he discusses a holistic or existential phenomenological conception of man which emphasises the importance of open and contemplative thinking (as against the now dominant calculative thinking) for man to manifest himself as a more genuinely human being. Lehtovaara sees a personally chosen, clear and well-argued conception of man as a necessity for any educated person. Because we always have some kind of assumptions about the nature of man – however we approach him – we as teachers need to be as consciously well aware of them as possible.

Grounding his treatise on a holistic conception of man Lehtovaara discusses central aspects of human existence, such as the three basic modes of man's existence (consciousness, bodily being and situationality), experiencing, understanding, primordial understanding, genuinely human learning, language, open dialogue and conditions fostering (foreign) language learning as learning of the art of open dialogue. He contends that, if we see the art of open dialogue as man's basic life skill, the most efficient way of teaching a (foreign) language (in the spirit of the ideas presented in his chapter) is *not teaching it as a language system*. If we take as our goal fostering the development of every person so that he or she can learn to actualise him- or herself as a fully human being, an ethical subject, the most genuinely human and, thus, the most efficient way of teaching a human language is *teaching it as the art of open dialogue*. Fostering the development of this skill would obviously be the main goal of all education, not only of foreign language education.

Chapter 2

Towards experiential foreign language education

Viljo Kohonen

2.1 WHY EXPERIENTIAL FOREIGN LANGUAGE EDUCATION?

In this section I discuss foreign language education in relation to the current changes in society, teaching, learning and communication. The developments suggest the need to redefine the traditional roles of teachers, learners and curricula and move towards a collegial institutional culture. Experiential learning provides new perspectives for the fundamental process of redesigning foreign language education.

2.1.1 Society developments

The school is obviously part of the surrounding society sharing its values and practices. It creates a community of its own that reflects the prevailing culture in society. Inevitably, learners bring society with them to school through their family and peer cultures. The school provides learners with an important experience of what it means to live as a member of society. I outline this social context of foreign language education in Figure 2.1.

It is consequently useful to consider what demands the developments in society seem to pose on education for the future. Due to recent political and social developments worldwide, new needs and tensions have emerged that require open discussion and cooperation between nations. Requirements for increasing efficiency in the competitive markets, coupled with economic depressions and automation in production, have caused a high proportion of labour to lose their jobs temporarily or permanently. For a number of people, the structural changes in society and work places are accompanied by feelings of inequity, insecurity and anxiety, even by threats of marginalisation.

The globalisation of the capital markets and the increased mobility of work force, students and specialists will increase cross-cultural contacts. In Europe, the current integration processes are moving the whole continent towards a multilingual and multicultural political and economic union. Contacts are facilitated enormously by the new information technology. It will make vast amounts of information services readily available to more and more people through international networks. The developments will create

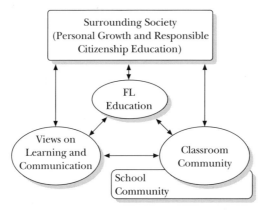

Figure 2.1　Social context of foreign language education

new demands for global communication and tolerance for intercultural diversity. They will certainly open new opportunities especially for language learning through an easy access to authentic data in a variety of languages (cf. Kaikkonen, in this volume).

High quality learning is commonly accepted as the goal of education on many international forums. In two recent European reports, for example, schooling, democracy and teacher education are linked together (White Paper 1996; Cochinaux and de Woot 1995). *New important skills in work life include flexibility in thinking, continuous learning, good communication, team work and taking the initiative.*

Such capacities are discussed in the White Paper (1996), emphasising the current shift towards the learning society. The document outlines an action plan for the European Community, including the following goals:

(1) Encouraging the acquisition of new knowledge
(2) Bringing school and business sector closer together
(3) Combating marginalisation, developing a sense of belonging
(4) Developing proficiency in three European languages
(5) Treating capital investment and investment in training on an equal basis

The second document (Cochinaux and de Woot 1995) is a report on the future of education in Europe. It describes Europe's future using the concept of the *learning society,* with the following important characteristics:

• Learning is accepted as a continuing activity throughout life
• Learners take responsibility for their own progress
• Assessment confirms progress rather than brands failure
• Capability, personal and shared values and team work are recognised equally with the pursuit of knowledge
• Learning is a partnership between students, parents, teachers, employers and the community, all of whom work together to improve performance

The learning society offers a broad vision of the future: everyone participates in education and training throughout life. The *main message is that learning empowers*. The learning society places the values and processes of learning at the centre and creates conditions for all individuals to develop their capacities.

The notion of *citizenship* in the learning society entails a *dual identity as individual persons and as members of the public*. Citizenship establishes the right for self-development but also the responsibility that the common resources should serve the well-being of the public domain, providing all individuals equally with reciprocal rights and duties, liberties and constraints, powers and responsibilities (Ranson 1994). Citizens have both the right and the obligation to participate in community life. To provide purposes and conditions of action, *new values and conditions of learning* are necessary. Values are considered at three levels:

- *Individual*: personal self-discovery and ethical views
- *Society*: mutuality within a moral order
- *General principles of participatory democracy*

The notion of democracy refers to a set of values that are commonly agreed upon in society. The values are obviously different in different cultural and political contexts and traditions. My perspective in this chapter refers mainly to developments in post-industrialised societies, with an emphasis on western societies. However, apparently similar processes seem to be under way world wide in a number of contexts, connected with society restructuring and emerging market economies.

Democracies aim at enabling the individual to live the best possible life or achieve the greatest possible measure of self-fulfilment, while allowing others to do the same. The implication is that citizens should not only be law-abiding, compliant and cooperative. They should also develop the skills of active, critical participation and involvement, and contribute voluntarily to developments in their community and society (Ranson 1994; Wringe 1996).

In accordance with these views, the structure of central administration in a number of post-industrial societies is being reformed towards more democratic principles and participatory practices. In many cultural contexts, the relations between central and local government are increasingly guided by the principle of decentralisation in order to allow greater participation and responsible action at the lower levels of administration.

In education, the trend is seen as the deregulation of power from central administration to the municipal and local levels. Its purpose is to give schools more freedom in designing their curricula and using the resources. In many contexts schools are expected to design their own site-based curricula, based on the national (or regional) curriculum framework and guidelines.

> *For your reflection.* Think of the current situation in your own society and personal context in the light of this discussion. (a) What processes and values are prominent in your society? (b) How do you understand the concept of citizenship education in your context? (c) Who designs school curricula in your setting? (d) How do you see your role as the teacher in the development of language-teaching curricula in your context? How do you find this role? How comfortable are you about it?

The site-based curricula emphasise the importance of the teachers working together to design their curriculum and develop it together with the stakeholders of the school. In this process it is necessary for teachers to consider the educational values and goals they wish to promote in school. This is a matter of making far-reaching value-based choices. Site-based curriculum development requires a fundamental understanding of a host of educational approaches and their theoretical underpinnings. It presupposes a wide professional knowledge base and collaboration. I examine this foundation in the following section.

2.1.2   Paradigm shifts in curriculum, teaching and learning

Three paradigms in education

The notion of *paradigm* generally refers to a systematic pattern of thought or a set of principles and basic beliefs for understanding and explaining certain aspects of reality. It is a belief system that guides action and provides an interpretive framework for inquiry. It can also be seen as a *worldview* of its holder that defines the nature of the 'world', the individual's place in it and the range of possible relationships to that world and its parts. The beliefs are basic in the sense that they must be accepted on faith, however well argued, as there is no way to establish their ultimate truthfulness (Guba and Lincoln 1994).

The history of mankind shows significant and dramatic revolutions of understanding that involve sudden intuitive leaps, insights and liberations from old patterns and limits of thought in many fields of inquiry. Since Thomas Kuhn's classic work on the structure of scientific revolutions (1970), the term *paradigm shift* has been used to describe the ways in which new belief systems emerge and how and why they are also resisted for some time. In a paradigm shift, the prevailing paradigm is pushed to a point of crisis because new observations emerge which fail to fit into the existing scheme. When a new insight offers a more powerful explanation for the phenomenon a new paradigm breaks through and is gradually advanced by its proponents. A new paradigm is a *distinctly new way of thinking, a more comprehensive theory than its predecessor,* opening new doors and means for exploration (Ferguson 1982).

Paradigm shifts usually extend over long periods of time. This is because the new paradigm cannot be embraced without rejecting old belief systems. As those who have worked successfully within the old paradigm are emotionally and habitually attached to it, it takes courage to challenge and replace old assumptions. Old beliefs must be reframed, put into a new context, and unwarranted assumptions must be given up. A paradigm shift is thus potentially threatening as it implies that part of our current understanding has become obsolete and needs to be restructured. This explains why new paradigms usually meet with suspicion, resistance and even hostility. The proponents may even be accused of heresy (cf. Copernicus or Galileo for historic examples; Ferguson 1982).

The beliefs and assumptions contained in a paradigm are basically of three kinds: ontological, epistemological and methodological. The *ontological* question is concerned with how we perceive the form and nature of reality and human beings: what there is that can be known about the phenomenon studied. The *epistemological* question is a matter of the nature of knowledge: how we know about the world, and what is the relationship between the inquirer and what can be known. The *methodological* question refers to how we gain knowledge about the world, how we find out what we believe can be known (Guba and Lincoln 1994).

While these three fundamental questions are interconnected, the *ontological assumption is of primary importance*, followed by the epistemological and methodological questions. *The ontological decision constrains how the other two questions may be answered.* For example, if a 'real' world is assumed, then the only admissible questions are those which relate to real, objectively discernible existence or real and concrete actions. Other questions (e.g. those concerning aesthetic or moral values) fall then outside the scope of legitimate scientific inquiry. (Cf. Lehtovaara, in this volume.)

Based on the ontological, epistemological and methodological assumptions, it is customary to distinguish between *three major educational paradigms*: the positivistic paradigm, the constructivist–interpretive paradigm and the critical –emancipatory paradigm. The paradigms need to be related to the teacher's professional knowledge and linked to classroom practices and the teacher's role as an educator. They suggest quite different roles for the teacher and consequently different goals for professional practice and development (Guba and Lincoln 1994; Tom and Valli 1990).

(1) In the *positivistic paradigm*, reality is seen as external and objective, summarised as time- and context-free generalisations which can be taken as causal laws (ontology). The epistemology is dualist and objectivist: the investigator and the investigated 'object' are assumed to be independent entities. The researcher is considered capable of studying the object without influencing it or being influenced by it. The methodology is experimental: the hypotheses are subjected to empirical testing based on quantitative data analysis.

The *way of knowing* in this orientation is *technical knowing*, consisting of 'facts and figures' which typically have right or wrong answers. We come to know them through observing and experimenting. Many things are obviously learned in this way. We have conventions of describing categories of objects or ideas by lexical labels (such as 'bus', 'car', 'tree'). We learn the spelling and pronunciation conventions as well as conventions of carrying out certain acts that require specific skills, e.g. driving a nail with a hammer, or hitting a forehand in tennis or squash. Technical knowledge thus has a legitimate place in curriculum contents (Smith and Lovat 1992).

The teacher's professional knowledge is objective, context-independent generalisations which can explain and predict human behaviour. The values are placed outside the realm of objective inquiry. The context-independent generalisations are considered useful for a variety of instructional purposes to improve teacher effectiveness. The *teacher's role* is to be a consumer of expert knowledge produced by educational researchers. Teachers are didactic implementors of the curricula and materials produced by outside experts, acting according to their guidance and inspection. The top-down management of administration restricts their growth as independent and autonomous professionals. Implicitly, this also encourages them to use a similar power relationship with their students. Based on Jürgen Habermas's influential theory of knowledge, Carr and Kemmis (1986) regard this interest of knowledge as the *technical interest* whereby knowledge is used as a guide to efficient action. It is assumed that the most effective means to a given end can be defined and controlled.

(2) In the *constructivistic–interpretive paradigm*, realities are seen as multiple and intangible mental constructions. They are local and specific and are socially and experientially based. The constructions are not true in any absolute sense; they are just more or less informed and more or less sophisticated. They are thus considered alterable (ontology). The investigator and the investigated object interact in the process. The findings are literally created as the investigation proceeds (epistemology). The methodology is hermeneutical and dialectical: individual constructions can only be elicited and refined through interaction between and among the investigator and the participants.

This dialectical interchange is aimed at elucidating a consensus construction that is more informed and sophisticated than its predecessors. As the aim is to understand others in their own terms, their values are implicitly accepted. Facts are therefore not so rigorously separated from values. The focus is on understanding cases which reveal local meanings in context, not on generalising across cases or contexts.

The *way of knowing* in this orientation is *interpretive, hermeneutical or communicative knowing*. New knowledge is gained through the negotiation of meanings in an interactive communication between the writer/speaker and the reader/listener. A great deal of learning in school is based on understanding through language, using language to learn. Developing relevant interpretive skills is therefore important for promoting self-directed learning. For such skills to develop, the curriculum needs to include opportunities for negotiated learning based on concrete experience (Smith and Lovat 1992).

The *teacher's role* is that of an understanding, reflective practitioner who can benefit from useful research-based knowledge and pedagogical suggestions (Schön 1987). To understand others, the teacher needs to be engaged in the process of reflective self-understanding. The interpretations encourage teachers to use their own judgement in pedagogical decisions. The teacher's position is thus more independent. More emphasis is placed on the teacher's own experiential knowledge and commitment in instructional development. For Carr and Kemmis (1986), this orientation is based on a *practical interest* of knowledge: understanding and clarifying the conditions of meaningful communication and grasping the social meanings that constitute social reality.

(3) In the *critical–emancipatory paradigm*, reality is seen as shaped over time by various factors (social, political, cultural, ethnic, gender) and crystallised into a series of structures that are taken as 'real'. They are natural and immutable, as part of the individual's historical reality (ontology). As the investigator and the respondent are interactively linked, the values of the investigator influence the inquiry. The findings are consequently value mediated (epistemology). The methodology is dialogic and dialectical, requiring a dialogue between the investigator and the subjects of the inquiry. The dialectical nature of the dialogue transforms ignorance and misapprehensions into a deeper awareness.

The *way of knowing* in this orientation is difficult to describe and prove. It is a feeling that something is happening inside us, a feeling of increased individual awareness. Such *self-reflective knowing* or knowing from inside can occur, to some extent, without the influence of others. It is called *tacit knowledge*, implicit in our spontaneous behaviour with others. For conscious awareness and control, however, it needs to be made explicit through a critical reflection on the experience. *Critical knowing* develops a greater understanding of the individual and his/her actions in terms of how these actions have been shaped and informed by the broader social, cultural and historical forces. Such an understanding develops in a collaborative inquiry process which involves critical thinking skills and challenges learners to engage in practical action for change (Smith and Lovat 1992).

Educational inquiry is motivated by an explicit commitment to particular values (such as equality, justice and self-determination). Knowledge is thus seen as a source for emancipatory actions. It needs to uncover the ways and circumstances which prevent the realisation of the preferred values. It also assesses the extent to which any existing forms of communication may be systematically distorted by prevailing political, social and cultural conditions. Unjust and unequal educational and social arrangements need to be reformed. People are seen as capable of acting upon and transforming institutional arrangements.

In this *emancipatory interest* of knowledge, the *teacher's role* goes beyond understanding the subjective meanings of the participants in a social context. By developing a critical understanding of their work, teachers can be emancipated from the routines, beliefs and assumptions concerning their work. They can take an active charge of developing their profession. Critical self-reflection permits teachers to understand why their work conditions may be frustrating and restricting and suggests a course of action to improve them. Teachers need to voice the disapproval of their contemporary social arrangements, instead of being just content with illuminating the problems and socially imposed constraints (Carr and Kemmis 1986).

The basic beliefs in these paradigms are summarised in Table 2.1 in terms of ontology, epistemology and methodology.

In classroom-based research, there has been a shift of emphasis away from positivistically orientated quantitative research towards the interpretive and critical paradigms. This involves qualitative research strategies and qualitative

Table 2.1 A comparison of three educational paradigms

Paradigm	Ontology	Epistemology	Methodology
(1) Positivistic paradigm	Realism; reality summarised as time- and context-free generalisations	Dualist and objectivist; the investigator and the 'object' as independent entities	Experimental, verification of hypotheses; mainly quantitative methods
(2) Constructivist–interpretive paradigm	Relativism; local and specific constructed realities	Transactional and subjectivist; created findings	Hermeneutical and dialectical interaction
(3) Critical–emancipatory paradigm	Historical realism; individual structures historically situated	Transactional, subjectivist; value-mediated findings	Dialogic and dialectical interaction

data collection and interpretation. The need for classroom-based research in instructional development is due to the following kinds of dissatisfaction with the positivistic research tradition (Tom 1992; Järvinen *et al.* 1995):

• Research was divorced from specific, relevant classroom realities
• It provided outsiders' advice, but fewer insiders' insights
• It forced the teacher into the role of a consumer of knowledge
• It ignored the individual learner's prior knowledge, skills, beliefs and attitudes by introducing the concept of the 'average' learner and 'standard' situations
• It ignored learner diversity and the differences in motivation and attention in a given educational context and setting

The critical–emancipatory paradigm is committed to the notion that classroom-oriented research helps teachers to interpret, understand and eventually transform the social life in schools. This goal gives an increased impetus for teachers to get involved in research which is geared to the classroom realities and is largely carried out by the teachers themselves. Teachers are seen as ethically committed change agents. They foster democratic procedures and principles both within the school and within the larger society. To do so, they need to be actively involved in developing their practical theories through continuing action, collaboration and reflection (Carr and Kemmis 1986).

> *For your reflection.* Think of the current trends in educational research and teaching practices in your context. (a) How could you describe them in relation to the three paradigms? (b) What shifts of emphases can you notice in language teaching? (c) Where do you stand yourself in your own educational thinking? (d) Where might you wish to proceed? (e) What constraints and obstacles can you identify? (f) How might you deal with them?

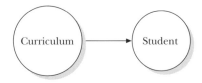

Figure 2.2   The transmission position

Three curriculum orientations

Curriculum represents a selection of the ideas, knowledge, concepts, skills, values, beliefs, norms and practices available in a society. By what is included in the curriculum and what is left out, curriculum creates a reality for learners. Curriculum design is thus essentially concerned with making decisions and choosing between alternatives. Curriculum is context-specific, i.e. the decisions and choices depend on the national and local context, and the available resources and traditions. The types of decisions to be made in curriculum work are those of selecting, sequencing, organising and structuring the knowledge and skills to be learned. Curriculum is targeted to an identified group of learners in a given cultural and educational context. Thus the decisions that are appropriate for one context may not be so in another (Smith and Lovat 1992).

The way the decisions about curriculum are made leads to basically *three different curriculum orientations* which are related to the three educational paradigms discussed above: (1) the transmission position, (2) the transaction position and (3) the transformation position (Leithwood 1986; Miller 1988). The positions should not, however, be seen as mutually exclusive. There is overlapping between them and each has its place in curriculum development, providing perspectives to classroom practices. They are outlined as follows.

(1) The *transmission position* is related to the positivistic paradigm. It aims at the mastery of discipline-based school subjects and social norms which are taught mainly through traditional, teacher-centred methods. The teacher is the expert who presents didactically the knowledge that the student is to learn. There is thus a one-way movement from the teacher to the student who is supposed to learn the facts, concepts, skills and values in rather a passive role as the recipient of information. It is the teacher's responsibility to control that the student has learned the knowledge. This position can be presented in Figure 2.2.

Underlying the orientation is the behaviouristic theory of learning, associated notably with the well-known work of B.F. Skinner. Behind the theory is an atomistic world view that sees nature as composed of isolated building blocks. Consequently human behaviour is also broken into isolated components that are carefully analysed, sequenced and presented to the learner. To ensure correct learner responses, the learning task is organised into small incremental steps. Correct answers are immediately reinforced, rehearsed and repeated (e.g. through pattern drills), aiming at automatised and error-free routine performance.

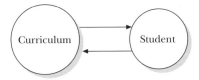

Figure 2.3   The transaction position

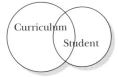

Figure 2.4   The transformation position

(2) The *transaction position* is related to the interpretive paradigm. Education is a negotiation process between the curriculum and the learner, a dialogue between the student and the teacher. In this orientation the individual is seen as rational and capable of intelligent problem-solving. The position consequently tends to stress inquiry and problem-solving skills and to facilitate democratic decision-making in social contexts. Teachers and learners are partners interacting with each other. Instead of right or wrong answers, knowledge is open to interpretive understanding in which the student constructs knowledge through an interactive process, as shown in Figure 2.3.

The world view underlying the transaction position focuses on solving a wide range of problems and helping the individual to deal constructively with the world. The position is thus connected with the constructivist learning theory. It sees human beings as intentional, goal-oriented and conscious actors who are actively involved in processing knowledge. Individuals construct internal representations or mental models of the surrounding world. These models help them organise the flood of information around them. New learning is based on prior constructions which guide perception and action. It is therefore important for the teacher to help the learner to make relevant connections by activating their prior understanding and guiding their attention to salient properties of the task at hand.

(3) The *transformation position* is connected with the critical paradigm. Its principal goals are self-actualisation and personal and social change, aiming to create a more democratic society. The position has a holistic emphasis, regarding the learner as a person with both the cognitive and aesthetic, moral, physical and spiritual needs. Consequently learning emphasises the integration of the physical, cognitive and affective domains. The learner and the curriculum are interconnected in a holistic manner, as seen in Figure 2.4.

The world view underlying this position is humanistic with a concern for the sense of individual identity and personal growth. Learning takes place as a gradual organisation of meanings into the individual's world picture. Human beings are seen as intentional and self-directed, capable of making choices and assuming an ethical responsibility for their lives in the social context. Personal growth extends throughout the entire human life cycle. In his well-known psychosocial theory of personality, Erik Erikson (1963) proposes that the maturation of the person, from infancy to old age, progresses through eight sequential stages. The stages unfold according to a universal plan. They have a specific developmental task to be dealt with at that particular time. Each stage is accompanied by a crisis, a turning point arising from psychological maturation and the social demands connected with that stage. The crises need be resolved adequately for a healthy personality and a greater maturity, trust and autonomy to develop further.

Transformative learning occurs when we work on our frame of reference. It has two dimensions: a *meaning perspective* and a *meaning scheme*. The former consists of broad and generalised orienting predispositions, while the latter is a cluster of specific beliefs, feelings, attitudes and value judgements. We elaborate existing meaning schemes, learn new meaning schemes, transform meaning schemes, or transform meaning perspectives. *Critical reflection* is essential for transforming the frames of reference. Another essential component is *action*. A transformative learning experience requires that the learner makes a conscious decision to act on the reflective insight and does so one way or another (Mezirow 1996).

Transformative learning is situated in the sense that learning is influenced by contemporary cultural and social forces. These forces impact on the individual's biographical and historical meaning perspectives and schemes which the learner brings to the learning experience. The educator has an important task of creating a supportive environment for learning. Under favourable conditions, participants are able to engage in a discourse that is free from coercion and enables them to weigh evidence and assess arguments. They are also open to alternative perspectives and a critical reflection on their presuppositions (Mezirow 1996).

Status of the teacher: two positions

To summarise the discussion, two pictures can be portrayed of the status of teachers based on the polar ends on the continuum between the technical and critical orientations to curriculum. The dimensions in Table 2.2 should not be seen as a dichotomous, either-or picture; various degrees of emphasis in either direction are possible. Neither should they be seen as any 'right' or 'wrong' ways of teaching and teacher education. They are just different ways of looking at the teaching profession and might provide some food for thought about the status of teachers in a given cultural context.

The teacher's role depends obviously on the traditions of teaching and teacher education in the different national contexts. The broad educational goals are usually a matter of national policy-making at the level of central administration, guided by prevailing theories of learning and teaching, and by the academic traditions. The teacher's role therefore needs to be examined

Table 2.2   Two contrasting views of the teacher's professional status

Dependent status	Independent status
• *Initial teacher preparation:* Minimal, practically orientated training	Longer preparation, attempting to integrate theory and practice
• *Control of teacher's work* Tight curricula, objectives and norms; inspection and control (e.g. through standardised tests)	More professional autonomy (e.g. through designing site-based curricula), less external control
• *Role of teaching methods* Emphasis on clearly structured, didactic methods; teacher-structured learning	More emphasis on principles and pedagogical choices; teacher as a facilitator of learning
• *Teaching culture* Teachers working in isolation	Collegial collaboration important
• *Learning materials* 'Teacher-proof' materials	More space for personal choices
• *View of professionalism* Teachers as technicians, implementing given curricula	Teachers as professionals, developing their own curricula
• *Orientation to process/product* Product orientation: goals are taken as given and are evaluated through outcomes; teachers are held accountable for the goals	Process orientation: goals are negotiated and specified during the process; emphasis on a more responsible learner role

with regard to the national policies, priorities, goals and traditions of teaching and teacher education. Thus options that work in one setting may not be applicable or even available in another cultural context.

In general, the status of a *profession* depends on several factors. For one thing, there must be an adequate knowledge base to ground the profession. Professional conduct must thus require a sufficient amount of specialised knowledge that makes its members uniquely capable of making competent choices. Secondly, the education of the members needs to establish a code of ethics for professional responsibility and client welfare, serving the public interest. Thirdly, professionals need to develop autonomy that entails a commitment for developing their expertise through a research orientation. Further, in addition to improving the capacity of its practitioners, the profession also needs to improve its image, appreciation and status in society (cf. Strike and Soltis 1992; Järvinen *et al.* 1995).

In the light of these criteria, the teacher's position in the left-hand column is a relatively low-status profession. This is surely due to several historical developments. Research and practice have been traditionally separate in teaching, with researchers being in charge of developing educational theories and assuming a status of theoretical experts. Consequently teachers are often seen as applying theories to practice. In a number of national contexts, their role is to implement centralised curricula and materials. When they do so teachers give away some of their intellectual power and responsibility. *This dependent position undermines the teacher's professional status and autonomy.* Regardless of the apparent methodological freedom that the teachers have in their classrooms, their work is controlled to a large extent by administrators, inspectors and researchers.

The right-hand column, on the other hand, emphasises the importance of seeing teaching as an autonomous, *ethical profession.* In addition to the classroom-specific instructional skills, teachers need sophisticated communication and collaboration skills to develop their schools. *They are committed to foster human growth in themselves in order to be able to foster growth in their learners.* The new role leads to extended goals for professional growth and a collegial institutional culture (Niemi and Kohonen 1995; Fullan 1996).

> *For your reflection.* Reflect on the language teacher's role and status in your own cultural context. (a) What trends and traditions can you identify in your setting? (b) Based on the above criteria, to what extent can language teachers be regarded as a profession in your country? (c) How would you describe your own stance as a language teacher in relation to the three curriculum orientations and the dimensions of the teacher's professional status? (d) What do you notice about your assumptions and beliefs as a teacher?

2.1.3   Implications for experiential foreign language education

These shifts suggest the need to develop foreign language teaching towards the notion of *learner education.* I use the term learner 'education' rather than 'training' to imply an educational, holistic goal orientation to learning. The two terms suggest a continuum from a narrower training approach towards the broader educational approach. The differences between the two notions can be examined using the dimensions suggested in Table 2.3.

In traditional foreign language teaching, language teaching was primarily aimed at developing the student's mastery of the grammar as the linguistic system as near as possible to that of a native speaker. Foreign language teaching now needs to have a *wider goal orientation of educating intercultural speakers* who are conscious of their social citizenship rights and obligations. A natural task for language learning is to connect people from various cultural backgrounds and to increase the tolerance for diversity and ambiguity. Language learning therefore has to be sensitive to the social dimension of language involving such factors as the setting, communicative intentions and relationships between the partners (Doyé 1996; Byram 1996; Kaikkonen, in this volume).

School is not just preparation for the life to come; it is also a community in its own right, with a specific culture. Learners practice living in community through the ways in which the teachers structure their learning experiences.

Table 2.3 Language teaching as learner training and learner education

Language teaching as learner training:	Language teaching as learner education:
Goal orientation: narrow, specific objectives, situations and tasks	**Goal orientation**: broad communication and personal growth
Syllabus contents: specific, clearly defined communicative skills	**Broader syllabus**: communicating in new, unpredictable contexts
Linguistic effectiveness: correct performance on limited tasks, learners working mainly alone	**Personal efficacy**: in addition to communication skills, emphasis on risk-taking, self-direction, learning to learn, and social skills
Teacher role: direct, frontal teaching; learners progress mainly at the same pace in the class	**Teacher role**: more indirect, individual guidance, negotiation, and contracts for learning tasks
Emphasis on external performance testing by specific criteria	**External evaluation, self-assessment and reflection** of processes

The development of autonomy in the classroom context requires a sufficient learning space and guidance provided and structured by the teacher. Developing a critical awareness of language and learning processes means that learners have opportunities to share in the decisions related to their learning. Language classroom practices should therefore reflect democratic procedures (Sheils 1996).

Professional success and personal satisfaction will increasingly depend on the ability to communicate competently with people from other cultures. The acquisition of appropriate linguistic knowledge and skills can be integrated with the learning of the self-reflective and interpersonal skills and attitudes that help language learners to deal with otherness and cultural diversity in constructive ways. Preparing young people for responsible citizenship entails that they develop an independence of thought and action that is combined with a sense of social and intercultural responsibility (Sheils 1996; Kaikkonen, in this volume).

The familiar concept of communicative competence in language teaching is related in critical social science to an ethical theory of self-realisation. The theory of communicative competence and *communicative action*, originally advanced by Jürgen Habermas, is connected with the emancipatory interest of knowledge. Communicative action is essentially concerned with *'stepping back' in order to understand our situation better and to listen to and understand others from their point of view*. It entails an attempt to aim at an unforced consensus with others through a genuine dialogue, respecting equally the rights of all participants (Carr and Kemmis 1986; Kemmis 1995).

We need to consider the properties of discourse and speech situations that foster the realisation of the individual's potential for learning. In an ideal discourse the participants have equal chances of initiating and perpetuating

discourse, of putting forward and giving reasons for or against any statements, explanations, interpretations, and justifications. They also have the
same chances to express their attitudes, feelings, intentions and the like. An
open speech situation ensures discussion which is free from constraints of
coercion or dominance. Such discourse aims at a dialogue between the participants (Carr and Kemmis 1986; Jaatinen; Lehtovaara, in this volume). In this
process the language classroom can become a truly communicative environment, a forum where 'knowledge may be jointly offered and sought, reflected
upon, and acted upon', as Breen and Candlin (1981: 98) point out.

Foreign language curricula are an important part of the institutional curricula in general education. They are variously based on the national curriculum framework and guidelines. The role of the national (or regional)
curriculum is interpreted differently in different contexts. While a large
number of countries have centralised curricula, some are currently aiming at
clearly decentralised curriculum strategies, while still others are shifting the
emphasis from decentralised curricula towards a more prominent national
control. Language curricula are thus part of this dynamic process, sharing
the tensions between the local design and implementation and the national
guidelines and evaluation. Consequently, what is seen as a desirable curriculum development strategy in one cultural context may be less desirable
in another context. As language educators we need to be aware of such
conflicting tendencies and avoid any dogmatism and imposition based on
our own context.

> *For your reflection.* Think of the dimensions of language teaching as learner train-
> ing and as learner education. (a) Where do your pedagogical choices stand
> along the dimensions? (b) In what ways are they supported and constrained
> by your national (or regional) contextual factors? (c) What possibilities can
> you discover for developing your language teaching? (d) What assistance can
> you find?

The varying perspectives and options need to be explored and reviewed
in language curriculum design, implementation and evaluation. This is a
question of an ongoing process of professional inquiry among language educators. To my understanding, the views discussed in this section pose a great
challenge to develop a new paradigm of foreign language learning as learner
education. Experiential learning provides significant concepts and means for
progressing in this direction.

2.2   WHAT IS EXPERIENTIAL LEARNING?

2.2.1 Role of experience in learning

The *basic tenet* in experiential learning is that *experience plays a significant role
in learning*. The term *experiential learning* is used to refer to a wide range of
educational approaches in which *formal learning* (in institutional contexts)
is *integrated with practical work and informal learning* in a number of settings:

industrial, business, government or service organisations, various public service internships, field placements, work and study assignments, clinical experience, overseas programmes, etc.

Experiential learning techniques include various interactive practices where the participants have opportunities to learn from each others' experiences, being actively and personally engaged in the process:

- personal journals and reflections
- portfolios, thought questions and reflective essays
- role plays, drama activities, games and simulations
- personal stories and case studies
- visualisations and imaginative activities
- models, analogies and theory construction
- empathy-taking activities, story-telling, sharing with others
- discussions and reflection in cooperative groups

All of these contain a common element of *learning from immediate experience and engaging the learners in the process as whole persons, both intellectually and emotionally.* Experiential learning involves both observing the phenomenon and doing something meaningful with it through an active participation. It thus refers to learning in which the learner is directly in touch with the phenomenon being studied, rather than just hearing, reading or thinking about it (Keeton and Tate 1978).

With the rapid development of the information superways and the internet, we are literally surrounded by overwhelming amounts of information readily available through modern information technology. These developments are undoubtedly offering qualitatively new learning experiences and opportunities. The possibilities seem particularly relevant for foreign language learning. Modern technology serves as a useful input for the individual and group learning processes. Sharing personal observations and reflections with other learners in small groups makes learning come alive and gives learners opportunities to compare their views with those of others (e.g. the use of authentic videos in intercultural learning; see Kaikkonen, in this volume).

In my view, however, the technological developments can also pose problems if they are used excessively by young learners. This is because technology entails a loss of touch with concrete reality and replaces first-hand experience by second-hand, electronically transmitted experiences (cf. TV, cartoons, comics, film, video, interactive computer games with 'virtual realities', etc.). While these advances open important new avenues for learning they can also separate learners from the responsibilities of real human encounters and relations in the present world. We learn life by living it rather than watching it on the screen.

> *For your reflection.* Think of an incident in your life in which you discovered something significant about yourself through a personal encounter with somebody else. (a) What happened? Who were the participants? How did you act yourself? (b) How did you feel about the incident? (c) What did you learn about yourself?

Important experiences can provide significant learnings for personal growth and they deserve to be reflected on with due care. This is what experiential learning is about: learning from actual experience through reflection.

2.2.2 Foundations of experiential learning

The roots of experiential learning can be traced back to John Dewey's progressive pedagogy, Kurt Lewin's social psychology, Jean Piaget's work on developmental cognitive psychology, George Kelly's cognitive theory of personality, and to humanistic psychology, notably the work of Abraham Maslow and Carl Rogers. More recent theories include the multiple intelligence theory advanced by Howard Gardner (1983; 1993) and the conception of emotional intelligence by Daniel Goleman (1995; 1998).

In his well-known progressive pedagogy, Dewey (1938) emphasized the importance of learning by doing: *experience acts as an organising focus for learning*. Dewey described his approach as cultivation of individuality, learning through personal experience, and as a dynamic, here-and-now view of learning for current relevance. *Learning is situated in concrete environments*. Dewey has the useful concept of *educative experience* whereby prior learning in one situation becomes an instrument of understanding and dealing effectively with the situations which follow through the principles of continuity and interaction among the learners. Care must therefore be devoted to the conditions which give each present experience a worthwhile meaning for the learner. Dewey also notes that the postponement of immediate action is necessary for observation and judgement to take place, but action is still essential for the achievement of the purpose.

Lewin's work (1951) on group dynamics and the methodology of action research has been very influential. In his encounter groups he made the important discovery that learning is best facilitated in an environment where there is a *tension between immediate, concrete experience and analytic detachment and reflection*. Lewin noted that learning must also include an element of concept formation, aiming at an integration of theory and practice. His famous saying, 'there is nothing so practical as a good theory', symbolizes his commitment to the integration of scientific inquiry and practical problem solving.

In the basic model of experiential learning advanced by Lewin, immediate personal experience is the focal point for learning. In his model, (1) *immediate concrete experience* is the basis for observation and reflection. It is accompanied by (2) *reflective observation* that leads to the (3) formation of *abstract concepts* and further to (4) *testing the implications* in new situations. There must, however, be a balance between observation and action: just as observations provide the necessary input for learning, action is necessary for testing hypotheses and obtaining further personal experiences. Lewin's four-stage learning cycle has been later elaborated by David Kolb (1984).

Piaget's classical work on developmental psychology led him to discover age-related regularities in children's reasoning processes, and *how intelligence is gradually shaped by experience*. Intelligence is a product of the interaction between the child and his environment. Thus the powers of abstract reasoning and symbol manipulation can be traced back to the infant's actions in exploring and coping with his immediate environment, whereby experience is translated into a model of the world.

Kelly (1955) proposed that we perceive and interpret the world of experience through personal constructs. The notion of *construct* refers to the categories of thought by means of which the individual interprets his personal world of experience. *Constructs are abstracted from experience and can be revised in the light of ongoing events in life.* Each individual views reality through his personal constructs that are unique to him. Reality is thus a subjective interpretation of the events, based on the individual's past experiences and history of life. Meanings of external events are open to interpretations from a variety of perspectives, and the interpretations are also subject to change. Learning cannot thus provide final answers as the individual can find new questions and discover new possibilities. Knowledge is ultimately governed by what Kelly calls *constructive alternativism*: the individual can revise his present interpretations of the universe.

Kelly's basic assumption is that the *individual makes sense of the world through his or her constructs.* As reality is a function of the way in which the individual perceives it, individuals respond to events in accordance with how they perceive and interpret them. They function in terms of their expectations about future events, making plans and choices on the basis of expected outcomes (Kelly 1955). This thinking entails what Rosenthal and Jacobson (1968) have later called 'self-fulfilling prophecies' in their classic study. The individual's anticipations of future events affect the choices that he makes, and may thereby lead to the anticipated outcomes. Thus success-oriented anticipations may lead to success, while failure-oriented ones are more likely to breed failure (Kohonen 1987; 1992a).

The importance of personal experiences for the growth of personality is similarly prominent in the humanistic psychology of Rogers (1975). He argues that the individual's *self-concept is a social product that is shaped gradually through interaction with the environment.* It is an organized, integrated pattern of self-related perceptions, becoming increasingly differentiated and complex. The development of a healthy self-concept is promoted by a *positive self-regard and an unconditional acceptance by the 'significant others'.* He notes that conditional acceptance, based on the desired actions or feelings, is detrimental to the development of a balanced self-concept.

For a healthy personality development, the child needs an atmosphere in which he or she is valued unconditionally. In such an environment, the individual can progress towards becoming a fully functioning person. This process of change is characterized by a widening range of human experience: an awareness of one's own feelings, openness to new experiences, tolerance, a basic trust in others, and an ability to listen to them empathically and perceive their feelings. It is an *actualising tendency towards maintaining and enhancing oneself as a human being.* Fostering such qualities is an essential goal in learning (cf. Kaikkonen; Jaatinen; Lehtovaara, in this volume).

The notions of dependence, independence and interdependence are significant concepts in personal growth. A learner with a *dependence orientation* relies on someone else telling him or her what to do or think and perceives learning as something that others do to him or her. An *independent learner* has grown out of external sources of action and self-worth and has taken the responsibility of making sense of life for himself, *relying on internal sources of motivation*. Independent learners perceive learning as something they do for themselves. However, self-actualisation is also a question of becoming an *interdependent learner*. In order to develop our maximum potential we need a relationship with ourselves in which we are able to reflect on our own learning and also recognise that we learn from others, just as they do from us. We realise that we are *partners and resources of learning for each other, responsible for fostering learning in a community of learners* (Kohonen and Kaikkonen 1996; Askew and Carnell 1998).

The importance of fostering the learner's holistic growth as a person has been emphasised in two recent theories of intelligence: Gardner's theory of *multiple intelligences* (1983; 1993) and Goleman's conception of emotional intelligence (1995; 1998). Gardner argues that there is no one monolithic kind of intelligence such as the standard IQ focusing on the verbal and mathematicallogical abilities. Rather, intelligence should be seen as a wide spectrum of human talents involving *seven key intelligences or 'frames of mind'* as he puts them: bodily-kinesthetic, musical, linguistic, logico-mathematical, spatial, interpersonal and intrapersonal intelligence.

I find it interesting that Gardner includes interpersonal and intrapersonal intelligences in his theory of multiple intelligences. He breaks *interpersonal intelligence* further down to the following abilities:

- *leadership*: organising groups and coordinating team efforts
- *personal connection*: recognising and responding appropriately to people's feelings and concerns, nurturing human relationships
- *negotiating solutions*: having talents of a mediator, preventing and resolving conflicts
- *social analysis*: being able to detect and have insights about people's feelings, motives and concerns

Intra-personal intelligence is a correlative ability, turned inward. It is a *capacity of self-knowledge, forming an accurate and realistic model of oneself*. It entails an *access to one's own feelings* and the ability to discriminate among them and draw on them to guide behaviour.

Emotional intelligence refers to our capacity to *recognise feelings and express them appropriately* and to engage in self-critique of our ways of feeling and knowing. It involves the following main domains (Goleman 1995; Askew and Carnell 1998):

- *knowing one's emotions*: developing self-awareness to recognise and name a feeling as it happens, having a surer sense about how one really feels about personal decisions

- *managing emotions*: learning to handle one's feelings, e.g. frustration, tolerance, anger and stress management
- *motivating oneself*: emotional responsibility and self-control, e.g. delaying gratification and stifling impulsiveness
- *recognising emotions in others*: developing empathy and sensitivity to others' feelings, learning to be a good listener
- *handling relationships*: developing social competence by analysing and understanding human relationships, being assertive and skilled at communicating

Emotional intelligence develops our awareness of emotions and helps us understand them and accept them. In addition to accepting our emotions we should, however, also be able to challenge our emotional reactions when appropriate. By questioning our attachments to a particular emotional experience we can reframe the experience and perceive it differently.

A central tenet in experiential learning is, then, that *learning involves the whole person, including the emotional, social, physical, cognitive and spiritual aspects of personality.* When we function as whole persons we have connection to ourselves, connection to other people and connection to a spiritual source of purpose and meaning in life. Capacity to whole-person learning is not fixed; it can be increased. Learning capacity increases as learning increases. Prior learning can be used as a resource for further learning. Emotional state affects the learner's capacity to learn. This capacity increases when learners understand themselves better. *Learning to learn is a capacity that can be enhanced by conscious pedagogical measures.* This perspective suggests a process-oriented view of learning (Askew and Carnell 1998).

2.2.3 Basic model of experiential learning

In experiential learning, immediate personal experience is the focal point for learning. As pointed out by Kolb (1984: 21), *personal experience* gives the '*life, texture, and subjective personal meaning to abstract concepts*'. At the same time it also provides 'a *concrete, publicly shared reference point for testing the implications and validity of ideas created during the learning process*'. Experience alone is not, however, a sufficient condition for learning. Experiences also need to be processed consciously by reflecting on them. Learning is thus a cyclic process integrating immediate experience, reflection, abstract conceptualisation and action.

Kolb (1984: 42) advances a general theoretical model of experiential learning as shown in Figure 2.5.

According to the model, learning is essentially a process of resolution of conflicts between two dialectically opposed dimensions, the *prehension* dimension and the *transformation* dimension.

(1) The *prehension dimension* refers to the *way in which the individual grasps experience.* The dimension includes two modes of knowing, ranging from what Kolb calls grasping via 'apprehension' to what he calls grasping via 'comprehension'.

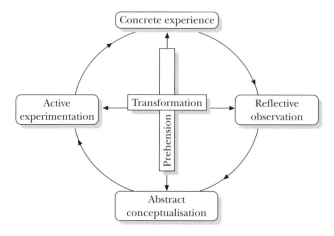

Figure 2.5   Model of experiential learning

Apprehension is instant, intuitive and tacit knowledge without a need for rational inquiry or analytical confirmation. The other end of the dimension, grasping via *comprehension*, on the other hand, emphasises the role of conscious learning, whereby comprehension introduces order and predictability to the flow of unconscious sensations. Reality is thus grasped through varying degrees of emphasis on unconscious and conscious learning.

(2) The *transformation dimension* refers to the *transformation of experience through reflective observation and active experimentation*. An individual with an active orientation is ready to take risks, attempting to maximise success and showing little concern for errors or failure. An individual with an excessive reflective orientation, on the other hand, may withdraw from risks in order to avoid failures, preferring to transform experiences through reflective observation.

The polar ends of the two dimensions thus yield *four orientations to learning* (Kolb 1984):

(1) *concrete experience*, learning by intuition, with an involvement in personal experiences and an emphasis on feeling over thinking. This is an 'artistic' orientation relying on sensitivity to feelings. The instructional activities that support this aspect of learning include discussions in small groups, simulation techniques, use of videos and films, and the use of examples, stories and autobiographies.

(2) *abstract conceptualisation*, learning by thinking, using logic and a systematic approach to problem-solving. Emphasis is placed on thinking and manipulation of abstract symbols, with a tendency to neat and precise conceptual systems. The instructional techniques include theory construction, lecturing and building models and analogies.

(3) *reflective observation*, learning by perception, focusing on understanding the meaning of ideas and situations by careful observation. The learner is concerned with how things happen by attempting to see them from different perspectives and relying on one's own thoughts, feelings and judgement. The instructional techniques include personal journals, reflective essays, observations, and thought questions and discussions.

(4) *active experimentation*, learning by action, with an emphasis on practical applications and getting things done. The learner attempts to influence people and change situations, taking risks in order to accomplish things. The instructional techniques include typically fieldwork, various projects, laboratory and home work, games, dramatisations and simulations, and the use of case studies.

Experiential learning consists of a four-stage cycle combining all of these orientations. Thus simple everyday experience is not sufficient for learning. It must also be observed and analysed consciously, and reflection must in turn be followed by testing new hypotheses in order to obtain further experience. I wish to argue, in fact, that *theoretical concepts will become part of the individual's frame of reference only after he or she has experienced them meaningfully at an emotional level.* Reflection plays an important role in this process by providing a bridge, as I see it, between experience and theoretical conceptualisation.

From the teacher's point of view, experiential learning means that opportunities are provided for the full development of the cycle. There are various instructional techniques to promote the different aspects of the learning cycle. The traditional academic setting has tended to emphasise reflective observation and concept formation at the expense of active experimenting and immediate concrete experiences. The model also cautions against the opposite extreme, the assumption that any experience can lead to learning. Only experience that is reflected upon seriously yields its full measure of learning. Reflection must in turn be followed by action for further experiences (Kohonen 1992a).

I find it interesting to relate the four learning orientations to the historical developments in foreign language pedagogy. The *grammar-translation method* was obviously strong on the *abstract conceptualisation* of the linguistic system of the foreign language, at the expense of spoken fluency. This is because it focused on elaborate explanations of grammatical rules, memorisation of vocabulary, analysing texts to consolidate grammar, and translating disconnected sentences for accuracy. The behaviouristic approaches, such as the *audiolingual method*, were strong on *concrete experience.* They emphasised oral communication skills which were built up in a carefully graded progression using a variety of pattern drill exercises. Grammar was taught inductively, avoiding theoretical explanations, and new vocabulary was introduced through demonstrations and visuals.

The *communicative approaches*, on the other hand, have shifted attention somewhat back on *abstract conceptualisation* and emphasised *active experimentation*, the communicative use of language in meaningful situations. Affective factors are also taken more into consideration. In the *intercultural learning approach*, emphasis is being shifted even further towards reflecting on the personal, emotional and social factors. Whereas communicative competence related primarily to the individual's knowledge and skills in communicative situations, intercultural competence also focuses on the learner's personal and social abilities, such as ambiguity tolerance and respect for diversity. Intercultural learning thus aims at an integrated and more balanced view of the different learning orientations in experiential learning, emphasising also the importance of *reflective observation* in language learning (cf. Brown 1994; Kaikkonen, in this volume).

> *For your reflection.* Think of your personal experiences as a foreign language learner. (a) To what extent and in what contexts can you identify the above shifts of emphasis on the different modes of language learning? (b) What effects have the various approaches had on your language learning? (c) What kind of positive experiences can you recall in your language learning autobiography? (d) How are these experiences related to the basic ideas of experiential learning?

To summarise the discussion in this section, experiential learning is characterised as follows:

(1) Learning takes place along a *continuum of meaning, ranging from 'meaningless' routine learning to 'meaningful', experiential learning that involves the* learner. It is a process where concepts are derived from and continuously modified by experience. Learning is the process of *creating knowledge through the transformation of experience.* All learning is relearning in the sense that previous experience is modified by new experiences.

(2) Learning is a continuous process that is grounded in experience. Thus *knowledge and skill gained in one situation become instruments of understanding and dealing with situations that follow.* Predictability is established on the basis of previous experience. While continuity and predictability provide security, learning also involves an element of ambiguity and risk-taking.

(3) The process of learning requires the *resolution of conflicts between dialectically opposed modes of grasping and transforming experience.* Learning is a tension-filled process, where knowledge, skills and attitudes are achieved through varying degrees of emphasis on the four modes of learning. The ways in which the tensions are resolved determines the quality and level of learning.

(4) Learning is a *holistic process of relating to the world. It involves feeling, observing, thinking and acting, as a cyclic process.* These modes of learning are integrated, and development in one mode affects development in others. Learning is active and self-directed and continues throughout life.

Traditional academic learning has been strong on theory but weaker on application and practice. On the other hand, focusing on the role of experience alone may run the risk of stressing practice at the expense of theory. If the element of reflection and concept formation is left out, learning remains rote imitation.

An interesting question is the role of intuition in experiential learning. In contexts of uncertainty, ambiguity and unpredictability we need to rely on intuition, particularly when we have to come up with a solution under a time pressure. Similarly, we use intuition when there are equally good alternative ways of acting, choosing a possible course of action on the basis of our tacit feeling of what might be wise to do, and see what happens (Niemi and Kohonen 1995). We need to act to obtain experiential data for reflection.

Consequently, experiential learning should not be seen as an attempt to substitute one mode of learning for another. It is a merger of the complementary modes of learning. What is thus needed is a balanced combination of the different modes.

2.2.4 Directions and settings in experiential learning

So far I have discussed experiential learning without reference to the settings where it is used. It is helpful to realise that experiential learning refers to a spectrum of practices in different settings from different walks of life. The techniques and applications of experiential learning are relevant to the challenges that people face in their personal lives, in education, in institutional development, in business life, in communities, and in society change. These settings entail different emphases and goals for experiential learning. Based on the notion of the four clusters ('villages') of experiential learning (Warner Weil and McGill 1989; Henry 1989), I make a distinction between four settings in experiential learning.

1. Assessment and accrediting of prior learning in adult education is concerned with the problems of assessing and accrediting learning from prior work experience. A central question in accreditation is how to make valid and fair judgements about prior learning as a basis for creating new routes into higher education, employment and training opportunities, and achieving professional status. The focus is on the outcomes of prior learning in terms of what counts as evidence for learning. There are several techniques which can be used in the assessment of prior learning. These include various performance measures, with competence checklists, discussions, tests and examinations for the learning outcomes. Portfolio assessment is another flexible instrument which can be used for reporting learning outcomes.

2. Pedagogical change in formal education concerns the learning processes in various institutional settings, from early learning to adult education, and the role of prior learning as a resource for further learning. Learning needs to be related to the learner's prior experiences which are activated for conscious access. Experiential techniques can be incorporated in traditional classroom and course work. The techniques include combinations of independent study, contract learning and project work, shared reflection, role plays, simulations, field trips and problem-based learning.

The experiential techniques are aimed at increasing the participants' involvement in their own learning by engaging their full attention in the process and increasing their control over their experiences. The techniques also emphasise the relevance of learning with regard to the world outside the classroom. Experiential learning thus serves as a link between formal learning, work experience and personal development.

3. Social change and community action uses learning from experience as a means for group consciousness raising, community action and social change. Individual experience is connected with the power relations in society. Individuals are encouraged to make links between their autobiography, group history and social and political processes. The techniques include personal reflection and various forms of group discussions and group projects utilising the diversity in the participants' experiential and social backgrounds. The variety of views stimulates understanding, empathy and attitude changes and helps people to recognise the dominant assumptions or ideologies in society.

Uncovering hidden assumptions is an emancipatory means towards personal and collective empowerment. People may become aware of the inadequacies, biases and oppressions of formal structures. The new understanding can lead to community action aimed at challenging or transforming the social structures, or it can entail transforming the group's relationship to them. In both cases it is necessary to understand the patterns and contexts that cut across individual experience.

4. Personal growth and development focuses on individual and interpersonal experiencing and thus affective learning. It is aimed at increasing personal and group effectiveness, autonomy, choice and self-fulfilment. These goals are usually explored in various group processes using stories, narratives, autobiographies, diaries and visuals (e.g. video, films) as inputs. Other techniques include the use of drama, guided imaging and visualisations, and creative arts approaches such as meditation, movement and drawing. Reflection on prior and the 'here and now' experiences provides the basis for insights and change. The experiential techniques foster empathy, risk-taking, feedback and constructive conflict resolution.

An important aim is to learn personal communication to develop authentic self-expression, empathy-taking and openness to the feelings, emotions and attitudes both within oneself and others. Experiential learning is a way of enhancing the individual's self-awareness, self-understanding and personal effectiveness. These properties are key elements for the development of autonomy.

2.2.5 Reflection and motivation in experiential learning

Experiential learning is centrally concerned with the role of experience and reflection in learning which is understood as the process of extracting personal meanings from experience through reflection. Transformative learning takes place when an individual revises his or her beliefs, assumptions or expectations into qualitatively new ways of seeing the world. The process is emancipatory in the sense that the individual feels free from forces that have constrained his or her options or have been taken for granted or seen as beyond control. Critical reflection is a key to learning from experience. A transformative learning experience requires that the learner acts on the new understandings (cf. Kaikkonen, this volume).

Learning is potentially threatening for the individual as it means entering into an unknown territory entailing the risk of failure. It is therefore important to ask also *why learning fails to take place, what kind of factors may impede and block learning.* Part of the factors are *inside the learner.* They depend on the learner's personal beliefs, assumptions and expectations. Low expectations, unfavourable comparisons with others and the task, fears, anxieties and negative self-attributions (like 'I'm no good at all') may cause the learner to slip into helplessness, withdraw from learning opportunities and give up the attempt, feeling discouraged. The energy needed for learning is taken up by self-reservations, doubts and the feelings of being confused. The learner loses his interest and curiosity for learning and lowers his expectations accordingly (see the notion of 'self-fulfilling prophecies', discussed above).

Learning is also a question of the *quality of the learning tasks.* For Rogers (1975), there is a continuum from meaningless to significant, meaningful learning tasks. The former end of the continuum refers to learning that has little or no personal meaning and does not involve the learner's feelings. The latter end of the continuum, on the other hand, is characterised by personal involvement, use of different sensory channels, a sense of self-initiation and discovery, and a tendency towards self-assessment by the learner. The essence of such learning is personal meaning (see Kaikkonen; Jaatinen; Lehtovaara, in this volume).

Similar ideas have been elaborated with reference to the notion of *control theory* by William Glasser (1986; 1990). The concept refers to the idea that human behaviour can be understood as an attempt to act so as to satisfy certain needs. In addition to satisfying the basic physiological needs, human behaviour is orientated to fulfilling the higher-order needs of love, belonging, power, fun and freedom. Human behaviour arises from stimuli within the individual. The individual acts, he does not react. This view is consequently in sharp contrast to the behaviourist theory which assumed that human behaviour is caused by external stimuli.

Learning can be impeded and blocked by the *peer culture in the social contexts and processes* of learning. Learners will find school motivating to the extent that it satisfies their needs. Satisfying work gives them feelings of belonging, sharing, power, importance and freedom regarding what to do, and it is also fun. *If they feel no belonging to school and no sense of commitment, caring and concern, they lose their interest in learning.* Discipline problems are less likely to occur in classes in which learners' needs are satisfied and where they have a sense of importance allowing them to feel accepted and significant. This suggests that school learning needs to be structured in a way that fosters learner commitment and is need-fulfilling for them. In such an environment it is also safe to take risks and make mistakes without feeling embarrassed or threatened by the peers (Glasser 1986; 1990).

Building a *community of learners* is promoted by the use of *cooperative learning* techniques. Cooperative learning teams provide an effective context for the development of belonging and new understandings. Learner talk can be harnessed to the exploration of dawning understandings and new learnings. At its best it can produce something quite different from traditional classroom discourse. In an affirming small group, learners feel free to talk in provisional, exploratory ways. They speak tentatively, trying out their ideas on each other. As there is no need to defend opinions or pretend certainties that are not felt, the mode of learner discourse can be one of 'perhaps'. Learners can voice uncertainties and try out rudimentary ideas (Salmon 1988; Kohonen 1992a). Such discourse is dialogue, a conscious effort to build new understandings together in an effort to find agreements and discover different syntheses of viewpoints (Lehtovaara, in this volume).

The cooperative learning teams are heterogeneous and consist of 2–4 members, chosen by the teacher after a careful consideration. The teams are responsible for learning the tasks together, helping each other. Learners are encouraged to explain ideas or skills to one another, each member being an active participant and an important resource person for the whole team. The discussions are beneficial for all: faster learners consolidate their own understanding of issues at hand when explaining them to slower learners. They engage in cognitive elaboration that enhances their own understanding. Similarly, slower learners benefit from peer tutoring by their mates who may have just passed the stage of understanding themselves and have the memory of discovery still fresh and alive in their minds. Sometimes learners seem to be more able to translate the teacher's explanations into a 'kid language' which is easier for their team mates to understand, being involved in the experience and sharing the same world picture.

An important advantage of heterogeneous learning teams is that they can be facilitated to work independently to an increasing extent, with learners helping each other. Thus valuable teacher time is released for individual or group tutoring, for observing learning in action and gathering information about individual learners and groups. In an important sense teaching is also a matter of professional observing of how students learn. Observation gives data about learner progress which the teacher can use as a basis for planning further instructional actions and interventions (Kohonen 1992a; Cohen 1994; Sharan 1994).

The notion of *ownership of learning* is a useful way of discussing learning from a number of perspectives. As a political term ownership refers to the *power relationships between teachers and learners.* In terms of the interest of knowledge, ownership refers to the ways in which learners make sense of their experiences and the world around them. *Meaningful learning requires that learners are facilitated to construct and interpret their own learning.* At an emotional level, ownership poses the question of who 'owns' the learning in terms of the right and responsibility for making the decisions about learning. It is a question of the extent to which learners feel that they have an element of choice, control and initiative. The three curriculum positions discussed above suggest varying degrees of balance between teacher and learner ownership, summarised in Table 2.4 (adapted from Collis and Dalton 1990).

However, learner ownership and independence should not be confused with the teacher withdrawing altogether from pedagogical decision-making in the class. *Developing responsible learning requires finding a careful balance between learner control and teacher support and feedback.* While too much control can stifle learner initiative, too little control denies learners the access to the support they need for their learning.

Table 2.4   Learner ownership in curriculum

Teacher ownership	Shared ownership	Learner ownership
• Strong teacher control: 'I decide what you do in this class'	• Shared control: 'Let's decide together how to proceed'	• Strong learner control: 'I make my own decisions'
• External control based on teacher authority	• Teacher encourages learner negotiation and helps them learn the appropriate skills	• Internal control by the learner, facilitated by the teacher
• Teachers see themselves as responsible for learning	• Shared responsibility through negotiation and learning contracts	• Learners see themselves as responsible for their own learning
• Encourages learner's dependence on the teacher	• Interactive, negotiable dependence, with more learner choices	• Learner independence, and responsible interdependence

For your reflection. Think of your own foreign language learning experiences in school in terms of the concept of ownership. (a) Can you recall instances in which you felt a strong personal ownership? (b) What happened in them? (c) What did you do and how did your teacher facilitate the process? (d) How might you provide similar experiences to your students as a teacher?

These considerations suggest important *qualities for the teacher* as a facilitator of experiential learning. The teacher needs to

- *establish and maintain collaborative, ethical norms in the learning situations* which reduce the negative effects on the learning atmosphere
- *recognise his or her own attitudes to learning and develop a reflective attitude,* modelling a collaborative learner and opening doors for personal growth
- *be able to tolerate ambiguity, uncertainty and conflicting feelings,* being ready to accept backsliding and mistakes in learning

Emphasis on the learning process is not, of course, a novelty in education. Good teachers have probably always realised the importance of the process for the outcomes of learning. Experiential learning theory, however, invites conscious attention to the importance of the learners' experiences, attitudes and feelings about their own learning (cf. Kaikkonen; Jaatinen; Lehtovaara, in this volume).

2.3   AWARENESS, AUTONOMY, AUTHENTICITY AND COHERENCE IN EXPERIENTIAL FOREIGN LANGUAGE EDUCATION

In this section I propose a theoretical framework of experiential foreign language education. I suggest the concept of coherence in experiential learning to link the notions of learner education, authentic assessment, teacher development and institutional culture.

2.3.1 Framework of experiential language education in context

My *first basic tenet* in the paradigm shift I am outlining in this chapter is that the *goal of autonomous language learning needs to be based on a broad experiential learning approach.* In terms of the conception of man, the learner is seen as a self-directed, intentional person who can be guided to develop his or her competences in three interrelated areas of knowledge, skills and awareness (Kohonen 1992b; 1996; 1997):

(1) *Personal awareness*: self-concept and personal identity, realistic self-esteem, self-direction and responsible autonomy
(2) *Process and situational awareness*: management of the learning process towards increasingly self-organised, negotiated language learning and self-assessment, including the necessary strategic and metacognitive knowledge and the self-reflective and interpersonal skills
(3) *Task awareness*: knowledge of language and intercultural communication: the meta-knowledge of language at the various levels of linguistic description, providing an unfolding 'map' of the whole language learning enterprise

My *second basic tenet* is that these components of learner development need to be accompanied by and consciously *linked to the teacher's professional growth* towards a critical and ethically based view of what it means to be a professional language teacher. Further, teacher development needs to be embedded in the context of a *purposeful staff development* towards a collegial institutional culture, connected with society developments at large.

Awareness, autonomy and authenticity in learner education

In addition to the intellectual capacities, school success depends to a large extent on the learner's *emotional intelligence*: being self-assured and motivated, being able to wait, following directions and concentrating on the task at hand, turning to teachers and school mates for help, and offering help to others. As noted above, learners need to develop the following kinds of capacities, all related to their emotional intelligence (Goleman 1995):

* *confidence*: sense of control and mastery of one's body, behaviour and the world
* *curiosity*: desire to find out about things
* *intentionality*: capacity to work with persistence and develop a sense of competence
* *self-control*: ability to modulate and control one's actions appropriately, developing a sense of inner control
* *relatedness*: ability to engage with others, developing a sense of empathy

- *communication*: ability to exchange ideas, feelings and experiences with others, developing trust in others
- *cooperation*: balancing one's needs with those of others in group situations

To develop these abilities, the teacher needs to facilitate learners to increase their self-understanding and awareness of themselves. A suitable metaphor for learner awareness might be the map and the terrain in orienteering. We need a map to guide our physical exercise, indicating where we need to go – and we must also be able to read and interpret the map with understanding. If there is a mismatch between the map and the terrain (e.g. due to a dated map) we must be able to recover from the information gap. We need to trust our interpretation of the terrain and be willing to explore the terrain and the map with an open mind. We must also be ready to change our interpretations as appropriate and be able to choose between alternative routes. Further, we must have the motivation, persistence and physical fitness to complete the task. Learner education addresses similar questions in facilitating a holistic learner growth.

1. Personal awareness develops in learning processes throughout the life cycle. The development can be facilitated in language education by a conscious design of the learning environment in a manner that fosters the learner's healthy personal growth. This is a question of developing a community in which the learner feels safe to explore the uncertainties involved in language learning. (See Jaatinen; Kaikkonen; and Lehtovaara, in this volume.)

Self-esteem refers to how a person feels and thinks about himself or herself. It is based on the appraisal of his or her past accomplishments, the evaluation of present actions, and on the perceptions of his or her ability to attain the goals set for the future. It basically means a feeling of self-worth. How a person feels about himself or herself affects how he or she lives. A healthy self-esteem means that the person appreciates his or her own worth, qualities and abilities in a realistic, but still basically positive way. Self-esteem affects learning in a variety of ways: how one relates to others, what kinds of risks one takes, how one tolerates uncertainty and anxiety, and to what extent one feels able and willing to assume responsibility for one's learning. Self-direction is based on intrinsic sources of motivation and growth (Kohonen 1992a; 1993).

A helpful framework to promote the learners' self-esteem is suggested by Reasoner and Dusa (1991), involving concrete learning materials. They discuss self-esteem in terms of the following five basic components: a sense of (1) *security*, (2) *belonging*, (3) *personal identity* (self-concept), (4) *purpose* and a sense of (5) *competence*.

Each component has an effect on the other ones. If a person generally feels safe, she is likely to feel closer to the others, and the feelings of belonging and connectedness increase her personal security. Similarly, getting support and realistic feedback has a positive impact on her personal identity. A positive self-concept allows the person to meet new challenges and set increasingly higher goals. Developing a sense of purpose in life helps her to become a more competent person. A person with a basically strong sense of

well being

competence is willing and able to take risks in language learning, rather than getting discouraged and withdrawing from the risky situations. She accepts mistakes and failures as an inherent part of learning, shares opinions and ideas, and cherishes her accomplishments and achievements (Kohonen 1993).

A teaching experiment. A few years ago we conducted a foreign language teaching experiment using the ideas of Reasoner and Dusa at the Teaching Practice School of the University of Tampere. We carried it through as an action research process extending over the academic year of 1991–92. The participating team of teachers divided the autumn and spring terms into five theme weeks according to the above five components. During these theme weeks, each of the elements of self-esteem was studied, discussed and practised consciously in two experimental foreign language classes (in English and Swedish), using cooperative learning techniques.

The findings indicated that a *conscious enhancement of learners' self-esteem can be integrated in foreign language learning in school.* This is a matter of both the contents to be studied and the learning processes. Relevant materials are available in existing textbooks to some extent, additional materials are readily available (such as Reasoner and Dusa 1991) for adaptation, and further tasks can, of course, be designed by the teachers themselves. The tasks need to combine the process and the personal experience. They need to be open-ended, leaving sufficient space for individual opinions and negotiations about different views.

We used, for example, tasks that involved shared decisions about the groundrules for classroom behaviour, justifying them as a negotiated process and agreeing upon a joint set of rules for the class. Further tasks invited learners to make action plans and set personal goals for themselves, and to evaluate their work during the term. Such tasks allowed learners to produce communicatively authentic and personal language texts, both spoken and written. The processes of completing the tasks involved the learners working together in small cooperative groups, with an explicit teaching of the social skills as necessary. A conscious work on such contents and processes increased the learners' awareness of themselves and the moral values in school to some extent (Kohonen 1993).

The learner's self-esteem and his view of himself as a person and language learner are important characteristics that correlate with successful foreign language learning. Language learning requires persistent efforts, an ability and courage to cope with the unknown and tolerate ambiguity. In a sense, the learner appears childish and makes a fool of himself when he makes mistakes. A person with a reasonably balanced self-concept can cope with these demands better. This point was already emphasised by Stern (1983), who notes that a person who is ready to accept with tolerance and patience the frustrations of ambiguity is in a better position to cope with them than a learner who feels frustrated in ambiguous situations.

Tolerance of ambiguity is necessary in foreign language learning which is bound to involve unpredictability and novelty because of the new linguistic and cultural system. New learnings and understandings are always potentially threatening. Learners with high self-esteem are less likely to feel threatened. They have the advantage of not fearing unfamiliar situations or rejection as much as those with higher anxiety levels. They are thus more willing to take risks and try new and unpredictable experiences. Cognitive factors are thus integrated with the affective elements in experiential learning (Kohonen 1992a,b; 1993; Horwitz 1996; Oxford 1996; Arnold 1998).

Autonomy is an elusive notion that is difficult to define. In the narrow sense it means the learners' right to choose the level of engagement appropriate to their own situations. As a personal property it means essentially the learner's capacity for detachment, critical reflection, decision-making and independent action. For autonomy to increase, the learner needs to develop a particular kind of psychological relation to the process and content of learning (Little 1991). With regard to the three paradigms in education discussed above, learner autonomy can be related to the *different interests of knowledge* on the learners' part (Benson 1997).

1. In terms of the technical interest of knowledge, autonomy means a technical ability to cope with the problems in communicative situations by using appropriate strategies and thus being able to manage on one's own. In this view language learning is reduced to a technical activity, subordinated to the goal of developing learning skills and applying them properly.

2. The practical interest of knowledge suggests a *psychological, innate capacity to self-direct one's own learning and take more responsibility for the decisions* about what contents to learn and how to monitor one's learning processes. The view of personal autonomy emphasises the sense of individual self-direction, developing and strengthening the confidence of the individual.

3. The emancipatory interest of knowledge suggests that learner autonomy grows as *learners become more critically aware of the social context of their learning and the constraints* involved in learning. They assume a *greater control over the contents and processes of their learning.* In this sense, I understand learner autonomy as basically an ethical and a political concept. It is part of the individual's moral growth and self-government to become a socially responsible person and citizen. *Being an autonomous person means respecting one's dignity as a moral person and valuing others by treating them with dignity.* An essence in human dignity is the notion of moral agency: being morally aware of one's conduct and its effect on others, and assuming an obligation to maintain and enhance human dignity through socially responsible conduct.

The perspectives suggest that *learners also come to language classes with different beliefs and assumptions of their role as language learners.* Based on their personal learning biographies and experiences, they have different notions about what is good language learning, how languages should be studied, what properties good language learners have, and how good they are themselves at language learning (Horwitz 1996; Oxford 1996; Jaatinen, in this volume). They are thus variously willing to be engaged in learning that poses demands on their own active role. While a number of students are comfortable with a responsible role as self-organised and autonomous learners, some prefer a more dependent role. They expect the teacher to give them the facts of the language and explain the mistakes directly rather than asking them to find them out for themselves. Teachers who work within the constructivist and critical paradigms thus need to be prepared to meet with suspicion and resistance from some of their students.

Consequently, in order to foster responsible learner autonomy, teachers need to teach their students to visualise for themselves the big picture of their whole foreign language learning enterprise. Students are encouraged to ask themselves the following kind of questions:

- What does it mean to be an intercultural communicator?
- How do I understand the concept of language for myself?
- What does the notion of communication mean to me?
- What kinds of smaller tasks does the big enterprise include?
- How are they related to each other in a systematic way?
- What beliefs do I have about myself as a language learner?
- How do I see my role as a member of the learning community?

Experiential learning challenges both language teachers and learners to work towards the emancipatory goal of language learning as learner education. In experiential learning *the teacher is a facilitator of learning, an organizer of learning opportunities, a resource person providing learners with feedback and encouragement, and a creator of the learning atmosphere and the learning space.* The relationship between teacher authority and the development of learner independence (and interdependence) is intriguing. It is different for learners who are at different stages of their personal growth. The essential question is how the teacher exercises his or her pedagogical power in the class.

The variety of learner beliefs and assumptions came up in our experiment of supporting the learners' self-esteem in foreign language learning (Kohonen 1993). A majority of the students found the open-ended group tasks and discussions satisfying and engaged in them responsibly, negotiating with each other. By the end of the school year (1991–92), there were clear signs of improved collaboration, which somewhat lessened competition and discipline problems. The results indicated that *autonomy and self-esteem can be supported consciously in language learning, using relevant contents and reflective learning processes.*

On the other hand, however, there were also some learners who felt bored about the group tasks and just disturbed the work of the others. A common attitude for these students seemed to be that language learning should take place without the learner having to make any big personal effort in order to learn. A number of learners seemed to think that they just sit in their groups and expect learning to happen and, if it did not happen, they could always blame the group, the subject, the tasks, or the teacher. A number of learners seemed to expect that it was the teacher's duty to teach the material to them by frontal instruction, and their role was one of being a recipient of the instruction. In other words they expected learning to be an easy way of getting the information in a digested form, rather than being involved in an active process of discovering and organising it for themselves. Their assumption of effective language learning was thus one of teacher-directed frontal instruction.

In our seminars with the participating teachers, we realised that self-esteem is a complicated phenomenon that depends on a number of factors. The children's feelings of security, self-acceptance and self-worth are profoundly shaped by their early childhood experiences in their families, by the quality of parenting they have been brought up with. Another source of influence is the friends and significant others outside school. The school certainly exercises a long exposure and direct influence over many years, both in terms of the learning experiences and social relations with the peers. However, it is not the only component in the young learner's life. It is thus understandable that the learner's attitudes, beliefs and social skills that have grown over the formative childhood years cannot be changed easily in school. If the efforts are made by just a few language teachers during a limited amount of curriculum time, the impact can remain rather small. Both learners and teachers need *time to work on their deep-rooted beliefs, expectations, attitudes and working habits.*

The big question is, then, *how to facilitate students to take an increasing charge of their learning and bring their full contribution to the work at hand.* This contribution entails taking responsibility both for their own and for the group's learning. The development of autonomy is thus a matter of both personal, social and moral education. Cooperative learning entails working responsibly together towards both individual goals (individual accountability) and group goals (positive interdependence in the group). This dual goal-orientation provides important pedagogical ways of promoting learner autonomy (Kohonen 1993; Sharan 1994).

Within the technical and practical views of autonomy, learners tend to accept established language teaching contents and methods as given. The critical view proposes emancipatory goals for language learning with respect to the decisions concerning the social context of learning, the power relationships in the class and the learning tasks. Learner autonomy can be promoted, and also impeded, by the ways in which the teacher makes these decisions. It is therefore important that *we as teachers clarify our own stance to the concept of autonomy and the pedagogical ways of dealing with it.* There are several ways of promoting greater learner independence (Dickinson 1992):

- encouraging learners to take a more independent attitude to their learning, thus legitimising independence as a learning goal
- providing them with opportunities to exercise greater independence in their learning
- convincing them that they are capable of assuming independence, by providing them successful experiences of doing so
- helping learners to develop their learning strategies to be better equipped to exercise their independence
- helping them to understand language as a system and develop their learning skills on their own, using reference books
- helping learners to understand more about language learning so that they have a greater awareness of what is involved in the process and how they can tackle the obstacles

Becoming increasingly skilful as a language learner is thus a question of educating students for more responsible learning, both alone and in different groups.

> *For your reflection.* Think of your own foreign language learning autobiography. (a) What instances can you recall of being an autonomous learner yourself? What kind of tasks or activities did you do (on your own or with somebody else)? (b) How did you feel about your learning? (c) How did your teacher help you to proceed? – (d) Can you identify autonomous learners in your own language classes now? (e) What do they seem to think of their role as language learners? (f) How might you facilitate their progress?

2. *Process awareness.* Raising the awareness of one's own learning and gaining an understanding of the individual and group processes involved is the second essential element in developing autonomous learning. Emphasis on the learning process calls attention to the following kinds of elements (Askew and Carnell 1998):

- explicit teaching of learning how to learn
- facilitating active learner participation and providing feedback
- developing understanding, constructing knowledge, making connections and taking control and action
- reflection on student role as a learner
- reflection on learning contents, processes and outcomes and on the context of learning
- group support for the individual; the group as a catalyst as well as a source for learning through a variety of perspectives
- learning about human relationships by practising them
- developing a feeling of social identity and belonging in the group, enhancing individual identity
- learning how to resolve conflicts and controversies arising in groups

Learner education involves knowledge about *strategies* of foreign language learning and language use. Strategies are problem-oriented, that is, learners utilize them to respond to an identified learning or communication need. Strategies are techniques of memory management used by learners in order to facilitate the storage, retention, recall and application of linguistic information. The element of a conscious choice and action is important in learning of strategies, distinguishing them from non-strategic processes. Strategies of language learning and language use thus constitute the actions which learners choose consciously in order to improve their foreign language skills.

At a higher level of abstraction, the metacognitive knowledge of learning helps learners to improve their ways of planning and organising their learning tasks and processes. While cognitive strategies are used to deal directly with incoming information, *metacognitive strategies* are used to regulate the various strategies of language learning and use. Recently Bachman and Palmer (1996) have conceived the well-known strategic competence as a set of metacognitive strategies which provide a cognitive management function in language use. The strategies are kinds of higher order executive processes and include the components of goal-setting, planning and assessment.

I find it interesting to note that the revised definition of metacognitive knowledge by Anita Wenden (1991) also includes the learner's knowledge or conceptions about language learning, entailing thus the *element of learner beliefs and assumptions as part of the learner's metacognitive knowledge.* This underscores the importance of working on the learner's autobiography and emotional intelligence as well as on the cognitive elements when enhancing metacognitive knowledge. A conscious teaching of these aspects and sharing the experiences in cooperative groups increases the learner's awareness of the processes. As I see it, then, this *'strategic' teaching also needs to involve an experiential learning element of personal and shared reflection and action,* accompanied by personal experiences and ways of conceptualising them. (See further in Bachman and Palmer 1996; Cohen 1998.)

Teaching reading strategies: a portfolio study. In a recent study of learning reading in ESL in the middle school (Smolen *et al.* 1995), ESL students were taught to assess their progress and identify specific weekly goals on small goal cards (index cards) every Monday morning. Establishing personal goals engaged them to make decisions about what to focus on during the week's time. The cards were on their desks to remind them of what they had chosen to accomplish. In addition to the goal cards they also had time planning sheets and daily learning logs to monitor the process. An explicit teaching of good reading strategies helped them to identify appropriate strategies in their reading, and when to use them. Discussions in cooperative teams helped them to classify their reading strategies (such as making predictions and confirming them) and focus on improving their performance, based on explicit strategies.

Learners were able to develop their metacognitive skills in analysing their reading behaviour. At the end of the week they wrote a reflective statement on the reverse side of the card describing how well they thought they had achieved their goals during the week. They used their time planning sheets and learning logs to negotiate with the teacher and to monitor their work. Each Friday they selected a sample of their work for inclusion in the showcase portfolio, with a reflective statement explaining why that piece was important for them and why they chose it for the portfolio. The reflections gave the teacher a window into her students' thinking and helped her to facilitate the processes, developing a partnership between the teacher and the students.

In a narrow sense, then, learning to learn means training learners for a limited set of learning strategies, language use strategies and metacognitive strategies. Experiential learning framework, however, suggests a broader goal orientation in terms of a conscious learner education. It means developing a motivation and commitment to continue learning and growing as a person throughout the life cycle. The learning tasks and processes are formative for learner development, providing the learner with contextualised feedback about who he or she is as a person.

3. Task awareness. An important part of foreign (and particularly second) language learning will obviously take place in informal contexts, outside the classroom settings. However, language classes still provide a powerful environment for learning. It allows language, communication and learning to be made explicit and discussed and explored together, with the teacher as a professional guide and organiser of the learning opportunities (Breen and Candlin 1981). The quality of this environment is a question of what learners do and how they are guided to work. As proposed by Candlin (1987), the teacher needs to pay conscious attention to the learning of

(1) *content*: what kind of tasks the learner works with, and
(2) *process*: how the learner is guided to work on them

Instructional decisions can be made so that they promote both the language learning aims and the educational goals for learning in general. This thinking combines, in fact, the *twin goals* of the learner-centred curriculum by facilitating language learners to develop:

(1) the language skills and attitudes, and
(2) a critical self-consciousness of their own role as active agents in the learning process, with an ability to assess their own progress, materials, activities and the learning arrangements (Nunan 1988)

The twin goal offers powerful pedagogical ways of developing language education. Developing foreign language and intercultural skills together with the goal of fostering active and independent learning requires attention to the following kind of task properties:

- how authentic and open-ended are the tasks?
- to what extent do the contents engage the emotions and imagination of the students?
- what opportunities are provided to develop the language needed to carry out and reflect on the tasks?
- to what extent are there problem-solving tasks and activities?
- what opportunities do learners have to reflect on and evaluate their progress and processes?
- do they have access to a variety of learning resources?

Using the metaphor of orienteering noted at the beginning of this section, students need a map of the *linguistic terrain* they are entering as language learners to be able to take charge of their orienteering task. The map needs to be gradually unfolding in terms of accuracy, having several scales from the broad atlas to a detailed street map. This awareness guides their work of putting together the different linguistic ingredients and elements in the language curriculum.

Becoming an autonomous language learner is a question of a conscious and ongoing reflection of the tasks, based on personal experiences of language use. Concrete experiences provide a shared point of reference for the reflection. Negotiating the curriculum contents and processes with the learners facilitates them to grasp the tasks for themselves. It is also necessary for them to see where they stand in relation to the goals and what progress they make in the goal direction. They need to see optional courses of action and make personal choices, taking responsibility for the decisions. Seeing options, making choices, reflecting on the consequences and making new action plans are essential elements for the development of autonomous language learning.

To use another metaphor, language learning can be seen as a long and demanding journey that the students are undertaking. Like any big journey, it needs careful preparation, knowledge and adjustments under way. To progress on their personal journeys, learners need to be involved in the process of planning their curriculum. This raises the concept of negotiated curriculum whereby the learners are actively engaged in the process of enacting the curriculum. Negotiation means bringing together the experiences and the intentions of the participants into a shared learning intent that is carried out and evaluated.

The process includes the following broad elements: (1) joint planning and negotiation, (2) setting the aims (teacher's and learner's intentions), (3) collaborative exploration (shared intent under the constraints), (4) achievements (core learning and products), and (5) evaluation (shared reflection). These elements are overlapping in practice and involve cyclical processes, but they can be discussed as stages (Boomer 1992):

(a) Preparatory unit design by the teacher – 'mapping the territory': the teacher makes the distinction between the core elements to be studied by everybody, and the optional elements for learner choices. The teacher might also consider the possibility of a learner-managed project as part of the unit completion requirements. She decides on the contents (learning materials) brought in by the teacher, and how to present them. *(b) Negotiating the tasks* – 'preparing for the journey': the teacher and the learners consider the task and the available resources together, working out what the learners already know and need to know. They plan the work in manageable stretches (e.g. weekly/ bi-weekly/ monthly action plans) and set the expectations (criteria for acceptable outcomes). They discuss together the responsibilities of the participants. *(c) Teaching and learning* – 'on the journey': the teacher presents the new knowledge and demonstrates the new skills. She arranges for resources and organises learning activities, answers questions and provides advice and guidance. *(d) Consolidating and documenting learning* – 'arriving at the (interim) destination': the learners present their products. The teacher acts as a critic, adviser and problem shooter, giving individual feedback to each learner. *(e) Evaluation* – 'reflecting on the journey': joint discussions and possible (formal) tests. The teacher facilitates learners to review their own work and set objectives for further action.

An action research experiment on negotiated learning. In a teaching experiment carried out in the Teaching Practice School of the University of Tampere, we used Boomer's model in the design of two foreign language units (in English and Swedish; Tervaoja and Tuukkanen 1995). The teachers wanted to explore how they could bring the negotiated curriculum to the grassroot level of their daily encounters with the students. The students were 9th graders in the Finnish comprehensive (lower secondary) school. The experiment consisted of teaching one unit in the spring term (some 35 lessons given daily during an intensive study period of seven weeks, from February to April).

The teachers chose the *core curriculum* with certain grammatical elements and textbook materials that were compulsory for all. In addition to this basic core they provided *optional texts* for individual choices. The students also made a *project work* as part of the unit requirements for which they could negotiate a topic of their own choice. We thus built varying degrees of learner choice among the tasks.

The teachers agreed on the working procedures and evaluation practices jointly with the learners. The basic texts were studied together as mainly frontal instruction, but in the optional contents the learners could proceed at their own pace in small groups with their class mates who had chosen the same texts. The teachers provided guidance regularly both personally and on separate sheets. The learners could listen to the audio tapes containing the texts independently when they wished. The teachers provided optional tasks and resource materials and were available for help and feedback. For the project work, they guided the learners to make a plan of their own, including time-tabling questions, cooperation in teams and the way of presenting the product to the whole class.

Unit evaluation consisted of the joint core unit test, a test on the optional texts studied, and the project work and other work samples, all documented in the learner portfolios. Learners were also instructed to carry out continuous self-assessment during the process, writing their observations in their diaries. A number of students were able to do this on their own, while some needed the teacher to remind them and give prompts and support. The teachers also discussed the learning contents and processes together with the class during the lessons and modified their pedagogical decisions on the basis of the comments. They guided learners to give feedback on their class mates' project works. They held a short personal portfolio conference with every learner at the end of the unit to negotiate the unit grade together, based on the learner's suggestion. The whole process was evaluated together after the unit completion.

The experiment showed that a negotiated curriculum is a possible way of redesigning work in language classes. The learners had great difficulties in identifying their aims in specific learning terms and they also had difficulties in linking their aims with the materials and techniques. Consequently they needed *a great deal of guidance and feedback by the teacher to organise their learning.* Some of them found the process quite difficult and expected a more direct teacher role, particularly in the teaching of the common core grammar. Students generally found it easier to make their own decisions about their working techniques (who to work with, how to proceed) than the contents. About half of the students expected the teacher to control that the homework assignments were done properly by all. The whole idea of responsible self-direction was quite difficult to accept for a number of students. This was obviously because the learners were not accustomed to planning their learning and working on their own. Giving the specific help, support and encouragement became a central element in the process for the teachers.

We discovered that the *essence of the whole experiment was how to support the idea of self-direction and ownership of learning.* This is primarily a question of justifying and legitimising the idea to the students and motivating them to assume increasing amounts of responsibility for themselves. The teacher needs to delegate some of her pedagogical power to the learners and help them to realise the importance of the idea for themselves. Secondly, the process needs to be facilitated with specific (and timely) *guidance and support,* tailored as far as possible to the varying learner needs. The process needs clear guidelines, agreements on the deadlines and a certain amount of firmness by the teacher, reminding learners and intervening as necessary. *The process also needs time and skill in sequencing learner responsibility as a gradual process, progressing in sufficiently small steps.*

The findings emphasise the *teacher's role as a significant resource for self-directed learning.* The teachers noticed that their role shifted towards becoming an observer, consultant and organiser of student learning. The process required a great deal of flexibility, sensitivity to learner needs, and tolerance of uncertainty when facing unanticipated and surprising situations. Preparatory work outside the classes was also increased. A central concern for the teachers was *how to learn to ask good, stimulating questions and give prompts and suggestions,* thereby *encouraging the students to proceed on their own.* The teachers felt that they had benefited from the experiment professionally, learning new skills of collaboration and learner guidance.

Negotiating the curriculum means deliberately inviting the learners to make a personal contribution to their language learning, so that they have a real investment both in the learning process and the outcomes. Negotiation also means making explicit the constraints in the learning context due to the curriculum framework with its goals. The elements that are compulsory in the curriculum are non-negotiable and everybody does them. In addition to this, the language curriculum needs to provide optional and open elements that give space for individually negotiated contents. *The actual journey of learning is the real curriculum experienced by the learner.* It entails the contents and processes of discovering the new language (Boomer 1992; van Lier 1996).

Quality of tasks and processes. Promoting learner autonomy is a complex process of designing the learning tasks and the learning environment so that learners have real opportunities to proceed from closed (or restricted) learning tasks structured by the teacher towards increasingly open-ended and communicatively meaningful tasks. The tasks have clearly less teacher structuring and control and thus provide more space for the learner's own engagement. There are several guidelines and taxonomies for the design of the language learning tasks on the dimensions of task openness and teacher control. (For a recent discussion on task-based language learning suggesting six types of tasks with interesting samples of the materials, see Willis 1996.)

Another kind of hierarchy of tasks is connected with the different interests of knowledge in the development of learner autonomy. Benson (1997) suggests the following areas of activity through which learner autonomy can proceed towards the critical (or political) engagement:

- authentic interaction with the target language users
- collaborative group work
- open-ended learning tasks
- learning about the language and the social contexts of its use
- exploration of societal and personal learning goals
- criticism of learning tasks and materials
- self-production of tasks and materials
- control over the management of learning
- control over the content of learning
- control over resources
- discussion and criticism of target language norms

These points offer different emphases for the teacher on the dimension towards an increasingly independent and critical orientation. *Fostering learner autonomy thus means encouraging learners to proceed from technical and psychological autonomy towards an increasingly critical position,* understanding language learning in its broader political context.

Leo van Lier (1996) discusses the development of language proficiency in terms of three successive, cyclical stages that involve certain *conditions* and yield certain learning *outcomes.* The process is fuelled by the dynamism of the *principles of awareness, autonomy and authenticity* and takes place in social interaction.

(1) Through the exposure-language to *language awareness.* At this initial stage the quality of the exposure is important for learning. It is determined by the characteristics of the language material and the interaction in the social setting. The learner needs to be receptive to the language data to develop a perception of language properties through attention-focusing.

(2) Through engagement in the learning process to *language autonomy,* developing a comprehension of the language as a system of communication. For the exposure-language to be comprehended and integrated in the learner's constructs as a personal *intake,* the learner needs to make an investment in the process and be engaged actively and meaningfully in it.

(3) Through a personal intake to *authenticity,* which entails proficient and creative communication. To develop a mastery (uptake) and creativity in the foreign language, the learner needs to be committed to the process, developing an intrinsic motivation to proceed.

There are thus a number of successive *conditions* for learning to proceed: learner receptivity, active participation, investment and commitment. It results in *learning outcomes* as a cyclic development from language perception, cognition and mastery to creativity. The end-result is language proficiency, which is still likely to be a proficiency-in-progress. The process needs to be designed and facilitated in terms of the characteristics of the exposure-language, the properties of learner, and the quality of the setting and social interaction in which the learner encounters the exposure-language and human otherness.

I want to emphasise the importance of considering the openness of the language learning tasks together with the quality of teacher structuring in the learning environment – in other words, examining the content and process variables at the same time. Teacher structuring is desirable in closed tasks where the emphasis is on accuracy and there is a right answer. However, a constraining way of teacher structuring can be even counter-productive in open tasks which call for learner creativity and involve higher-order thinking skills (such as reasoning, making inferences and judgements, considering alternatives, elaborating and justifying cases). In fact, to maximise learner interaction in small groups, it is beneficial to design tasks that are 'ill-formed', containing an element of ambiguity and the possibility of several justifiable solutions.

There is a tricky dilemma between the amount of teacher structuring and the quality of learner interaction, as pointed out by Elizabeth Cohen (1994: 22): 'If teachers do nothing to structure the level of interaction, they may well find that students stick to a most concrete mode of interaction. If they do too much to structure the interaction, they may prevent the students from thinking for themselves and thus gaining the benefits of the interaction.' For meaningful and productive interaction, learners need communicative space and a safe environment to explore the shared meanings through the language (Kaikkonen, in this volume).

> *For your reflection.* Review some current learning materials in a group that you are teaching in terms of the openness of the tasks. Think of the processes that you design in your class. (a) What do you notice about the learning space and environment that you provide for your students? (b) How might you wish to improve your language teaching practices?

Summary diagram. To summarise the discussion in this section, I propose the following holistic framework for experiential foreign language education (Figure 2.6).

To promote experiential language education we need to consider the learning processes at the levels of the individual learner and teacher, the student groups and teacher teams, the school organisation and the surrounding society. This entails redesigning the language teaching profession and reculturing the schools as collaborative work places.

As shown by the cyclic process in the middle of the diagram, experiential learning constitutes the reflective core orientation at each level. Intuitive experiences are grasped and made sense of through the prehension dimension in Kolb's model. This involves a tension between unconscious and conscious learning. The experience is transformed into personally meaningful learning through the transformation dimension, ranging from a detached reflective orientation to an action orientation. There is thus another tension on this dimension between the elements of reflective observation and active risk-taking. Both are necessary for the development of authenticity in language use.

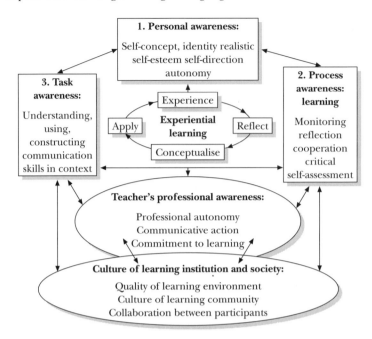

Figure 2.6   Experiential language education in the institutional context

Authenticity in experiential language learning calls attention to the role of evaluation in promoting learning. Authentic assessment provides new ways of fostering authentic language learning. It emphasises evaluation in the service of learning, in the first place for classroom purposes. I discuss this concept briefly in the following.

2.3.2   Developments in evaluation: authentic assessment

Authentic assessment refers to the procedures for evaluating learner perform-ance using activities and tasks that represent classroom goals, curricula and instruction in as realistic conditions of language use as possible. It emphasises the communicative meaningfulness of evaluation and the commitment to measure that which we value in education. It uses such forms of assessment that reflect student learning, achievement, motivation and attitudes on instruc-tionally relevant classroom activities. The use of self-assessment promotes the learner's direct involvement in learning and the integration of cognitive abilities with affective learning (Hart 1994; O'Malley and Valdez Pierce 1996; Kohonen 1997; 1999).

Authentic assessment includes communicative performance assessment, language portfolios and various forms of self-assessment by learners. The following summary provides a list of the basic types of authentic assessment in language learning (O'Malley and Valdez Pierce 1996):

- oral interviews (of learners by the teacher)
- story or text retelling (with listening or reading inputs)
- writing samples (with a variety of topics and registers)
- projects and exhibitions (presentation of a collaborative effort)
- experiments and demonstrations (with oral or written reports)
- constructed-response items (to open-ended questions)
- teacher observation (of learners' work in class, making notes)
- portfolios (focusing on learner progress over time)

Essential to the different forms of authentic assessment is that they (1) focus on important curriculum goals, (2) aim at enhancing individual competence, and (3) are carried out as an integral part of instruction.

Portfolio assessment is discussed briefly in the following as it combines several types of authentic assessment. A *portfolio* is defined as a *purposeful, selective collection of learner work and reflective self-assessment that is used to document progress and achievement over time with regard to specific criteria.* The language portfolio thus promotes the twin goals of the learner-centred curriculum noted by Nunan (1988): learning communication and developing a critical awareness of language learning. It serves two main functions in the total learning process:

- *pedagogic function*: a tool for self-organised language learning. Learners learn to collect authentic data of their own work, record it in suitable ways and reflect on their language learning biography
- *reporting function*: a tool for reporting language learning outcomes to teachers, institutions and other relevant stakeholders (parents, administrators, other educational institutions, employers, etc.)

As far as I can see, the *foremost purpose of the portfolio is the pedagogic function: enhancing student learning* and assisting learners to develop their learning skills. The documents in the learning portfolio are personal learner property, tied to the learner's life world. Their ownership belongs to the learner. Learners are taught to reflect their learning history through personal learning logs and diaries. Reflection ties together the documents in the portfolio and helps the learner to track the progress in his or her language learning (Wolf *et al.* 1991; Wiggins 1993; Hart 1994; Kohonen 1997; 1999; Gottlieb 1995; McNamara and Deane 1995).

A useful distinction is made between the learning portfolio and the showcase portfolio. The learner uses the *learning (working) portfolio* to store relevant, authentic documentation of language learning processes over time. In addition to the authentic documentation, learners are also guided to reflect on their learning and to assess their learning contents and processes. For self-assessment to be meaningful, it is essential that there is an element of learner choice regarding the learning process. This entails the idea of at least a partially open, negotiated curriculum, e.g. through learner-monitored project work, as discussed above. The learning portfolio constitutes an interface, as it were, between learning and evaluation. It helps learners to develop a reflective orientation to their learning and assess their own progress in language learning, aiming at increasingly autonomous learning.

The *showcase portfolio* is extracted from the learning portfolio for the purposes of reporting learning, e.g. for evaluation and grading, or for transition to another stage of schooling or a further education institution. A showcase portfolio can also be prepared for employment purposes. Depending on the purpose, it contains different elements to document learning and reflect on the choices (Gottlieb 1995; McNamara and Deane 1995; Kohonen 1997; 1999).

In a *portfolio experiment* in an upper secondary school in Finland (Pollari 1997), portfolios were used as a means for learners to negotiate their own syllabuses within a given framework in English. The contents of the six-week intensive course dealt with culture (Landeskunde) in English-speaking countries. A central goal in the project was to promote self-directed learning as part of a language course in English. The author made a distinction between personal empowerment and lingual empowerment. The former referred to learners' active role in, and control of, the process. The latter concept referred to the learners' ownership of their language knowledge and skills, taking charge of their ability to use the language for a variety of communicative purposes and functions in different contexts.

The learners had the freedom to make decisions concerning their own learning and thereby develop an ownership of their learning. Self-assessment was taught explicitly, and regular class conferences (about 15 lessons) were organised to supervise learner work. Each learner was expected to choose two or three pieces of work for their showcase portfolios, which were presented in the class. The pieces of portfolio work were expected to be diverse both in content and in form, including both oral and written documents. The products were evaluated holistically by the teacher for the grades on that particular course; no other language tests were used. The assessment criteria emphasised learner effort, responsibility, involvement and the ability to communicate meanings, regardless of language errors.

An analysis of the learner portfolios (about 100 learners) indicated that nearly 80 per cent of the students had taken an active and responsible learner role. They set their own goals and generally worked hard to reach them. They generally had a positive attitude to portfolios as a vehicle of their learning. Self-direction enhanced the meaningfulness of language learning for them. Feelings of personal satisfaction and accomplishment were evident in a number of learners' comments on their own work, as in the following (Pollari 1997: 48–9):

> . . . I enjoyed writing and doing the portfolio . . . I have already given myself a 10 [highest grade] from trying and crossing my limits. And the most important thing is that I am satisfied with my works and proud of them.

In the teacher's assessment, these students also learned English at least as much as on the earlier, more traditional courses. However, 14 students (all boys) did not assume an active role during the course and they also found the portfolios too distressing or too demanding, requiring too much work.

They considered teacher-directed work more effective and suitable for them (Pollari 1997).

The findings suggest that we need to be sensitive to the diversity of learner beliefs, assumptions and expectations, as discussed above. Facilitating autonomous language learning is a question of fostering learner development towards an increasing capacity for self-assessment, accepting that the learners are at different stages with regard to their autonomy. What is possible and stimulating for some learners may be less so for some others in the same group. However, if we wish to promote autonomous language learning in a serious way, we should offer (and justify) the possibility of authentic assessment for all learners and accept the diversity in learner readiness and motivation.

In the light of this discussion, then, authentic assessment provides new possibilities for enhancing learning and instruction. The following points summarise some of the possibilities:

- encouragement of complex reasoning skills (e.g. making judgements and considering evidence)
- focus on educationally and communicatively worthwhile tasks that promote learning skills
- multiple sources of data on learner progress over a period of time
- learners are treated as unique persons; learner diversity is recognised
- support for learner strengths, initiative and capacity for learning
- collaboration between learners, with an emphasis on social skills
- procedures and criteria are known to learners in advance
- learner guidance can be based on specific information
- intrinsic learning motivation and learner involvement are supported

While authentic assessment provides new possibilities for language evaluation, it also poses a number of problems. Learning documentation provides rich data about learning, but it is labour-intensive for the teacher to analyse thoughtfully in order to give accurate feedback to the learner. This is a problem particularly in classes with large numbers of students. Another problem of time and resources is connected with the learner guidance. To become more skilful in learning, students need a great deal of personal supervision and clear guidelines. As noted above, they may also resist the new practices, being accustomed to more traditional language tests. They certainly need time, guidance and encouragement to learn the skills of self-assessment. Common groundrules need to be negotiated for the work to be done, specifying learner responsibilities, support and the deadlines.

These views pose new challenges for the teacher's professional competence. There is an integral connection between language learning, teaching, evaluation and the teacher's professional growth. Working towards coherence in experiential language learning means investing in the teacher's professional development.

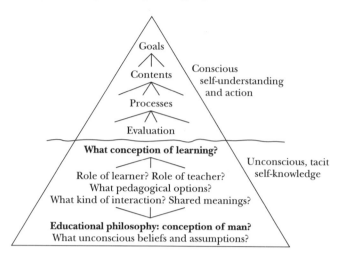

Figure 2.7   Conscious and unconscious teacher knowledge

2.3.3   Coherence in language learning through teacher development

Coherence in curriculum entails an effort towards a consciously designed balanced relationship between the learning experiences and the desired learning outcomes. It can be seen as the degree of consistency between what is said in public documents, what is done in actual practice in school, and how it is experienced by the participants. The concept can be illustrated by the metaphor of putting together a pile of jigsaw puzzle pieces. Anyone who has tried completing the puzzle knows how important it is to have a picture of the whole puzzle available. Otherwise fitting in the pieces can become an exercise of frustration. None of the pieces is important alone, but together they constitute the picture, and the completion process is meaningful intellectual work. When doing the puzzle, it is a good idea to form larger chunks of the pieces by attaching new pieces to partly completed sections. Looking at the big picture helps to see where the different pieces might fit in (Beane 1995).

Professional thinking is based on an understanding of the values and assumptions that underlie a given pedagogical approach. This includes an understanding of the theoretical principles that constitute the framework of the approach and how they manifest themselves as classroom activities and teaching techniques. Such understanding contains both tacit and conscious knowledge. Our tacit knowledge entails unconscious beliefs and assumptions that guide our action in fundamental ways. Our conscious understanding and awareness, and conscious action based on them, constitute as it were the tip of the iceberg of our pedagogical choices. I illustrate this distinction between unconscious and conscious teacher knowledge in Figure 2.7.

Teaching involves making choices and decisions all the time, both consciously and unconsciously, and under the pressure of frequently having to respond quickly (cf. Jaatinen, in this volume). The choices need to be based on an examination of one's own beliefs and views of learning and teaching, and an awareness of the possibilities and the likely consequences of the various options.

These views, then, underscore the *significance of the teacher in the choice of the teaching techniques and the ways of actually using them and relating to the students in language classes.* The teacher needs to clarify for herself her fundamental educational orientation, i.e. what constitutes 'good' language learning and teaching for her and to what extent this is in accordance with the educational goals and instructional aims as she understands them. This is a question of the *teacher's professional growth towards greater authenticity as an educator.*

Teacher development is thus an ongoing effort to improve one's professional understanding. Teachers need to engage in professional discourse with each other and support and challenge one another as colleagues. In so doing they support their own professional learning processes and learn to honour everybody's learning in school. By focusing on learners, they learn how to make explicit connections between their teaching and student learning, thereby getting new perspectives to their work. Working together teachers establish a culture of inquiry in their schools and learn to frame and reframe the issues. *For practices to change, the teacher beliefs and assumptions behind them need to change.* The goal is a greater professional authenticity (Grimmett 1996).

Pursuing this search for professional growth frequently involves teachers in a struggle because the conditions and settings in which teachers work pose obstacles for professionalism to obtain its rightful recognition. *The teacher's work is constrained by situational and social factors.* Frequently these factors offer teachers the technical curriculum implementor's role, rather than invite them to work towards an educational innovator's position. Dealing with such obstacles requires great commitment, effort and persistence. As Grimmett points out (1996: 303),

> It is a struggle for authenticity in which teachers attempt to discover both their true selves as responsible professionals and the new knowledge that enables them to see possibilities in teaching that will lead to a redefinition of classroom realities and roles and an enhancement of student learning. Ultimately, it is a struggle for teachers to find their motivational and inspiring forces of moral leadership in a constantly changing educational context.

The struggle for professionalism can be related to three kinds of *reward motives for teacher development,* corresponding to the three interests of knowledge discussed above. The *extrinsic motive* ('what is rewarded gets done') is *based on external incentives and control.* When they strive to be less controlled by extrinsic gains, they become more *personally involved* in their work and do *what they find relevant for themselves* ('what is rewarding gets done'). To become *moral agents,* however, teachers need to grasp the *ethical commitment as the basis for their work* ('what is good gets done'). This incentive derives from authentic motivation to enhance learning in the given context and set of circumstances, regardless of external rewards or self-oriented agendas: 'Authentic motivation, by contrast is essentially moral; it is caught up in a struggle to do what is necessary and of value, not just for the organisation nor just for oneself, but ultimately in the important interests of learners' (Grimmett 1996: 303).

2.3.4   Coherence through collegial school culture

Developing responsible, autonomous foreign language learners and interculturally competent language users is a matter that goes far beyond the traditional language teaching objectives emphasising communicative knowledge and skills. No single subject (such as a foreign language) alone can do much to promote the broad educational goals within the limited amount of curriculum time in school. It is a matter of the different subject teachers committing themselves to work together in order to improve the educational atmosphere of the whole school, *reculturing the school as a community of learners.*

Developing the teachers' personal and team skills, attitudes and beliefs entails a *shift from the traditional school culture based on teacher isolation towards a new, collegial school culture.* It involves professional collaboration among teachers and the various stakeholders of school, and between the learners and teachers in classes. Active, collaborative learning provides a way of integrating school work across the curriculum as a conscious effort towards a new school culture.

The *commitment of both learners and teachers to growth is an essential part of collegial school culture.* Involving learners to take responsibility for their own learning as well as for their community is a necessary condition for language teaching as learner education. We need to aim at creating a learning culture that supports the development of socially responsible learners. The teaching of the collaborative attitudes and interpersonal skills clearly emphasises the importance of teacher cooperation (Niemi and Kohonen 1995).

I see the struggle for authenticity as a moral quest that involves teachers in *redesigning their classes as revitalised places of learning and reculturing their schools as professional work places.* While these goals may seem demanding, I wish to conclude this chapter with a note of hope. Caring teachers may have to accept anxiety in their lives, but there is a two-way link between emotion and hope, as Michael Fullan (1997) points out. Understanding this link is a powerful insight. Hope is not a naive, sunny view of life. It is the capacity not to panic in tight situations, to find ways and resources of addressing difficult problems. Hopeful people have a greater capacity to deal with interpersonal discomfort and persist in what they wish to do. *Hope is a powerful resource in its own right, and it can be amplified in communities of teachers working together* and sharing the big picture of their professional efforts.

2.4   REFERENCES

Arnold J (ed.) (1999) *Affect in language learning.* Cambridge: CUP
Askew S and Carnell E (1998) *Transforming learning: individual and global change.* London: Cassell
Bachman L F and Palmer A S (1996) *Language testing in practice.* Oxford: OUP

Beane J A (1995) Conclusion: toward a coherent curriculum. In Beane J A (ed.) *Toward a coherent curriculum*. Alexandria, VA: ASCD, pp 170–6

Benson P (1997) Philosophy and politics of learner autonomy. In Benson P and Voller P (eds) *Autonomy & independence in language learning*. London: Longman, pp 18–34

Boomer G (1992) Curriculum composing and evaluating: an invitation to action research. In Boomer G, Lester N, Onore C and Cook J (eds) *Negotiating the curriculum. Educating for the 21st century*. London: The Falmer Press, pp 32–52

Breen M P and Candlin C N (1981) The essentials of a communicative curriculum in language teaching. *Applied Linguistics* 1(2): 89–112

Brown D (1994) *Principles of language learning and teaching*. 3rd edn. Englewood Cliffs, NJ: Prentice-Hall

Byram M (1996) Introduction: education for European citizenship. *Evaluation and Research in Education* 10(2–3): 61–7

Candlin C (1987) Towards task-based language learning. In Candlin C and Murphy D (eds) *Language learning tasks*. Englewood Cliffs, NJ: Prentice Hall, pp 5–22

Carr W and Kemmis S (1986) *Becoming critical: knowing through action research*. Victoria, Australia: Deakin University Press

Cochinaux P and de Woot P (1995) *Moving towards a learning society*. Brussels: CRE-ERT Forum Report on European Education

Cohen A (1998) *Strategies in learning and using a second language*. London: Longman

Cohen E (1994) Restructuring the classroom: conditions for productive small groups. *Review of Educational Research* 64(1): 1–35

Collis M and Dalton J (1990) *Becoming responsible learners*. Portsmouth, NH: Heinemann

Dewey J (1938) *Experience and education*. London: Collier Macmillan

Dickinson L (1992) *Learner training for language learning*. Dublin: Authentik

Doyé P (1996) Foreign language teaching and education for intercultural and international understanding. *Evaluation and Research in Education* 10(2–3): 104–12

Erikson E (1963) *Childhood and society*. 2nd ed. New York: Norton

Ferguson M (1982) *The Aquarian conspiracy*. London: Paladin

Fullan M (1996) The school as a learning organisation: distant dreams. In Ruohotie P and Grimmett P (eds) *Professional growth and development*. Vancouver, Canada: Career Education Center, pp 215–26

Fullan M (1997) Emotion and hope: constructive concepts for complex times. In Hargreaves A (ed.) *Rethinking educational change with heart and mind*. Alexandria, VA: ASCD, 1997 ASCD Yearbook, pp 216–33

Gardner H (1983) *Frames of mind: the theory of multiple intelligences*. New York: Basic Books

Gardner H (1993) *Multiple intelligences: theory in practice*. New York: Basic Books.

Glasser W (1986) *Control theory in the classroom*. New York: Harper & Row

Glasser W (1990) *The quality school*. New York: Harper Perennial

Goleman D (1995) *Emotional intelligence*. New York: Bantam Books

Goleman D (1998) *Working with emotional intelligence*. New York: Bantam Books

Gottlieb M (1995) Nurturing student learning through portfolios. *TESOL Journal* 5(1): 12–14

Grimmett P (1996) Teacher development as a struggle for authenticity: implications for educational leaders. In Ruohotie P and Grimmett P (eds) *Professional growth and development*. Vancouver, Canada: Career Education Centre, pp. 291–316

Guba E and Lincoln Y (1994) Competing paradigms in qualitative research. In Denzin N and Lincoln Y (eds) *Handbook of qualitative research*. London: Sage Publications, pp 105–17

Hart D (1994) *Authentic assessment: a handbook for educators.* New York: Addison-Wesley

Henry J (1989) Meaning and practice in experiential learning. In Warner Weil S and McGill I (eds) *Making sense of experiential learning.* Milton Keynes: Open University Press, pp 25–37

Horwitz E (1996) Student affective reactions and the teaching and learning of foreign languages. *International Journal of Educational Research* **23**(7): 573–9

Järvinen A, Kohonen V, Niemi H and Ojanen S (1995) Educating critical professionals. *Scandinavian Journal of Educational Research* **39**(2): 121–37

Keeton M and Tate P (eds) (1978) *New directions for experiential learning.* San Francisco, CA: Jossey-Bass

Kelly G (1955) *The psychology of personal constructs.* New York: Norton

Kemmis S (1995) Action research and communicative action. Invited address to a meeting of the Innovative Links Project, Melbourne, May 1995

Kohonen V (1987) *Towards experiential learning of elementary English. A theoretical outline of an English and Finnish teaching experiment in elementary learning.* Reports from the Department of Teacher Training in Tampere University A 8. Tampere: University of Tampere

Kohonen V (1992a) Experiential language learning: second language learning as cooperative learner education. In Nunan D (ed.) *Collaborative language learning and teaching.* Cambridge: CUP, pp 14–39

Kohonen V (1992b) Foreign language learning as learner education: facilitating self-direction in language learning. In North B (ed.) *Transparency and coherence in language learning in Europe.* Strasbourg: Council of Europe, pp 71–87

Kohonen V (1993) Language learning as learner education is also a question of school development. In Löfman L, Kurki-Suonio L, Pellinen S and Lehtonen J (eds) *The competent intercultural communicator.* Tampere: AFinLA Series of Publications 51, pp 267–87

Kohonen V (1996) Learning contents and processes in context: towards coherence in educational outcomes through teacher development. In Niemi H and Tirri K (eds) *Effectiveness of teacher education: new challenges and approaches to evaluation.* Reports from the Department of Teacher Education in Tampere University A 6. Tampere: University of Tampere, pp 63–84

Kohonen V (1999) Authentic assessment as an integration of language learning, teaching, evaluation and the teacher's professional growth. In Huhta A, Kohonen V, Kurki-Suonio L and Luoma S (eds) *Current developments and alternatives in language assessment. Proceedings of the LTRC96 in Tampere.* University of Jyväskylä: Centre for Applied Language Studies, pp 7–22

Kohonen V (1998) Authentic assessment in affective foreign language education. In Arnold J (ed.) *Affective language learning.* Cambridge: CUP, pp. 279–94

Kohonen V and Kaikkonen P (1996) Exploring new ways of inservice teacher education: an action research project. *European Journal of Intercultural Studies* **5**(3): 42–59

Kolb D (1984) *Experiential learning. Experience as the source of learning and development.* Englewood Cliffs, NJ: Prentice Hall

Kuhn T (1970) *The structure of scientific revolutions.* Chicago, IL: University of Chicago Press

Legutke M and Thomas H (1991) *Process and experience in language classroom.* London: Longman

Leithwood K (1986) *Planned educational change.* Toronto, Ontario: Ontario Institute for Studies in Education

Lewin K (1951) *Field theory in social sciences.* New York: Harper & Row
Little D (1991) *Learner autonomy. Definitions, issues and problems.* Dublin: Authentik
McNamara M and Deane D (1995) Self-assessment activities: toward autonomy in language learning. *TESOL Journal* 5(1): 17–21
Mezirow, J. (1996) Contemporary paradigms of learning. *Adult Education Quarterly* 46(3): 158–73
Miller J (1988) *The holistic curriculum.* Toronto, Ontario: OISE Press
Niemi H and Kohonen V (1995) *Towards new professionalism and active learning in teacher development: empirical findings on teacher education and induction.* Tampere: Reports from the Department of Teacher Education in Tampere University A2
Nunan D (1988) *The learner-centred curriculum.* Cambridge: CUP
O'Malley M and Valdez Pierce L (1996) *Authentic assessment for English language learners.* New York: Addison-Wesley
Oxford R (1996) When emotions meet (meta)cognition in language learning histories. *International Journal of Educational Research* 23(7): 581–94
Pollari P (1997) Could portfolio assessment empower EFL learners? In Huhta A, Kohonen V, Kurki-Suonio L and Luoma S (eds) *Current developments and alternatives in language assessment: proceedings of the LTRC 96 in Tampere.* University of Jyväskylä: Centre for Applied Language Studies, pp 37–54
Ranson S (1994) *Towards the learning society.* London: Cassell
Reasoner R and Dusa G (1991) *Building self-esteem in secondary schools.* Palo Alto, CA: Consulting Psychologists Press
Rogers C (1975) The interpersonal relationship in the facilitation of learning. In Read D and Simon S (eds) *Humanistic education sourcebook.* Englewood Cliffs, NJ: Prentice Hall, pp 3–19
Rosenthal R and Jacobson L (1968) *Pygmalion in the classroom.* New York: Holt, Rinehart and Winston
Salmon P (1988) *Psychology for teachers.* London: Hutchinson
Schön D (1987) *Educating the reflective practitioner.* San Francisco, CA: Jossey Bass
Sharan S (ed.) (1994) *Handbook of cooperative learning methods.* London: Greenwood Press
Sheils J (1996) The Council of Europe and language learning for European citizenship. *Evaluation and Research in Education* 10(2–3): 88–103
Smith D L and Lovat T J (1992) *Curriculum: action on reflection.* Wentworth Falls, NSW, Australia: Social Science Press
Smolen L, Newman C, Wathen T and Lee D (1995) Developing student self-assessment strategies. *TESOL Journal* 5(1): 22–6
Stern H H (1983) *Fundamental Concepts of Language Teaching.* Oxford: OUP
Strike K and Soltis J F (1992) *The ethics of teaching.* 2nd edn. New York: Teachers College Press
Tervaoja M and Tuukkanen R (1995) The teacher and the learner as curriculum developers and implementors (in Finnish). Unpublished minor graduate thesis, University of Tampere, Department of Teacher Education
Tom A (1992) In what sense does knowledge base determine the professional curriculum for teachers? In Ojanen S (ed.) *Nordic Teacher Training Congress: Challenges for Teacher's Profession in the 21st Century.* University of Joensuu: Research Reports of the Faculty of Education 44, pp 9–35
Tom A and Valli L (1990) Professional knowledge for teachers. In Houston R (ed.) *Handbook of research on teacher education.* New York: Macmillan, pp 373–92
van Lier L (1996) *Interaction in the language curriculum. Awareness, autonomy and authenticity.* London: Longman

Warner Weil S and McGill I (1989) A framework for making sense of experiential learning. In Warner Weil S and McGill I (eds) *Making sense of experiential learning.* Milton Keynes: Open University Press, pp 3–24

Wenden A (1991) *Learner strategies for learner autonomy.* New York: Prentice Hall

White Paper on education and training (1996) *Teaching and learning: towards the learning society.* European Commission, Luxembourg: Office for Official Publications of the European communities

Wiggins G (1993) *Assessing student performance.* San Francisco, CA: Jossey Bass

Willis J (1996) *A framework for task-based learning.* London: Longman

Wolf D, Bixby J, Glenn III J and Gardner H (1991) To use their minds well: investigating new forms of student assessment. In Grant G (ed.) *Review of Research in Education* (Vol. 17). Washington DC: American Educational Research Association, pp 31–74

Wringe C (1996) The role of foreign language learning in education for European citizenship. *Evaluation and Research in Education* **10**(2–3): 68–77

Chapter 3

Intercultural learning through foreign language education

Pauli Kaikkonen

3.1 TOWARDS INTERCULTURAL FOREIGN LANGUAGE LEARNING

3.1.1 Linguistics and foreign language teaching

The widening scope of linguistic research has been accompanied by significant developments in foreign language teaching, with a shift in emphasis from linguistic competence towards broader definitions of communicative competence.

The communicative approach to foreign language teaching, based on the concept of communicative competence (Austin 1962; Searle 1969; Hymes 1972; Habermas 1971), brought into focus the importance of communication skills. The goal of language study included both receptive and productive language skills. The learners had to be able to understand and produce the language, both oral and written. But it is important to note that foreign language study was, however, still strictly directed by textbooks, which in a way took the place of the curriculum. Foreign language education still neglected the learner's point of view. The starting point was the language and the analysis of how the language is used.

To be sure, sociolinguists have also drawn attention to the social character of language and to cultural background; but this knowledge has often been simplified to the teaching and study of stereotyped images of the behaviour of people in the target culture. Moreover, sociocultural and geographical information has often been introduced at times when the teacher deems that the concentration of students is not good enough for studying grammar, texts, vocabulary or pronunciation, with the result that culture-orientated study is shrunk into a fill-in programme in the late afternoon, just before the weekend, or at the end of term. In general, language teaching pedagogy has tended to concern itself exclusively with the picture of language provided by linguistics and linguistic research. Indeed, it can even be seen as harmful to foreign language learning that linguistics did not pay sufficient attention to calls for a wider definition of language, such as that made by Eco (1976). Instead, it continued to see language only in terms of the communication systems traditionally identified – the spoken and written forms. Non-verbal communication, for example, had practically no place in foreign language teaching despite the new emphasis on communication function.

If we think for example about Habermas's view of communicative competence (cf. Kaikkonen 1991) and his definition of language, we must conclude that foreign language teaching has preferred first and foremost the elements which refer to the external side of communication. Factors arising from within the learners themselves and their sociocultural interaction were not taken sufficiently into consideration because this was perceived as too difficult. The objective paradigm of linguistics still held sway. Similarly, as regards theories of learning, learner qualities were considered only if they could be measured in cognitive ways, so that the emphasis was on developing cognitive models of learning, researching the mind, its capacity and information processing, researching cognitive learning strategies, styles and techniques.

3.1.2   The intercultural and the holistic approach

The learning of a foreign language depends essentially on its starting point, the learner's basic culture. Several researchers have emphasized that the learning of a foreign language means different things for a Frenchman, a German, an Englishman, a Chinese, a Finn, a Brazilian or a Senegalese (cf. Neuner and Hunfeld 1993). The learner's basic culture determines what kind of primary goals are set for foreign language teaching. A culture which generally sets great store by the written word will not primarily value the spoken form in foreign language learning. Conversely, a society which values individual oral communication ability will see spoken fluency as the principal goal of foreign language learning. In addition to these goals set by society, the goals of foreign language education, especially the goals of primary teaching, have to be considered from the learner's point of view. We have to examine first what the learner's particular cultural background holds important and in high esteem, especially in elementary learning.

The communicative approach in foreign language teaching proceeded from the starting point that oral communication has primacy in human interaction. It was logical enough to concentrate on typical communicative situations and skills, and on basic phrases used in everyday life. However, while the shift of focus in foreign language teaching on to communication was necessary and proper, the ways in which textbooks and workbooks were designed in many countries oversimplified the situation. Often, the foreign language was taught for communication regardless of the learners' basic culture.

The communicative approach has also been criticized for being too sterile: the common communicative situations dealt with are commonplace, the textbook vocabulary chosen by frequency of use, the language typically studied through written dialogues and so on. Equally, in spite of the clearly communicative goals, foreign language learning is guided by grammar learning, and the texts are constructed from the point of grammar progression. Authentic use of language, often expressed as being an important goal, fails to materialise in the textbooks. As a result of 'cleaned' language and standardised communication use, the foreign language learned may become like a lingua franca which does not have the typical characteristics of a language with a cultural background any more, such as the English spoken in Great Britain or the USA. Christ (1991) calls this kind of language without national cultural background 'help language' and asks whether foreign language teaching is doing learners a favour by teaching them a language with a limited authenticity.

The goal of foreign language teaching is that the learner learns to use a foreign language for communication with other people. In recent years there have been increasing demands that the foreign language speaker should have an intercultural communication ability. The scope of foreign language education is thus widened to include the cultural background of the foreign language in order that one learns to communicate in a culturally appropriate and acceptable way. The communication goal can be described as extended, and foreign language teaching aims at taking into account non-verbal communication in addition to the traditional verbal communication. This means, in particular, that the learner should be able to note and understand how

- gestures
- facial expressions
- body language
- signals arising out of clothing, hygiene, hairstyles and other fashion styles, etc., and
- symbols specific to a particular culture, such as the use of wedding rings, finger signs, etc.

transmit information between people.

The extended communicative approach to foreign language teaching also embraces such issues as how people express or conceal their feelings and how near it is possible to come to the communication partner without violating his or her space. True, violations of this kind in intercultural communication are often forgiven of foreigners, especially if they do not speak the common communication language as their mother tongue. Nevertheless, it is useful if the communication radius of the foreign language learner can be widened. The focus of foreign language teaching is thus transferred to foreign culture education.

The concept of intercultural learning appears frequently in research literature. It is an interdisciplinary concept recognising that there are many differences between cultures and therefore many misunderstandings and other difficulties between people, despite which the people of these different cultures have to live together and interact. In foreign language education literature, the concept of intercultural learning has become a common one. On the one hand, there are increasing demands for intercultural learning to enrich foreign language teaching. On the other hand, there has been much discussion of the possibilities of using foreign language teaching to promote intercultural learning. Intercultural learning has been regarded as such an important concept that it has become a cross-curricular issue affecting many school subjects and has come to be seen as a part of learning in general.

Historically, we can see the different concepts of competence adopted by foreign language teaching as a continuous chain. At one stage, the goal was to develop linguistic competence. In the 1970s, the goal became communicative competence, which included linguistic competence. Since the late 1980s, the target has become intercultural competence, including naturally both linguistic and communicative competence.

Seen in this way, the task of foreign language education calls for a holistic approach, aiming at the development of this competence through a meaningful process of learning. The task is by no means easy. First of all, we must go beyond the traditional borders of linguistics, including applied linguistics, and move into a cross-disciplinary area. The holistic view of learning means that learners are involved in every learning situation with their whole personality: as knowing, feeling, thinking and acting individuals. Foreign language education thus needs to move in the direction of experiential learning, learning which involves the individual's unique personal experience (cf. Kohonen, in this volume). Intercultural learning relates to experiential learning in various ways, notably because the experiences we have are related to our culture(s) and represent culture-based learning. This culture-bound character of human beings sets many limitations and boundaries which are not simple to cross.

3.1.3 The shell of the native language and culture

Because our cultural background sets certain limits to our behaviour, and our mother tongue forms our conception of language, the learning of a foreign language and culture is significantly affected by our own culture and our mother tongue. It is not at all extravagant to say that the most important goal of foreign language education is to help learners grow out of the shell of their mother tongue and their own culture (Kaikkonen 1991). For it is clear that we live in a kind of cultural shell, even though we sometimes reach out to encounter other individuals, groups, and societies who behave in different, unusual ways. We have acquired, through the socialisation process in our own culture, a way of thinking, a way of shaping the world around us, a way of speaking, writing, listening, acting, etc. We have learned right from early childhood how to think of ourselves and to relate to others, especially to people who look or conduct themselves differently. Many preconceptions, stereotypes and prejudices about our own nature and the characteristics of foreigners are already in place before school age, formed by the child's own home and neighbourhood environment (cf. Schmitt 1989). Thus, when children begin to learn foreign languages at school – the age varying from country to country – they already have many preconceptions and fixed views about the world and their own language.

Our mother tongue is connected with our way of thinking. Even the reason why our language uses certain words and idioms to express certain meanings is related to the culture behind the language. Expressions used do not have their origin in emptiness, but are based on the experiences of a number of generations before us. Normally, users of the language are not conscious of the old cultural origins of words. Nevertheless, preferred words and expressions have certain associations, influencing the nature of the speaker's interaction with other people in a culturally typical way. Thus, culture has an influence on the way the individual thinks, communicates and distinguishes between the familiar and the foreign.

Why, for example, is the word 'citizen' in English *citizen*, in French *citoyen* and in Italian *cittadino*? And why is the same word in German *Bürger*, in Swedish *medborgare*, in Finnish *kansalainen*? English *citizen* basically refers to people living in a city (Italian *città*). Inhabitants of a city or town holding a certain social position were called citizens. The situation was similar in the case of German and Swedish citizens, too, but the term used has a special association: these citizens lived in walled cities or towns, whence the name Bürger (< German *Burg*, Swedish *borg* = *castle*). A particular characteristic of Swedish culture, the strong expression of the social interdependence of its citizens, is reflected in the prefix *med-* (English *co-*). The Finnish word *kansalainen* derived from the word *kansa* (= 'nation') means 'a member of a nation'. The word reflects the shared feeling at the time of the word's origin that there was a Finnish nation and that its people were essential parts of this nation. The word may indeed have a somewhat nationalistic emphasis.

> *For your consideration.* How does your own mother tongue (or any other languages you know well) express the meaning of the word *citizen* or other words like it? What does this reveal of the ways of thinking in the language concerned?

The different linguistic means used by different languages can be seen as essentially a part of the foreign culture. Foreign language teaching and learning – at least in the traditional school context – are influenced heavily by the learners' own linguistic and cultural ways of building sentences and constructing texts. Consequently, as far as grammar is concerned, the general task of foreign language education – to help learners grow out of the shell of their mother tongue and their own culture – is central. From the point of view of grammar the main goal of foreign language education is to develop a feel for the foreign language, so that they gradually learn how the foreign language combines words into sentences, sentences into bigger units, texts, etc. It is important to help learners notice how differently – or perhaps in some cases similarly – the foreign language functions in relation to their mother tongue. This requires

- sensitisation to diversity
- the ability to make conscious observations about both the native and the foreign language, behaviour and environment and
- a readiness to seek and gather information about linguistic and cultural standards in both cultures

3.1.4   Intercultural competence

In the research literature of the 1990s, there has been a clear demand for intercultural learning and education. This has been especially the case in the area of foreign language education. The concept of intercultural learning, however, is understood in very different ways. Röttger (1996) has summarised the use of intercultural learning in German pedagogical literature and says that the term seems to be vague, even disputed. This may be only natural because what is being investigated is a new foreign language pedagogy, with a clearly interdisciplinary point of view, and a far greater emphasis on subjectivity than in the foreign language education of the 1970s and 1980s.

Although there has been increasing interest in intercultural comparative studies among linguists, and intercultural learning is a concept often met in pedagogical literature, the concept of intercultural competence has rather come out of the sciences of persons and societies. The notion emphasises the diversity of human beings and considers individuals as knowing, feeling, thinking and social beings. The view of learning involved sees the human being as a multi-gifted and unique learner (cf., e.g., Gardner 1983; 1993 and Goleman 1995). As regards the intercultural element, such concepts as diversity, otherness, foreignness, own and foreign culture are terms that feature prominently in thinking on intercultural education and intercultural learning. The value of each culture and language is clearly recognized. Every language is somebody's mother tongue, and therefore as valuable as any other language. In this respect even the smallest language has the same value as widely used world languages.

The process in which human beings grow up differently from representatives of other cultures is bound up with the culture of origin in very important ways. All people learn a mother tongue and use it as a natural medium of verbal communication and self-evident interpreter of thoughts. Equally, they are used to communicating non-verbally and to considering things right, good or beautiful according to norms in their basic culture. Their environment constitutes a familiar world and gives them security. They are 'products' of their cultural background. Later, when they encounter foreignness, become familiar with a foreign language, learn new and other ways to communicate, visit foreign environments, and encounter other self-evident behaviours than their own, they start to cross the limits and boundaries of their own culture. They begin to grow out of the shell of their mother tongue and their own culture. This is a matter of the process that can be called the widening of one's picture of culture (cf. Kaikkonen 1995; 1996; 1997b; see also section 3.3.3 below). One important consideration is the individual's personal identity or personality. The idea of developing someone's personality raises ethical questions; a human being's personality is, at least according to western ways of thinking, in many respects inviolable, almost sacred, and must therefore be respected.

> *For your consideration.* How, then, are learners to reach out to become 'intercultural actors', people who do not cling frantically to their starting point – the

automatic, self-evident behaviours of the mother tongue and their own culture – but both strengthen their cultural identity and learn new information about foreign cultures, new languages and new ways of thinking?

If we are to guide children, young people and adults, too, so that they can encounter diversity, otherness and foreignness in a significant way, we have to consider what intercultural competence means and what it includes. Only then is it possible to set more accurate learning and teaching goals, to understand what qualities are worth developing in the pursuit of these goals, and to devise suitable tasks to train these qualities. The point of view has thus shifted from that of language learning to that of intercultural learning.

Lustig and Koester (1993; cf. also Kaikkonen 1996 and 1997a) suggest eight subgoals or subcompetences which contribute to the development of the learner's intercultural competence. This model includes the following behavioural dimensions of the good intercultural actor:

(1) the ability to show respect for a person of a different cultural background, i.e. the ability to express respect and positive regard for another person
(2) an appropriate interaction posture, meaning above all the ability to respond to others in descriptive, nonevaluative and nonjudgemental ways
(3) a new orientation to knowledge, especially to the terms people use to explain themselves and their world
(4) the all-important quality of empathy, the capacity to behave as if one understands the world as others do
(5) knowledge of task role behaviour, i.e. behaviours that involve the initiation of ideas in the context of group problem-solving activities
(6) similarly, knowledge of relational role behaviour, i.e. behaviours associated with interpersonal harmony and mediation
(7) the ability to manage interaction, requiring skills in regulating conversation and managing nonverbal communication
(8) last but not least, tolerance of ambiguity, i.e. the ability to react to new and ambiguous situations with little visible discomfort

When considering which of these subcompetences traditional foreign language school education has aimed to develop consciously, we find that foreign language teaching has often dealt with largely different kinds of goals. In fact, traditional foreign language teaching has hardly been able to promote significant intercultural learning. The goals of study were language and the fourfold division into communicative language skills: listening and reading, speaking and writing. Guidance on other important factors in communication and interaction has mostly been excluded from foreign language teaching. Cultural diversity and its influence on ways of thinking, intercultural communication and language use has seldom been efficiently dealt with.

Intercultural foreign language education focuses on learners as individuals and on their relation to languages and other individuals. This perspective differs from the traditional model of foreign language education. The idea of intercultural learning through foreign language education is based on treating the learner as a feeling, knowing, thinking and interacting person; working and studying in the classroom are no exception. Of course, school has been criticised since Seneca's day for ignoring real life. This criticism is still valid in our own day; but the concept of intercultural learning promises to provide one answer to demands for real life by opening up possibilities for intercultural encounters and communication.

Developing teaching and learning according to the aims of intercultural competence is rather complex and difficult, involving many personal qualities and the emotional and social life of the learners. In particular, showing respect to others, the capacity for empathy, and the tolerance of ambiguity as subcompetences of intercultural competence are very closely intertwined with personality. There are also some other factors dealing with the learner's emotions and social abilities. Moreover, different people, even when very young, have different starting points for growing as intercultural actors. None of this, however, argues against the case for making intercultural competence the goal of foreign language education.

3.2   DIVERSITY AND OTHERNESS – THE BASIC CONCEPTS OF INTERCULTURAL LEARNING

3.2.1   The need for intercultural learning

The need for intercultural learning arises from the basic fact that cultures are different, and these different cultures come into contact and communicate with each other. This is hardly a new situation, of course; it has been the case ever since human beings have existed. Encounters have not always been a matter of peaceful understanding and people learning from each other, but rather have often been experienced as dangerous and threatening. Diversity and otherness are not accepted, because they challenge the well-known and familiar.

Two commonly used terms when cultural encounters are discussed are internationalism and multinationalism. These basically refer to the nature of international affairs or any situation which involves the participation of representatives of different nations, of different people speaking different languages and with different cultural backgrounds. Understandably, intercultural learning is often identified with growth towards internationalism. But it is important to recognise that internationalism may have a different meaning from the political point of view than from the point of view of the individual.

Sociocultural thinking has been particularly affected by the historical development of nation states. Many societies became established as nation states relatively recently, with factors such as national language and culture playing a significant role. The resulting constellation of nation states into which the world is divided may be a relatively new situation, having mainly developed in the nineteenth and twentieth centuries, but defines commonly what we understand by internationalism. Internationalism has to do with such things as the political, commercial and exchange-of-information interests of states and the communities within them. As a result of the extensive intercourse that arises in maintaining relationships between states, all societies need members who are used to acting on the international stage, crossing easily from one country to another, understanding and speaking foreign languages fluently. This worldwide situation has increased the significance of intercultural communication. Small national cultures are often at a disadvantage in comparison with larger, more dominant cultures. Nations that communicate with one of the major languages take it for granted that it is their language that has to be used and learnt by other people. In smaller countries that have extensive international dealings, therefore, foreign languages are studied to a greater extent than in more dominant language cultures.

Different nations are international in different ways. Some nations have long traditions connected with minority cultures as an essential part of their identity. For such nations, mixing of cultures is a natural or readily recognised phenomenon. In fact, during their history all national cultures have involved intermingling in many different ways. The perspective of the individual human being, however, is mostly so short that it is difficult to perceive and understand the wide variety of origins from which national cultures have taken their form.

In the world of today, it is more and more important to consider interculturalism and language ability from the individual's point of view. Just as people's perspectives on their own culture vary, so too does the view of foreign languages and cultures vary from individual to individual. One person's perspective may be entirely professional; another's point of view may be that of the tourist. For the tourist, interculturalism is often more superficial, if there is no other dealing with foreign people except in the role of a tourist. Indeed, popular sun-worshipping tours can be described as travel to a country that does not really exist. Many on such tours travel together with fellow nationals and spend their time with people speaking their language, possibly participating in cultural activities that maintain national cultural stereotypes, and often eating in restaurants serving food they are familiar with from home. Intercultural encounters may thus be very superficial, if they count as intercultural at all.

There are also people in many countries who may never have been in contact with foreigners at all. To be sure, this group of people is dwindling all the time and may disappear entirely in industrial countries. One factor contributing to this development is educational policy. For example, foreign language education in schools in many countries has adopted a conscious commitment to promoting interculturalism among students and the understanding of foreign cultures and their special features. The foundations for intercultural learning in foreign language education have thus been laid.

Whatever the perspective of the individual, it is always different. People's attitudes to diversity, otherness and foreignness, which are essential elements of interculturalism, develop differently according to whether they live in an area with a large population made up of different basic cultures and languages, in a big city or in the countryside, and whether they have been conditioned to be afraid of foreigners or people experienced as strange and so on. In the development of interculturalism, a major concern are the fears, threats and doubts towards foreigners and foreign cultures currently experienced in many areas of the world. The feelings of the masses may be exploited for political purposes. Althaus and Mog (1992) state that where fear is the prevailing feeling, people tend to distance themselves from each other in intercultural encounters.

Clearly, intercultural learning is necessary today, although it can be seen to involve many complications. An attempt to chart the factors playing a role in the need for intercultural learning and education in the world of the late 1990s is presented in Figure 3.1.

Among the factors that bear on intercultural learning, the question of a person's own cultural identity and its strengthening is a very important one. Consciousness and self-esteem of one's own identity are a kind of foundation for intercultural learning. It is important to consider and clarify what makes an Australian an Australian, a Greek a Greek, a Finn a Finn or a Korean a Korean. Consideration of one's own cultural identity can be put to use in foreign language education, as this may help in the consideration of foreign cultural identities. Haarmann (1993) discusses national identity, and in particular what makes a German a German. He points out three aspects: (1) roots, (2) cultural mould and (3) perceptions and value judgements. The idea of roots basically has to do with the ethnic origins of one's parents, grandparents and ancestors. The individual's cultural mould is formed by the environment, especially by social contacts of the family and close relatives, by relationships to the neighbours, by language, by lifestyle and behaviour, by regional·traditions, by religion, or some other characteristic feature of the environment. Perceptions and value judgements are divided by

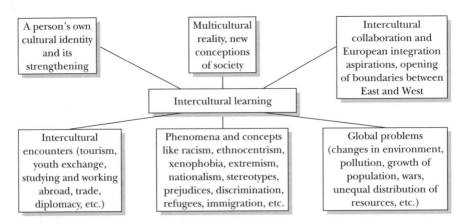

Figure 3.1   Reasons for intercultural learning

Haarmann into three groups: (1) perceptions of oneself and of one's own culture: self-understanding, view of the world, esteem for one's own culture, national pride; (2) perceptions of others outside one's own culture: classification of foreigners, attitudes to encounters with people of other nations; and (3) others' perceptions of one's own nation or culture, and projections of these views onto one's own self-understanding.

Awareness of the characteristic features of one's own culture develops naturally against the background of foreign language cultures. Learners notice gradually that the foreign language is the same kind of communication medium as their own mother tongue and that any ideas of the superior role of one's own culture are relative.

The need for intercultural learning also arises from the fact that the world around us is already quite multicultural. The picture of society in Europe, at least, is partly changing in this direction. It is possible, however, to observe opposing trends. While the European Union aspires towards a stable partnership of states and perhaps later a federal union like the USA, there is at the same time a trend towards new, small, nation states in the Balkans. We must therefore recognise differently directed aspirations in national policies. Also, with the dissolution of the old East–West divide we find ourselves in a new situation, where intercultural understanding and learning are more important than ever. In this changed situation languages play a very important role, for it is unrealistic to think that nations – even small nations – would not wish to hold on to their own languages and their rights to use them. The language policy of the European Union is a notable example of how this has been recognised.

In the 'global village' world of today, multinational connections abound. For example, economic changes in one part of the world are reflected immediately in other parts. There are probably very few countries which can act and work independently of others. Many companies earlier identified as belonging to a certain nation or state (e.g. General Motors, Philips, Benetton, Nokia) function today on a completely international basis. Due to this internationalisation labour forces have become more mobile than ever. This mobility of people and the multinational connections of companies clearly increase the need for intercultural learning.

When considering the need for, and the nature of, intercultural learning, a number of phenomena such as racism, xenophobia, discrimination, etc. need to be recognised and considered. The existence of such phenomena of course underlines the need for intercultural education. *Racism* is a particularly pervasive phenomenon; it needs to be recognised, as Lustig and Koester (1993) point out, following Taylor (1984), that 'racism can occur at three distinct levels: individual, institutional, and cultural'. It is also to be noted that the term racism, though strictly a concept associated purely with race, has sometimes become a broader concept with a range of meanings involving discrimination and inequality. In Finnish, at least, there is such a term as 'age racism', for example, meaning social discrimination on the basis of ageism.

Ethnocentrism has to do with one's own culture and the opinion that one's own culture is somehow especially better than other cultures. Lustig and Koester (1993) state that 'each nation now regards itself as the leader of civilisation, the best, the freest, and the wisest. All others are inferior. All cultures have a strong ethnocentric tendency, that is, the tendency to use the categories of one's own culture to evaluate the actions of others.' For example, products made in one's own country are considered better, more valuable or robust than foreign products.

> In the hotel that evening they began to quarrel, because Grooch wanted the French models while MacHeath advocated the English. 'We are in England, Grooch,' he reminded him angrily. 'Englishmen use English instruments! What would it be like if French products were given preference over here? That would be a fine state of affairs! You have no realization of the meaning of the word "patriotism". These instruments are devised by English brains, manufactured by English industry, and therefore good enough for Englishmen. I won't take anything else.'
> (Bertolt Brecht, *Threepenny Novel*)

It may be surprising to notice that most nations claim that they produce the cleanest food, make the best machines, and that their language is the most beautiful. But ideas of one's own excellence are as deep as prejudices towards diversity and foreignness. It is very important to understand that all people have prejudices with regard to their own and foreign cultures; the concept of *prejudice* is relevant to both. Mostly, prejudices are connected with foreignness, as Lustig and Koester (1993) point out by stating that prejudice refers to a negative reaction to other people based on a lack of experience or firsthand knowledge. According to de Haen (1994) prejudices are the conceptions existing in individuals that direct their acting, thinking and emotions towards another human being or group of human beings as if they were not unique persons at all, but faceless members of a negatively defined group of people.

The concept of *stereotype* is closely connected with that of prejudice. According to Scollon and Scollon (1995) it is an excessive generalisation of something that is one's own and something that is foreign. Lustig and Koester (1993) state that 'stereotyping is a selection process used to organise and simplify perceptions of others. Stereotypes are therefore a form of generalisation about some group of people'. Stereotypes of a nation in most cases develop outside the nation, but seem to be maintained very effectively by the nation itself. Italians are uncontrolled, Danes are indiscreet, Spaniards are arrogant, Brits cannot cook, Germans have no humour, Finns are not talkative, etc. are stereotypes which are maintained internationally, but are also fed by the nation itself, who accepts the common use of these stereotyped perceptions, uses them in jokes, and propagates them further in its own description of the nation's typical characteristics. It is typical of human beings' thinking to use categories and classifications such as stereotypes, but with regard to intercultural learning we have to consider how we are to deal with them.

In recent years there has been increasing discussion of the idea that people and nationalities are mixed. It may be reported, say, that nearly 10 per cent of the population in some countries are foreigners. However, it is not a simple matter to define who is a foreigner and who is not. The fact is that nearly all our ancestors may have been foreigners in some period of history, so great has been the mobility of tribes and nations over the past hundreds and thousands of years. The 'foreignness' of some individuals rather than others seems to be a function of the period of time concerned. We must keep this fact in mind when considering intercultural learning. The term foreigner comes up frequently in connection with such concepts as xenophobia, extremism, nationalism, immigration, asylum and refugee.

Human beings derive a significant part of their identity from the group and groups which they identify with. The shaping of identity and thereby a person's relationship with the familiar and the foreign is part of the process of socialisation. In this process fears and anxieties in the face of diversity and foreignness are entirely natural. The purpose of intercultural learning is to prevent these naturally existing feelings growing out of control by developing a healthy curiosity towards diversity. I think that curiosity is such a deeply rooted property in human beings that it ought to be possible to put it to the service of intercultural learning. This can be done most effectively by increasing the learners' opportunities for personal experience of diversity and foreignness and for reflecting on, analysing and evaluating one's own and other people's experiences. In this area foreign language education can do much; and there is indeed much to be done, for most foreign language teaching consists of the sterile studying of language systems and skills offering learners only very limited opportunities for authentic experience.

> *For your consideration.* How does your foreign language education promote your students' opportunities for authentic experience? How do you use your own and native speakers' experiences in your teaching?

3.2.2 Encountering foreignness: what makes foreign foreign?

Perhaps some of you, you young Swedish people I'm addressing this evening, will one day set out on travels to distant lands which you do not know. I can tell you that it will be a remarkable experience. You will discover to your astonishment not only that your surroundings change and everything appears strange and unknown, but that you yourselves also change before your own eyes in such a way that before long you will ask: 'Who am I? What am I like?'

As long as we are children at home, this question is of no importance; our whole environment gives us the answer, everyone shares the same view, and this shared view largely forms the basis for our own judgement of ourselves. As long as we remain in our native country, we are also in certain ways still at home; everyone we meet has approximately the same background, and if they do not know us we can nevertheless introduce ourselves to them without difficulty and tell them what they need to know in order to get to know us.

(Karen Blixen, *Collected Essays*)

What makes foreign foreign is an important question in intercultural learning. We all have our own perspectives we have grown up with in our process of socialisation. This process is unique for the individual, but shares similar properties across individuals. We are all born into a family, and this guides the direction of our development. The family's language and culture gives us a shared foundation with those people who have the same language and a similar cultural background. But we can justifiably say that within the same family the socialisation of children is different depending on when someone was born, whether that person is a boy or a girl, whether the first boy or the first girl, how old the parents are at the time of the birth and so on. We note thus that individuals who grow up in basically very similar circumstances nevertheless have a different sociocultural background. We indeed encounter many experiences of otherness in childhood. And yet we behave as if – and allow people to understand that – we are similar; possibly because if there are enough common factors and feelings of familiarity between people, there is also the feeling of security.

The feeling of foreignness can be aroused by all kinds of things around us; something is foreign if it is different from the familiar. From birth onwards, we come to perceive certain things as familiar; this is not only a cognitive process, but is a very deeply rooted experiential one. We acquire knowledge as feeling individuals. Our emotions play a very important role in this learning process. By going out of our homes and making observations about the surrounding world we encounter a great deal of foreignness. As we grow older we change much from what we were as children. We have always grown up as members of some community and society where there is a certain culture and where people speak a certain language. As part of our growth we acquire our mother tongue and the background culture. It builds a circle around us, like a protective shell. Intercultural learning, therefore, and foreign language education as part of it, means growing out of this protective shell (cf. above). It means a shift from the familiar towards the unfamiliar. Since it is evident that foreignness is often surprising, disconcerting and even frightening, we have good reason to consider what makes foreign foreign, to try and uncover those factors which especially arouse feelings of foreignness and otherness.

Let us first consider the role of nature in our experience. The kind of nature surrounding us is familiar, and forms our relationship to nature and the environment in general. Writers, as no doubt other artists, seem to be very sensitive to foreignness, and eager to describe the familiar.

> Over 225 pages we have said No, No out of sympathy and No out of love, No out of hate and No out of passion – and now for once we want to say Yes. Yes to the country and to the land of Germany. The land in which we were born and whose tongue we speak. Let the state go where it will; all that matters is that we love our country. Why this one – why not some other country? There are so many beautiful countries. Yes, but our heart does not speak there. Or when it does speak, it is in a different language. We address the ground in polite forms, we admire it, we treasure it – but it is not the same. There is no need for us to

sink to our knees before every patch of Germany and to lie: How beautiful! Yet there is something that is common to all regions of Germany – and each one of us experiences it in a different way. The heart may be uplifted in the mountains, where field and meadow overlook the little streets, on the shores of the mountain lake, where water, wood and rock scent the air, and where one can be alone. If that is one's native country, then there one hears its heartbeat. This has been so distorted in bad books, in even more stupid verse and in films that we are almost ashamed to say: I love my country.

(Kurt Tucholsky, Deutschland, Deutschland über alles)

In literature we can find many descriptions of how the familiar environment delights, and how the foreign environment surprises and intimidates.

> *Consider* in your mind for example what *forest* means for you. What kind of a personal relationship do you have to forest?

Our relationship to forest depends on our own home environment. For the individual who was born in a well-wooded area, forest can mean a home and a safe place into which he or she can go for shelter. For someone who has grown up in a place without forests, going into a forest can be a terrifying experience; likewise, for someone whose picture of forests is formed by the illustrations in Grimm's fairy tales. For people from certain cultures, it may well be impossible to understand or even imagine that some people go into the forest for a couple of days simply for relaxation and recreation.

The environment influences the individual: the inhabitant of a noisy city differs from the dweller of the wilderness who is used to silence. The environment has shaped him, his mentality, his way of thinking and communicating, his language. It follows that English *forest* does not mean the same as German *Wald*, Swedish *skog*, Italian *silva* or Finnish *metsä*. We can go through our whole environment finding phenomena which significantly influence what we do and do not experience as foreign. They are important factors for understanding the behaviour, communication and interaction of people from different cultures. Thus they are essential elements in the process of intercultural learning.

> *Consider* your own growing and living environment. What phenomena can you discover that are familiar and self-evident? What kinds of phenomena arouse feelings of foreignness in you?

All human beings undergo a socialisation process in the society into which they are born and in which they live. Our behaviour is always influenced by the values of the society, whether pluralistic or monistic. We are shaped by our culturally influenced perceptions about people (attitudes to and roles of children, old people, men and women, equality, social class, etc.); by our conceptions of knowledge, language, communication and interaction; our ways of living, residing, eating, drinking, getting dressed, moving around, etc.; by our national and social traditions; and by ideas connected with race, nation, tribe and so on. (These concepts have intentionally been listed separately, but they are in many ways integrated; separate phenomena are usually easier to consider, but we must also keep in mind the danger of over-simplifying them.) The point is that any of these factors may be the source of feelings of foreignness when we come into contact with people from other cultures.

We may at this point consider two phenomena which are in many respects culture-orientated, and which shape our perceptions of what is familiar and what is foreign: our *conception of space*, and our *conception of time*. Our conception of space is culture-related, depending as it does on how our ancestors have lived in the past. We can make a distinction between an *open conception of space and a closed conception of space*, which can be considered as polar opposites. Conceptions of space in different cultures are usually located clearly between these poles. Althaus and Mog (1992) mention that German experience of space is rather closed and American conception is considerably more open. According to them, the more closed German conception of space is largely attributable to the fact that the area that is now Germany consisted for a long period of time of small principalities, i.e. states which all had their own boundaries. People had the experience that moving from one place to another was not easy and simple. People were separated by boundaries; their own space was small. By contrast, in countries and areas in which there were no such problems, in North America for example, the conception of space was shaped in a different way. Immigrants settling and populating America were in a position to form a wider conception of space.

The conception of space influences how people live and make decisions, even on their everyday behaviour. In some countries large public spaces are preferred, in other countries everyone has their own small space and compartment. The door also plays a role with regard to the conception of space. In societies with an open conception of space the door invites you to go in, and is therefore mostly open. In societies with a closed conception of space, the task of the door is to close and separate, and the door is usually shut. We all have a certain conception of space arising from our own culture. Consequently, space-related conceptions and actions, communication, verbal behaviour, etc. that are different from our own cause feelings of foreignness in us.

> *For your consideration.* What space-related conceptions are there in your culture? Does the door, for example, invite you to enter, or is its function to separate and keep someone in or out?

Imprisonment, he says slowly, in a little soundproof room with no windows is, I've been told, particularly uncomfortable for somebody who grew up in Greenland . . . There are no prisons in Greenland. The greatest difference in the administration of the law in Copenhagen and in Nuuk is that in Greenland the punishment is more often a fine for offences which in Denmark would have resulted in imprisonment. The Greenlandic hell is not the European rocky landscape with pools of sulphur. The Greenlandic hell is the locked room. As I remember my childhood it seemed as though we were never indoors. Living in the same place for a long time was unthinkable for my mother.

(Peter Høeg, *Miss Smilla's Feeling for Snow*)

Althaus and Mog (1992) note that the closed German conception of space is evident in trains, for example, where the cars are traditionally divided into small compartments, resembling small 'states'. Every group of passengers has its own compartment. In some other countries, there used to be a two-way or three-way division of compartments primarily reflecting a socio-cultural class division only – the compartments themselves were rather large. Visiting different countries, it is possible to observe differing conceptions of space on camping sites, for example. In holiday periods and at other busy times these differences result in clashes between campers coming from different nations. Does it not reflect a more closed conception of space, if certain nationals have a clear tendency to mark off their own area on a common camping site with boundaries, as if it was their territory to which other visitors are not welcome without an invitation? And is it not a sign of a more open conception of space if people make no such territorial demands and accept new tents close to theirs? In any case, our conception of space has developed over a long period of time and is connected with many factors in everyday life, for example how we live, what kind of houses we build, how we relate to our neighbours, how we tolerate closed or open space, etc.

> Two passengers in a railway compartment. We know nothing of their history, their origin or their aims. They have made themselves comfortable, availing themselves of the folding tables, the coat hooks, and the luggage racks. On the unoccupied seats they have strewn newspapers, coats, handbags. The door opens, and in walk two new passengers. No greeting is offered. There is a distinct sense of reluctance to move, to clear the unoccupied seats, to share any of the storage space above the seats. At the same time the two original passengers, even though they do not know each other, behave with a peculiar solidarity. They put up a united front against the newcomers. It is their territory that is to be shared. Each new passenger is regarded as a trespasser. Their presumption is that of original inhabitants who assume that all the land is theirs. This is a view without rational justification, but seems all the more deeply rooted.
>
> (Hans-Magnus Enzensberger, *Die Große Wanderung*)

Our *conception of time* is likewise closely connected with what makes foreign foreign, with why certain ways of behaviour are considered by us as strange and foreign. It can reasonably be argued that people in western cultures have a rather similar conception of time in general. Our originally *cyclical conception of time* was based on the cycles of nature. This has changed into a *linear conception of time*. Our sense of time is no longer as strongly influenced by natural forces as before. We are no longer directly affected by heat or cold, for example, because our houses, cars, etc. are so well constructed. Neither do we depend on farming and other basic production of food, because we can import food that we are short of from countries with better agricultural conditions. We can thus easily bypass the cycles of nature.

We may consider our approach to time with the help of the calendar. Our calendar is basically for one year, but that limitation does not hinder us. We make plans for years to come, our calendar can have a number of exact times for meetings next year and in the year after that, and so on. The days, weeks, months and years of many westerners are organised according to an almost minute-by-minute timetable. They know exactly where they will be next year, on 21 May, at 3.30 pm! Time is either a linear progression in the past – a list of years with important events in history – or is thought of as a linear progression into the future. This western conception of time, the result particularly of industrialism and modernism, seems to be so dominant that it may well replace the earlier cyclic conception of time even on a global scale.

Despite this general trend, conceptions of time may differ between cultures and be the source of feelings of foreignness. For one thing, there are still many people in the world, even today, who may live with a more or less cyclic view of time. But even within the context of the prevailing western linear conception of time, there are different attitudes to time, and failure to understand how these attitudes inform the way people think, act and speak may, in intercultural encounters, lead to many kinds of misunderstandings, and even culture-based clashes and conflicts.

> The movie is supposed to start at 9 pm, but if there is one thing subject to change it is this hour. Even the vaguest formula for an appointment, as when one says 'around nine', is by comparison a term of utmost precision, for 'around nine' is over by half-past nine, when 'around ten' begins; this '9 pm', the unadorned precision with which it appears on the poster, is a snare and a delusion. The strange thing is that no one is in the least annoyed at the delay. 'When God made time', the Irish say, 'He made plenty of it.' There is no doubt that this saying is as much to the point as it is worth meditating on: if we imagine time to be a substance that has been given to us in order that we may settle our affairs here on earth, we have certainly been given enough, for there is always 'plenty of time'. The man who has no time is a monster, a fiend: he steals time from somewhere, secretes it. (How much time must have been wasted, how much must have been stolen, to make the unjustly famed military punctuality so proverbial: billions of stolen hours of time are the price for this prodigal kind of punctuality, not to mention the monsters of our day who have not time! They always seem to me like people with not enough skin . . .)
>
> (Heinrich Böll, *Irish Journal*)

Our relationship to time is inherent in culture. In our own culture, we are used to decisions connected with time. We seldom even notice them, so automatically do they function in our life. It is only natural, therefore, that we should transfer them to our behaviour in a foreign culture and to foreign language communication. We do not easily stop to think, for example, whether it is appropriate to visit someone exactly at the arranged time or a few minutes early or late. Misunderstandings of time on the part of foreigners are forgivable. They are also probably forgiven and accepted, but can also cause a number of surprising and irritating situations. An excellent example of an easily misunderstood concept of time is the Spanish *mañana*. At least to Finns, this basically suggests 'tomorrow'. But in Spanish communication it can refer to a much bigger and vaguer span of future time. It is also a conventional way of parting with a good feeling from somebody else – looking forward to a possible meeting sometime in the future, not necessarily the following day. It can even be a courtesy phrase to break a discussion, indicating that the proposed issue, question, agreement, etc. is in itself interesting and worth considering, and will be returned to later. The meaning of *mañana* thus becomes understandable only through a culture-based interpretation.

> *For your consideration.* How does your own culture understand the concept 'tomorrow'?

In western industrial countries, time is connected with certain established points, repeated rhythms and rituals which structure the daily use of time. Such common established points are for example annual vacations, festival days, week-ends, tea-breaks, lunch-time, regular TV viewing times (news, current affairs programmes, children's programmes, daily sports reviews, TV quizzes, etc.). Moreover, we have a number of hidden time-tables that make us do something on certain days, at certain hours. Becoming aware of such agendas may be eye-opening to us.

> *For your consideration.* Has your culture certain days or times when it is customary to do something? Is there, for example, a regular visiting day, a day for going out with the family, a laundry day, a shopping day, a car-washing day, etc.?

The conceptions of time and space are in many ways related to each other. Time-saving technology in modern transport, in particular, is bound to have affected our conceptions of space, which can hardly remain unchanged when we can move so rapidly from one country or continent to another. With such development human beings have naturally changed and will continue to change.

When we encounter people from other cultures and speak foreign languages, cultural differences are bound to cause a great deal of *verbal and nonverbal misunderstanding in communication*. Verbal misunderstandings are usually considered self-evident and readily clarified, but nonverbal communication and its culture-based characteristics, often involving deeply rooted emotions, may easily remain unnoticed and misunderstood.

The understanding of foreignness and otherness occurs through understanding one's own, familiar behaviour in the cultural context. Intercultural learning, therefore, always involves both sides: *identifying and reflecting on one's own behaviour*, and perceiving and understanding foreign behaviours. Aspects relating to anything other than verbal behaviour are often excluded from traditional foreign language teaching. This is hardly justified from the point of view of *intercultural competence* (cf. section 3.1.4 above). For the promotion of intercultural learning and communication, it is essential that there should be a more holistic and experiential approach to foreign language education.

3.3 CULTURE AND LANGUAGE

3.3.1 The concept of culture

> I stood for a moment on the scent, smelling this shrill and blood-raw music, sniffing the atmosphere of the hall angrily, and hankering after it a little too.

One half of this music, the melody, was all pomade and sugar and sentimental-
ity. The other half was savage, temperamental and vigorous. Yet the two went
artlessly well together and made a whole. It was the music of decline. There
must have been such music in Rome under the later emperors. Compared with
Bach and Mozart and real music it was, naturally, a miserable affair; but so
was all our art, all our thought, all our makeshift culture in comparison with
real culture. And this music had the merit of a great sincerity. Amiably and
unblushingly negroid, it had the mood of childlike happiness. There was something of the Negro in it, something of the American, who with all his strength
seems so boyishly fresh and childlike to us Europeans. Was Europe to become
the same? Was it on the way already? Were we, the old connoisseurs, the reverers
of Europe as it used to be, of genuine music and poetry as once they were,
nothing but a pig-headed minority of complicated neurotics who would be
forgotten or derided tomorrow? Was all that we called culture, spirit, soul, all
that we called beautiful and sacred, nothing but a ghost long dead, which only
a few fools like us still took for true and living? Had it perhaps indeed never
been true and living? Had all that we poor fools bothered our heads about
never been anything but a phantom?   (Hermann Hesse, *Steppenwolf*)

As culture is perhaps the most crucial concept in our research, it is necessary
to define how we have understood it. We have tried to see culture both from
the perspective of different disciplines and from the point of view of the
learner's everyday life. As a consequence we have come to a broad description of culture which combines both social and communicative aspects and
the theory of learning. Culture as a concept derives its force from the fact
that there is communication and interaction between individuals on the one
hand, and communities resulting from this activity on the other hand. Culture can in this way be defined both from the individual's and the community's point of view. Adopting this approach, we can describe culture as in
Figure 3.2, which shows the behaviour patterns resulting from interaction
and communication and the meanings which result from common norms
within a community. Communities that are organized in the form of a state
are called societies.

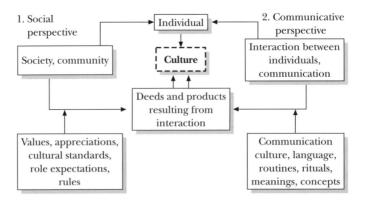

Figure 3.2 Culture: community, communication and individual

The concept of culture should be approached from two angles. First, there is the perspective of the theory of society which seeks explanation for cultural phenomena in the social order of society. This view is represented, among others, by Durkheim, Weber, Parsons, Habermas and Münch. Secondly, we should always study culture from the perspective of action and communication theories. Culture guides the individual's action through the interactive process and offers him an orientation in the form of background expectations and cognitive models. Phenomenology, ethnomethodology and cognitive anthropology represent this viewpoint. Concepts, meanings and communication are not just linguistic activity. They also result from a wider semiotisation which has many other components besides the verbal communication system (Loenhoff 1992). This view acknowledges the role of norms, rules, expectations, routines and ritualised behaviour. There are cultural standards of commonly accepted good behaviour within a community, applying to both verbal and nonverbal communication. In addition, prejudices, stereotypes and clichés, relating both to how people view their own culture and how foreigners see that culture, form a part of social reality.

Culture is learned largely through communication, in interaction with other people. Similarly, the individual also learns the fundamentals of culture such as language, cultural standards, behaviour routines and communication rituals in interaction with others within the community. It is a question of the communication strategies and behavioural norms that the members of a community have adopted, and which become automatised by their use. Because people act as members of society, culture also has its manifestations in behaviour and language use governed by social convention. It is clear that the interactive relationship between the individual, society, culture and language is so complex that it is difficult to divide it into parts.

The individual is always a member of a community or society and its subcommunity. In this community he has a need to interact and communicate with other members. All this goes to make up the kind of activity that we are here calling culture. It is defined by the two factors – community and the need for interaction. The situation gives rise to communication in many forms (including the everyday use of language, literature, art as a form of visual communication, etc.) and also to cultural institutions, such as home, family, school, church, etc. There would be no culture without the individual, communication and the community. Culture can thus be defined, in accordance with Nicklas (1991) and Kaikkonen (1991), as follows:

> Culture is a common agreement between the members of a community on the values, norms, rules, role expectations and meanings which guide the behaviour and communication of the members. Furthermore, it includes the deeds and products which result from the interaction between the members.

It is as a member of a community that the individual learns his culture. But even within the community, individuals experience the surrounding world differently. Their interpretation of the surrounding reality is different, even though they are representatives of the same community. This is why their learning, i.e. the process of making sense of and mastering their world, takes different forms and meanings. Therefore our starting point in foreign language education is the individual learner's previous knowledge, experience, beliefs and ideas. But the whole picture entails that learners are members of a special community and they have a special mother tongue. Their picture of the world is influenced by their own society, its cultural standards and language(s).

3.3.2 Widening the concept of language

Two factors motivate the view taken here of language as more than a linguistic code. One has to do with the relation of language and culture. According to Byram (1989), this relation is always psychological, sociological and political in nature. Human beings cannot help but express their cultural backgrounds in their use of language. The second concerns the nature of communication and interaction. Eco (1976) pointed out that those communication systems which do not operate through the verbal systems of speech or writing do not generally have the status of language because linguists do not accept them as belonging to language. It is because of this that they have almost automatically been excluded from foreign language teaching. But the view taken here is that it is not meaningful to separate verbal communication from other, non-verbal, forms of human interaction.

We can say that language achieves its significance ultimately in interaction. Meaning in language is jointly constructed by the participants in communication. In recent years conversational analysis has been an active and important area of linguistic research. Four general conclusions about the properties of language in communication have been drawn from this research (cf. Levinson 1990; Scollon and Scollon 1995):

(1) Language is ambiguous by nature
(2) Inferences have to be drawn from meaning
(3) Inferences tend to be fixed, not tentative
(4) Inferences are drawn very quickly

It is especially important to recognise that ambiguity is an inherent characteristic of language, and therefore part of all language use. If we ask someone for example *What time is it?*, the answer depends on the context in which the question is asked. There is a big difference between asking *What time is it?* of a stranger in the street and asking the same question of your spouse, say, when visiting friends. The answer depends totally on the context. The communication situation defines the meaning. When we communicate with people who are very different from us, it is difficult to know how to make inferences about what they mean. That is a very common situation when speaking a foreign language because we do not have the shared knowledge and cultural background necessary for our interpretation. Communication naturally works better if we share assumptions and knowledge of the culture and world. Scollon and Scollon (1995) state that there are two approaches which are useful to adopt in order to succeed in ambiguous intercultural communication situations:

(1) Increasing shared knowledge: knowing as much as possible about the people with whom we communicate, and about their culture
(2) Being prepared to deal with miscommunication: making the assumption that misunderstandings are certain to occur in intercultural communication

Both approaches are certainly important in intercultural encounters and for learning intercultural competence through foreign language learning. The latter approach is connected with the tolerance of ambiguity, which is an essential component in intercultural competence (cf. section 3.1.4 above). It is usually less discussed and taught in foreign language education; we are more used to teaching and transmitting various culture-based knowledge.

In normal communicative situations, the written and spoken language are only part of communication. The fact that school has traditionally concentrated on practising written and oral skills and on the instruments required for them (vocabulary, grammar, pronunciation and spelling) has set very concrete limits for foreign language teaching and learning in school. Such simplification has restricted opportunities for personally meaningful experiences in foreign language communication and has led to rather mechanical forms of practice. Although it is well understood that language is a far richer medium than the exercises done in school suggest, and that human communication involves more than verbal communication, there has been a lack of ways and ideas for improving foreign language education qualitatively. We can develop new and better study practices and a wider theoretical background to foreign language teaching and learning by looking closely at the connections between language and authentic communication.

Foreign language teaching has traditionally emphasised the prevailing view of communication as a verbal exercise. But there are a large number of nonverbal messages which human beings exchange. Gestures, facial expressions, body language, and various symbols and signals are the most common forms of nonverbal messages. In addition, there are a number of so-called paralinguistic phenomena (pitch and colour of voice, pauses, etc.) which are essential factors in communication. Especially body language, as the form of communication that is most independent of our will, needs serious consideration in foreign language education. How we use body language depends on our communication culture. Like verbal language, our body language is formed by the long history of our sociocultural behaviour. Our emotions are largely expressed by body language and paralinguistic means of communication. Sometimes body language messages are connected with culture-based taboos and easily lead to misunderstandings.

Human beings send signals in different ways, and we have to learn to read them. It is important to become sensitive to the role of non-verbal messages in communication. We send and receive these signals for example through our clothing, hairstyle, odour, our use of colours or other things we wear or use (badges, eyeglasses, hats, bikes, cars, etc.). Many signals have the value ·of symbols; they have developed into conventional forms of behaviour. An example of a sociocultural symbol is the use of the wedding ring, which varies from culture to culture. Similarly many gestures, for example various finger signs, have become symbols that are strongly culture-based. It is worth considering how finger signs are used outside the boundaries of one's own culture. Among paralinguistic phenomena, the use of pauses is particularly worth discussing. We need first to consider the meaning and uses of pauses in our own communicative behaviour and then turn to their uses in foreign language education. The use of pauses is related to the tolerance of silence.

> *For your consideration.* What nonverbal messages and ways of communicating can you identify in your own culture? Are they typical of your culture? Can you think of messages transformed into symbols in the culture you teach? What typical paralinguistic phenomena do you have in your own language culture?

Teaching nonverbal and verbal communication together offers opportunities for learning intercultural communication in such a way that learners participate in the process in a holistic way. This kind of practice requires tasks and behaviours which combine cognitive and affective processes and exploit the techniques of experiential learning. Nonverbal communication is of particular importance because *interpretation is usually based on the nonverbal message if there is a discrepancy between verbal and nonverbal information.* In one's own culture verbal and nonverbal communication are learned together. The reciprocal nature of the two communication systems is manifest in many old expressions and phrases, such as *cross your fingers, turn a blind eye to, do an about-face, get the boot* (= 'get fired'), etc. The close connection between verbal and nonverbal communication suggests that both of them have to be considered together in foreign language education.

3.3.3 Intercultural learning and foreign language education

Educational institutions in many countries make efforts to guide their students to an understanding of foreignness and dissimilarity in societies. The importance of peace education and international understanding at all levels of education and in all school subjects has long been recognised (cf. Byram and Zarate 1998). It is in this context that new concepts like *intercultural learning, intercultural education, intercultural understanding* and *interculturalism* have been developed. The concepts of intercultural learning and intercultural education are closely related to the pedagogical concepts concerning the recognition and understanding of what happens when different cultures come into contact in one way or another. The former concept refers primarily to learning, the latter to teaching processes. Paige (1994) notes that intercultural education differs from conventional approaches to education because it includes very personal behaviour and affective learning, self-reflection and direct experiences of cultural differences.

Intercultural learning has been interpreted variously in different national cultures. It may also mean different things within the same national culture. In multicultural countries with a number of cultural minorities (native minorities, other older ethnic groups, immigrants or refugees), *intercultural learning often aims at the integration of different cultures* and at improving their quality of life. In countries with a relatively homogeneous cultural background, *intercultural learning is principally concerned with the education of citizens towards internationalism or multiculturalism.* The concept 'intercultural learning' is a good one because of its explicit meaning of mutual or reciprocal understanding. Intercultural understanding always depends on the willingness and ability of all participants to make their best effort in an intercultural encounter.

Intercultural learning always has to deal with dissimilarity and foreignness. In intercultural encounters people have to tolerate foreign behaviour. Fortunately, however, human beings have a natural, built-in tendency to be orientated towards the future. People anticipate other people's behaviour wherever possible. This is manifest, for example, in the way people communicate in their mother tongue. They use totally automatised routines and rituals in their own communication (verbal and nonverbal), and understand with ease the routine discourse of other people of the same culture. The behaviour of their partners in interaction is thus largely predictable. However, any encounter also involves many chances of misunderstanding. Even representatives of the same national culture with the same language sometimes fail to understand the intentions of their communication partners. For this reason, intercultural learning is an important concept even within the same national community.

In all cultures, human growth towards the tolerance of ambiguity or the ability to cope with dissimilarity begins when the young child becomes aware of the family environment. But development towards becoming an interculturally competent person begins to take place when that person consciously begins to perceive and reflect on different behaviours and wants to learn more about them. As we express ourselves very much through the language we use, personal growth towards intercultural competence is not possible without encountering and learning a foreign language and the foreignness it entails. Personal contacts with a foreign culture and the study and use of the language of that culture are essential elements in intercultural learning.

In the process of intercultural learning, the learner constantly compares new experiences with old ones, new linguistic phenomena with those of his mother tongue, and new information with old information, etc. In other words, *intercultural learning is a process whereby the learner's picture of culture grows wider*, with the help of new information about the foreign culture and language. At the same time this increases the learner's consciousness of the special features of his own culture and language (Figure 3.3). Therefore, both the learner's basic culture and the foreign culture are important elements in foreign language education. In addition to both languages,

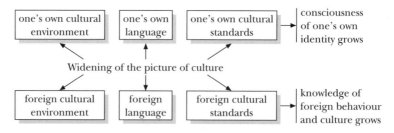

Figure 3.3 Widening the learner's picture of culture

all other elements of the learner's own and target culture need to be considered.

If the learning process can be directed so that the learner perceives behavioural and speech routines in foreign interaction and compares them with his own, this enables him to become conscious of his own behaviour. This consciousness in turn helps him to understand that his own behaviour may seem just as strange to the foreigner. In this way it is possible gradually to gain an understanding of things that are taken for granted in the foreigner's and in one's own behaviour.

In order to increase predictability, every culture has a well-developed set of mechanisms for relating to foreignness. Among these mechanisms are stereotypes relating to foreign cultures and foreignness. Since stereotypes are formed early in the child's development and are thus deeply rooted, it is important to take them seriously (Schmitt 1989). Understanding dissimilarity and foreignness presupposes that one is ready to problematise one's own stereotyped thinking. A consideration of stereotypes is thus a natural element in the process of intercultural learning and intercultural education.

Languages differ in nature in many respects. Traditionally, however, the differences between languages have been approached primarily through linguistic systems, such as pronunciation, vocabulary, or syntax. Thus, for example, vocabulary has been studied by contrasting the words of the foreign language with the meanings of the mother tongue. In such tasks learning has not gone beyond formal learning. Intercultural learning means, however, that the individual should learn to understand the intentions and expectations of the representative of a foreign culture. The learner should realise that any linguistic communication is just part of human communication which goes on all over the world, and that every language has elements which belong to the automatic, ritual and routine component of the native speaker's behaviour. It is these elements that learners should learn to analyse. In addition to this, they should gradually know how to express their own meanings and intentions in a foreign language. It makes little sense to limit foreign language learning simply to the study of the language system, for example, because we are dealing with a very complex learning process that is associated with social and communicative dimensions.

3.4 TOWARD CULTURE-BASED EXPERIENTIAL FOREIGN
      LANGUAGE EDUCATION

3.4.1 Curriculum development through teaching experiments

New curriculum thinking requires teachers to be ready to examine the theoretical underpinnings of their teaching critically and to be open to new perspectives. In this way their relationship to their work becomes more dynamic. *Conducting a teaching experiment is a good way to scrutinise well-established routines.* Such an experiment does not need to have the same goals as a traditional scientific experiment; it is enough for teachers to begin to consider their practices, aiming at a new approach to teaching. Teachers who dare to do this will be rewarded in many ways. This kind of spirit is very important in teaching and education, where we are working with human beings. But how is it possible to start an experiment and to benefit from other teachers' experiences?

Modern pedagogical literature maintains that teachers should be professionals who reflect on and investigate their work seriously and act ethically. Acting ethically in this context has to do with teachers' educational practices. Can teachers act ethically, indeed, if they are not willing to develop their work? Can teachers work ethically if they pursue their own goals, allowing their own preferences and prejudices to affect their teaching? Or if they are indifferent to the younger generation? Clearly, teachers are ethically required to develop themselves as personalities, educators and members of their work communities. In the context of foreign language education, this includes developing an understanding of the kind of holistic experience that foreign language learning involves for learners of different ages and backgrounds.

Teachers with an ethical orientation to their work are prepared to develop their work in new ways. We would like to encourage teachers to undertake small studies and experiments to research their existing practices. The word *research* might be off-putting here, since it is often so readily associated with the traditional quantitative orientation in educational research (cf. Kohonen, in this volume). Modern literature on school development, however, argues mostly in favour of school-based research approaches using mainly qualitative data. In these approaches, teachers relate to the development of their work professionally, critically and seriously, like researchers (cf. Altrichter, Posch and Somekh 1993).

When designing teaching experiments in schools, teachers create the foundation for permanent development in their own school curriculum. They discover that the curriculum is not a static model or a system created by researchers and educational planners outside the school, but rather a question of an ongoing thinking process relating to their own work and their own pupils in a dynamic way. The written curriculum thus comes to life, and develops year by year, becoming more and more satisfying to teachers and learners alike. The curriculum is best developed through the teacher's personal experiences and experiments in collaboration with colleagues and pupils. In foreign language education, it is particularly important to consider what practices can lead into intercultural communication and learning. Obviously, any teaching experiment needs to be based on the teachers' readiness to undertake the project.

3.4.2 Research project: 'Culture and foreign language education'

The teaching and research project entitled 'Culture and foreign language education', one of three large teaching experiments we have planned and conducted during the last ten years (Kaikkonen 1991; Kaikkonen 1993 and 1995; Kohonen and Kaikkonen 1996; Kaikkonen and Kohonen 1997), set out to explore

- how the students' picture of culture develops
- how culture-based teaching influences the students' foreign language communication abilities, the students' views of foreigners and foreign cultures and
- how culture-based teaching is connected with the students' abilities to encounter different people from different basic cultures

The teaching and research project was carried out in collaboration with the Department of Teacher Education at the University of Tampere and the Upper Secondary School *Tampereen normaalikoulu* (Kaikkonen 1993 and 1995). Students of 16–17 years of age studied German and French for two years with the cultural background of the language and its speakers being an integral part of their studies. The two-year programme consisting of five theme-oriented courses (of 38 lessons each) formed the curriculum for the study of language and culture.

The teaching experiment had the following common targets:

(1) Learners should deepen their knowledge of themselves and their cultural background, and learn to understand that because of background and world experiences a member of a foreign culture can be very different
(2) Learners should understand what multiculturalism and intercultural encounters entail, and how they are becoming 'intercultural actors'
(3) Learners should develop the ability to seek knowledge of a foreign language and culture autonomously
(4) Learners should learn to communicate in the foreign language so that they understand the foreigner's ways of thinking, and the foreigner understands their meanings as foreign language speakers

In a deep intercultural learning process the goal is that individuals aim at a constantly improving mutual understanding. The more the people involved differ as regards their cultural backgrounds, the more challenging is the encounter. The development of communication between people from different cultural backgrounds is central in intercultural foreign language learning. This is a question of foreign language learning in its broad meaning (including both verbal and nonverbal communication systems). It is thus important to *teach the foreign language in close association with its sociocultural background.* This was indeed the basic idea of our teaching experiment. We tried to consider the basic culture of the learners and then widen this starting point gradually so that aspects of the foreign culture could be noted step by step (cf. widening of the learner's picture of culture, section 3.3.3 above). The aim was for learners to become more and more able to understand the foreign culture and its members, and more willing to look for explanations for foreign cultural behaviours and accept diversities.

The process by which foreign language education can widen the learners' picture of the world *formed by their own culture* in the direction of a multicultural picture of the world can be described as proceeding through different stages. We defined four such stages for our teaching experiment that are relevant to interculturally orientated foreign language learning:

(1) Learners should be sensitised to foreign phenomena
(2) Learners should be instructed to observe phenomena in the foreign culture and compare them with those in their own culture
(3) Learners acquire information about the foreign language and foreign cultural standards and compare them with how their own language and their own cultural standards function
(4) New meanings are shaped, based on the first three stages, and this eventually leads to successful communication and interaction with the representatives of a foreign culture

This process has to be understood as ranging over a long period of time. Becoming multicultural is actually a life-long process, with the learner's ability to communicate with foreign language speakers always developing. There are so many different languages and cultures and so many levels in communication with members of one and the same culture that we can really speak of a life-long sensitisation to understanding foreign phenomena. Knowledge and experience of foreign languages and foreign patterns of behaviour are so various and complex that a good communication ability presupposes numerous opportunities for observation, exercise and experience of interaction with native speakers in social contexts. Our four-stage process applies basically to a whole lifetime of foreign language and intercultural learning.

We have used the same stages in planning and conducting different projects, units and single lessons. Foreign phenomena nearly always differ from the phenomena in one's own culture, so it is useful to have sensitising activities in every lesson. The students' stereotyped opinions and views, for example, can be brought to awareness and discussed, opening the way for changes in thinking. *Sensitisation also helps learners to activate their previous experiences and views* of the foreign language and culture. This enables new information of foreign phenomena to be linked with the learners' knowledge structures better than they would be without sensitisation. We believe that sensitisation also stimulates the development of one's ability for empathy. This ability is important for understanding foreign behaviours from the point of view of foreigners (cf. intercultural competence, section 3.1.4 above).

3.4.3   Intercultural learning from the student's point of view

We consider learning primary and teaching only secondary. Foreign language education in school has been based too much on the idea that learning is caused by teaching. Traditional teacher-centred school education has preserved this myth. For the various school subjects, levels, classes, students, ages, etc. particular teaching methods, materials, and tests have been developed, reducing learning into a one-way and similar cognitive event for all learners with teachers believing that learners shape the world, receive and process information and remember things in the same way. Perhaps teachers have not considered enough that their ways of shaping the world, language and communication and making decisions on learning materials and working methods are based on their own preferences and are not necessarily suitable to all learners.

In order to understand their learners' learning processes, *teachers should gather information about the learners' prior knowledge, experiences, opinions, personalities, etc.* Getting this information admittedly requires a great deal of effort. But guiding and facilitating the learning process meaningfully requires an understanding of the learner's situation. In intercultural foreign language learning, it is important to know and understand the learners' cultural and linguistic backgrounds. We can of course infer a lot from the fact that all our students are, e.g., Canadian, Greek, Japanese or Norwegian. They share a certain common picture of the world due to their national culture and mother tongue, their ways of interacting, and basic concepts by which they understand each other and help other people to understand them. But this is only a foundation on which foreign language education can be planned. In any national culture there are a number of subcultures all of which guide their members' behaviour. In addition, international and hidden influences (for example through TV) direct each individual's life and consequently his way of interacting and communicating. The more foreign language education encourages students to grow out of the shell of their own culture and mother tongue, and the more foreign language education fosters the growth of the student's whole multicultural personality, the more complex are the processes and events that the teacher has to deal with. *Foreign language education must include this multidimensional learning process* if we wish to consciously develop the learners' picture of culture (cf. widening of the learners' picture of culture, section 3.3.3 above).

In a new class it is useful to *make learners aware of their views and opinions of the target language and culture,* as well as of themselves as foreign language learners. This gives us a starting point for thinking about the learners and creating a foundation for individual experiential learning. In our teaching experiment the students completed a questionnaire with a number of open questions. To this interesting, but often insufficient, information we added personal discussions and interviews of the students. In this way we were able to get more detailed information about each student's views and opinions, as well as their former experiences and knowledge. The first lessons were planned so that the students were encouraged to ask the teacher about foreign language and culture. After that we started the study of new materials.

Such a step is important if teachers want to understand their students' learning process. Regardless of teachers and teaching methods, every student integrates new experiences and knowledge into his information structure, which is different from that of other students. Every student's understanding of the world develops in connection with his prior understanding. Students learn according to their own conditions. It is important from the instructional point of view that the teacher should know a lot about the students' learning processes and understand them as well as possible. This brings a new and demanding dimension to the teacher's role: the foreign language teacher needs to understand the learners' own cultural backgrounds, language usage, communication abilities and the experiences that they already have about the foreign language and culture. But the task has to be taken seriously if we wish to focus more on the individuality of learning.

At the beginning of our experiment, we encouraged students to ask their teachers about new and important things in the foreign culture. After a short period of hesitation the students were very keen to ask for information. This interaction is something that continued after the project too, and students have asked questions whenever they have wanted to. Mönninghoff (1992) points out that the prevailing model of school teaching is that knowledgeable teachers ask their less-knowing students. Transferred to a real-life context, this is like experts asking novices for information! This is not the norm in real life, and Mönninghoff suggests that the same ought to be true in the classroom as well: the one who asks questions should not know the answers.

Learners have a natural ability to make hypotheses. Human beings are used to making hypotheses about the surrounding world, seeking information, verifying, falsifying and revising their hypotheses. Intercultural foreign language education should support this very natural process by allowing learners opportunities to *make observations about the foreign culture and interaction and communication situations* in the foreign language. We decided that the units in our teaching experiment should include a project for every student about a certain topic in collaboration with some other students, and that this project should further be planned in such a way as to take into account both the cognitions and emotions of the participants. Also, it was important to *guide students to reflect on their own action and learning* both alone and in small groups. The idea was that learners should not only meet relevant phenomena in the foreign culture and learn words and meanings by heart, but also have opportunities to *connect them with their previous experiences and knowledge*, as part of their widening picture of the world. In this way, learners become the owners of new knowledge, and acquire knowledge better suited to them individually.

3.4.4   Intercultural learning: learning materials and methods in foreign language education

In our experiment we also wanted to reduce the traditionally routinised use of foreign language textbooks: we used only part of the text and exercise material contained in the students' school books. One important reason for this decision was the fact that *textbooks generally give a superficial and stereotyped picture* of the target culture and the sociocultural functions of the language (Grothuesmann and Sauer 1991). In addition to the text material, the *students also used folders* in which they collected the written and printed materials that they produced or received from the teachers. The students were instructed to file information, materials and work they produced in the folders, according to certain themes, for example. They also kept *personal journals* in which they were asked to make notes and reflect on their learning experiences and findings during a certain period of time. In this way traditional texts and exercise books were partly replaced by materials that teachers and students considered most helpful in the course of the teaching experiment.

In the latter phase of the experiment, the *students created a significant proportion of their learning materials* by conducting a large project, working in small groups, with partner classes in the foreign country, thus collecting a large body of authentic material and personal information about young people's opinions and problems in the target culture. The students found this material more authentic than the printed material in their text books, magazines or other papers. It is our view that *meaningful learning is promoted by learning materials that learners themselves regard as authentic.* Modern information networks like the Internet certainly offer new possibilities for working with authentic learning materials in foreign language education.

> *For your consideration.* How do you or could you use the wide range of electronic media with your students? How best can the Internet be exploited in creating contacts with people from other countries?

The teaching experiment made extensive use of *visual materials*. In particular, efforts were made to collect video tapes (lasting 3–8 minutes) of everyday life in the target culture. Partly authentic, partly prepared for language teaching purposes, these tapes proved useful for the purpose of *observing and making notes on communication in the foreign culture*. They generally dealt with matters of topical interest in the target culture, so student observations were very intensive and offered a solid foundation for discussions.

About once a month a native speaker visited the classroom. These visits were always planned so that they could be integrated with the normal study programme. The *visits always included discussion of the students' observations of foreign linguistic and cultural behaviour* in certain communication situations. The role of the native speaker in the classroom was that of a discussion partner and teacher, and also that of a foreign observer, i.e. one who could offer a native speaker's view of how our students behaved as foreign language speakers. After the scheduled work of the visit, the native speaker discussed his observations and findings with the students and gave critical feedback on how the students behaved when they were simulating foreigners. These encounters gave students a *real opportunity to test their interaction abilities.*

In traditional foreign language teaching it is customary to sequence the syllabus according to grammar progression. In our experiment we dealt with grammar by pointing out possibilities for observation in the authentic materials and situations. It is our view that *spontaneously acquired and reflected experiences and knowledge are in better accordance with the students' individual learning processes* and are retained in mind more effectively. The students were therefore encouraged to collect a lot of information and experiences in the classroom in a variety of ways. Hypotheses thus formed were later tested (i.e. verified or falsified), supplemented and modified during the study visits to Germany or France. Students' personal journals and their comments when interviewed demonstrate that the learning process progressed according to this principle.

The students did seem to be able to *build up meaningful hypotheses about the foreign culture and sociocultural language use through observation* (authentic texts, films, video clips, other pictures, experiences related by the teacher, etc.). But the *verification (or falsification) of hypotheses is difficult to achieve* in the classroom. It is also difficult to give students appropriate feedback on their FL communication and interaction abilities. Such feedback is, however, essential for their preparation for real intercultural contacts.

In our teaching experiment we developed a number of small projects and activities which were carried out regularly at certain periods of time. The students concentrated on some culture-based themes from different points of view. Our goal was also to *set problems involving students on both the affective and the cognitive level,* thus helping them to reflect (both alone and in small groups) on their experiences and learning processes. Project themes included such things as food (dining and eating customs); the environment (living conditions and life circumstances, living and housing), visits (being a visitor in a foreign family, preparing for a visit); the arts (painting as a group activity and its evaluation with a native artist); and planning a public area.

In a German project activity based on the last-mentioned theme, the students worked in small groups to make five plans for the use of the former Berlin Wall area and presented their ideas and plans to the other groups. Such fairly long projects (4–6 lessons) that simulate real life and offer scope for students to use their imagination were received very positively. Such work combines cognitive and affective experiences, and also integrates a number of important linguistic elements and skills. The Wall project was realized in small groups each of which formed a kind of a citizen movement (*Bürgerinitiative*). The task of the group was to suggest solutions for the Wall area that would satisfy all the parties concerned. According to their individual roles, each student assumed a certain imagined family background, occupation, political opinion, need, or a goal. In the process of making a common plan, the students learned a lot of linguistic elements in a highly motivated situation, particularly the vocabulary and concepts needed for planning and presenting the project results.

Now, some years after the pulling down of the Berlin Wall, it is known what has been built or planned in this area. We believe our students follow these developments with genuine interest, having actively worked on the same task in school.

> *For your consideration.* What might be appropriate themes, activities and projects in the teaching context in your own country? How could your students assume the roles of people in the target cultural environment, and how could their existing ideas and experiences be activated and used in the project?

Another example of our *simulation tasks* is the activity in which students planned and composed a curriculum vitae of an imagined German, Austrian, Swiss or French person. During the project the students read excerpts of a book and newspaper articles as input material on the life circumstances of different foreign people. The students created stories about their role persons using these printed materials together with their experiences during the study visits to Germany and France, and during the reciprocal visits of German and French school classes to Finland; and, of course, using their own experience of the world and their imagination. The task was carried out along with other foreign language activities over a period of six weeks.

The students wrote three stories about their role person, each from a different point of view. During the school lessons they interviewed each other about the life of their role persons, considered their cultural authenticity and developed their own role person's curriculum vitae further. The students thus had extensive practice in writing and speaking the foreign language. Again, the project required much energy and time and long-term concentration, but the students produced very creative work and their motivation was extremely high. Many students indeed reported after this activity that they had worked very creatively and activated their imagination more than is usually the case in school. Moreover, they mentioned that this activity had also increased their ability for empathy (cf. intercultural competence, section 3.1.4 above).

Our overall goal was to redesign our whole foreign language education programme in such a way that its subelements would be significantly connected with each other. We cannot say definitely to what extent our **holistic idea** was understood and put into practice by the different students. But we believe that we were able to make progress towards more coherent learner experience as a result of a deeper processing of certain culture-based phenomena and the exercising of foreign language skills in the context of the cultural background. Progress towards the goal was also furthered by the very personal student experiences on encounters with foreignness and otherness, and the conscious reflection on them in the students' journals. We are convinced that projects and activities that combined cognitive, affective and social goals similarly contributed towards development in the direction of holistic foreign language learning.

3.4.5   Intercultural learning: the site visit and student exchange in foreign language education

To become international, we need to make contacts abroad. Nowadays many young people already have contacts with foreign people during their time at school. Modern electronic communication media offer enormous opportunities for increased contacts. There are also institutions which operate youth exchange schemes for various purposes. These services are necessary and help individuals to become international. But however important such experiences may be for a given individual, for a whole school class, or all the students in the school, they are marginal. They help individuals to become intercultural learners, but to promote intercultural learning in the whole school it is necessary to develop teaching, syllabus contents, classroom activities, study materials, etc. In short, it is necessary to *proceed in the direction of intercultural learning becoming a value in itself.* In many countries, intercultural learning is already a common goal of school education. In our own present projects, international networking has functioned well in the participating schools. It is indeed a matter for serious consideration how intercultural learning can proceed in schools which are not in a position to offer opportunities to encounter foreign cultures or representatives of the foreign culture as part of the organised curriculum.

A well-prepared site visit to a foreign country is without doubt a significant way of stimulating intercultural encounters and learning processes for young people (cf. Byram 1997). Where such visits can be developed in the direction of student group exchanges, there is even more scope for learning both cultures (native and foreign). A *site visit in the school context should always be part of the curriculum*; in this way it forms a sound basis for designing a long-term learning process in which the visit plays a central role. If the visit is made within the framework of foreign language education its goals will naturally serve those of foreign language learning. The visit provides a *context for testing out knowledge and beliefs about the foreign culture and communication abilities in the foreign language.* At the same time, new information and experiences of foreign conditions and lifestyles are naturally gained, of a kind which it is probably impossible for normal school work to provide at all (cf. Christ 1991).

It was from these ideas that we proceeded in our own teaching experiment. The site visits to France and Germany were essential parts of the language curriculum, and we were able to prepare learners for them well in advance in a variety of ways. The learning tasks and activities in school were easily seen as personally important by all students. Besides considering features of the foreign culture, the students had to reflect on their own culture from many perspectives, including from the point of view of foreign people. The site visits thus had the *role of testing school knowledge and experiences in the relevant cultural context.* They were also an important interface for directing foreign language learning and teaching for the future. After an intensive visit to the foreign country, students have a very concrete idea of their language and communication abilities and their level of competence in the foreign culture.

The teaching experiment aimed at creating a process of intercultural foreign language education in terms of the following four stages: (1) sensitisation to foreign culture, (2) perception of foreign phenomena, (3) learning foreign cultural standards, and (4) learning foreign meanings and developing foreign linguistic and cultural communication (cf. above). In the experiment, learners were guided to consciously observe foreign phenomena both linguistic and nonlinguistic, to practise them in communication situations, and to reflect on the foreign culture and on how the foreign language functions. In this way *learners built up a number of hypotheses about the foreign language and culture.* They were able to form tentative answers to their hypotheses in school through teaching and authentic school materials. Really significant answers, however, they received through the intensive individual activities during the visit to the foreign country. Our basic hypothesis about the site visit was that it *allows learners to verify or falsify their beliefs, knowledge and conceptions about foreign behaviours, to widen and deepen them through their authentic experiences, and to consider how their experiences could be generalised.*

The site visits provided important opportunities for intensive learning and for flexible behaviour. This demanded openness on the part of the students – openness to the foreign culture and its people, and open-mindedness to consider their behaviour and learning processes. While the site visit was planned so as to provide intensive learning experiences, the programme also included some flexibility so that students had time for their own arrangements with their host families and school mates. Both *intensiveness and flexibility were thus key elements* in the programme.

The site visits included the following procedures for promoting intercultural encounters and learning:

(1) The students were given tasks involving the observation of family life, school work assignments, and free time activities in the foreign country. Each student stayed with a host family for one week, living as a member of the family and spending the weekend with them.
(2) The students carried out observation tasks every day and practised communication in the foreign language, for example through guided interview tasks. They also had a video camera at their disposal for recording their interviews and experiences.
(3) They discussed their observations and experiences and reflected on their tasks and on the programme as a whole together with their Finnish school mates every day. They were also asked to write down their experiences in the personal journals that were given to them before the visit.

The success of the programme naturally depended on how well the host families and schools understood our aims. According to student feedback and interviews, the planning of the interactive programme was moderately successful.

The following *observation tasks*, given before the visit, helped the students to progress in the desired direction: 'Write down in your personal journal every day how the people act and why you think that they act in this way. Make notes especially on things that you find surprising. To what extent do you think they are similar to your own practices. Write in your own language.'

Specific tasks students had to do during the site visit were as follows:

Task 1 (the same for all students):

1. Observe your host family. (What kind of family is it? What can you say of the family's living standards? What are the relationships between the family members, especially the children's relationship to their parents? What things are valued in the family? What is important for the family? Does everybody in the family have the same rights? How do the family relate to their guest? etc.)
2. Interview your host family. Plan the questions in the target language with your partner and report your results in your personal journal. Add some brief information about the family members.
3. Observe especially the way the family lives and what the home is like. Write down your observations about living customs, rooms, furnishings, domestic appliances, etc.

Task 2 (each pair had their own theme):

Choose one theme of the list below with your partner and observe and investigate it: (1) school, (2) environment, (3) youth cultures, (4) free time activities, (5) consumer habits and shopping culture, (6) transport, and (7) media and advertising.

1. Observe and make notes on what you observe, and collect different printed materials relating to your theme. You can also use the video camera.
2. Use the foreign language to explain what things interest you especially and what you want to know more about.

The implementation of the site visit was clearly successful. The students were accommodated alone in the foreign families. They had a free weekend with the host family for doing things that the family considered useful. They had enough time to meet with local young people in the afternoon and evening. Furthermore, they had a joint programme every day for observing the town, its inhabitants and their way of life. The students reported and discussed their findings together. They visited the schools of their French or German friends on two days. The programme also included an excursion day and a party one evening with local young people. We did not want to put together too strict a programme; rather, it was considered important that the visit was in accordance with the young people's own needs for socialisation as far as possible. According to the student feedback, these aims were very successfully achieved. The programme provided plenty of opportunities to communicate in the foreign language in different ways.

3.4.6 Intercultural learning: reflections on student experiences

The purpose of the site visits was to provide a variety of encounters and experiences with French and German native speakers, which were reflected on together afterwards. *Each student was also required to consider his own experiences in writing in a personal journal.* What the students wrote in their journals represented very mature reflections on the foreign culture and indicated that they were able to make interesting and informed comparisons between their own culture and the foreign culture.

One of the most important goals of our experiment was that the students could also explore the process of their own foreign language learning. Foreign language teaching has traditionally aimed at learning the linguistic system and communication skills, with the learning process being strictly linked to gradual progress in grammar and vocabulary. Learners' own experiences of the foreign language and culture and individual learning processes have been ignored in such approaches. *If the learning model is given and the process is strongly directed by the teacher and the study materials, individual learning remains superficial and the individual learning process cannot be observed properly or guided significantly.* There are obviously problems with supervising each student's individual learning process, but in the long run such work proves the best way of helping learners towards independent, autonomous and experiential learning.

The students were required to consider their experiences and learning processes regularly from their own learning perspectives. The teaching involved experiences of the whole foreign culture, not just of the foreign language. One important perspective in student reflections, therefore, was the *comparison of phenomena in the foreign culture with those in their own culture.* The understanding and learning of culture-based phenomena progressed through the processes of sensitisation, observation, learning of foreign meanings and conventions, and communication described above, with the themes of the lessons and units planned for this purpose. Reflection on learning experiences was also connected with these themes, activities and learning events.

By reflection in this context we understand a process where learners analyse and evaluate their own learning either on their own or together with other learners. We think it is important that reflection has both these elements: the learner as an individual and as a member of a group. Every learner needs to confront his experiences and analyse and evaluate them individually. But discussing them in a group provides an opportunity to view these experiences in proportion and from new perspectives. The group functions thus like a mirror, reflecting the experiences back to the learner. This is reflection in the original sense.

In learning a foreign language and culture, an important method is the *comparison of new experiences and conceptions with old ones* deriving mainly from the learner's own culture and native language. It seems our students' reflection indeed proceeded through such a process of comparison. In their reflections after the study unit, they discussed whether the language learning methods employed possibly neglected something that was aimed at earlier when different tasks and methods were in use (especially learning grammar).

They also considered what the new activities brought with them in comparison with earlier methods (for example in learning oral skills and communication). Moreover, the students compared foreign cultural behaviours with their own behaviours and discussed the possible changes in their foreign language behaviours. This brief discussion is sufficient to demonstrate that comparison plays a significant role in reflective activities.

The most efficient form of individual reflection was *keeping a personal journal*. Many young people of 16 or 17 proved to be capable of deep reflection when asked to write down what they did, observed and experienced and how they felt in the different situations. It is important to ensure that young people get enough freedom to act and their reflection tasks are not too strict. For example, exact questions tend to make learners answer only those questions, in which case reflection remains superficial. The *open personal journal functioned very well during the site visits*. Although the students often mentioned that they did not have enough time to write down their experiences, they were able to describe and reflect on their experiences at surprising length in just half an hour. Furthermore, they mentioned that writing the personal journal was helpful because they could return to their earlier thoughts and opinions later on.

Reflections in small groups seem to be most fruitful *when the students have already considered individually* how they have acted and what they have possibly learned. In face-to-face situations ready-made questions seem to help the structuring of the reflections: because of the interactive situation, there is less tendency for the activity to be reduced to just answering certain set questions than there is in the case of individual written reflections. Face-to-face reflection did, however, cause initial difficulties as the students had no experience of reflection as a group activity. It took a great deal of time to get such activity going, and the situation was often perceived to be unnatural. Nevertheless, the students mentioned that these group reflections were useful.

Our reflection activities were experimental in many ways. Although we had had a reasonable amount of previous experience in the use of reflection as a working method (cf. Kaikkonen 1991), our practices of reflection with young learners were mainly limited to getting feedback from them. This aspect was naturally important in our experiment, too, but we now wanted first and foremost to get the students reflecting on their own learning processes. It seems that we did attain this important goal in a satisfactory way. While we were aiming at the goal of intercultural competence, we learned more and more about the students' problems in learning a foreign language and culture. Moreover, we now understand the individual character of the learning process far better.

It is the *growth of the teacher's professional understanding* that we want to emphasize as a personally important outcome of the experiment. In intercultural learning, *teachers are also learners* of their own profession, and this experience has been very rewarding for all of the participating teachers.

3.5   CONCLUSION

When the question 'What is the task of language teaching?' is asked, the answer frequently given is 'Just teach the language'. Such an answer is simplified and expedient. By appealing to the traditional conception of language, teachers' willingness and motivation for change can be efficiently stifled. We therefore place great emphasis on the importance of ongoing discussions about language and the role of intercultural learning in the present and future world. Language teaching has to accept the challenge posed by such issues in the near future. As human life becomes more international in many ways, language teaching must aim at facilitating learners to live and succeed in an international and multicultural world. Here we wish to summarise some of the most important factors that make it important to go beyond the simple communicative approach in foreign language teaching, and argue for a kind of foreign language education that promotes intercultural learning.

Foreign language learning is a different process for each individual learner. This is true not only in a cognitive sense, but very deeply in a cultural sense, too. The ways in which Americans think about the world and use their language differ from those of the French, Brazilians or Japanese. Why then should language teaching be similar in these countries? The teachers have their own conceptions of language, language use, communication and the world, and the students and their parents also have different views. These conceptions may indeed be so convergent in one and the same language culture that we can speak of a typical German or Spanish way of thinking about the world and using language. Language teaching ought not to be anything global, provided for all learners in similar ways.

The target must be to achieve a level of competence in the foreign language that enables communication partners to understand each other's meanings and intentions well enough despite their different national and cultural backgrounds. What constitutes 'well enough' is like a line drawn on water. There are no absolute and easy criteria for the good-enough language ability. All descriptions are limited in some respects. Difficulties of reciprocal understanding in foreign language interaction have to be experienced in order to be learned well. The problems are experienced only in actual, meaningful language use, i.e. in communication and interaction with others.

Human beings are products of their own cultures, and can by nature understand the people of other cultures to a limited extent. Therefore, intercultural learning, as an essential part of foreign language learning, is a long process where one's own cultural background plays a fundamental role. The horizons of one's own culture broaden as a consequence of foreign language learning. Learners grow out of the shell of their mother tongue and their own culture. Their experiences of the world become both wider and deeper. How wide and deep one's picture of the world can become in the process of foreign language education is an interesting educational question. The pedagogical processes involved in intercultural foreign language education are based on more comprehensive principles and teaching practices and on more individual work than in traditional cognitive foreign language teaching, which emphasises the learning of linguistic systems and communication skills.

Intercultural foreign language education needs to be shaped as holistically as the learning conditions permit. It is necessary to give the learners opportunities for personal experiences with authentic foreign language use because this ensures an emotional involvement in the learning process. Naturally, foreign language education aims at processing and organising knowledge. It guides learners to perceive the world in a conscious way. It helps learners to become sensitive to phenomena often taken for granted and behaviours automatised in their own culture and language. Through this they become sensitive, too, to the nature of foreign phenomena. To support this kind of foreign language education, it is important to strive for authenticity in materials and encounters. The more learner emotions and feelings can be involved in the process, the deeper the learning experiences are.

The learning process is also supported by the understanding of psychological factors. The ability to be sensitive to both familiar and foreign phenomena, the ability for empathy, seeing things from the others' point of view, and to share feelings with others are essential for intercultural foreign language learning. Another very important individual quality is respect for diversity. Diversity is something alien and hard for human beings to accept, and its acceptance has to be learned. Tolerance is a matter of growing out of the narrowness of one's own social behaviour, growing out of the belief that the behaviours that are typical of one's own national or cultural group are somehow better or more natural than the behaviours of others.

As intercultural learning deals with encounters between different people with different cultural backgrounds speaking different languages, another very important factor is tolerance of ambiguity, tolerance of uncertain and conflicting situations. Tolerance of ambiguity can only be developed in real encounter situations. Tolerance of ambiguity and tolerance of diversity are closely connected, but they are also different in many ways. As we understand it, diversity derives from cultural origins, whereas ambiguity seems to be more of a psychological matter. When encountering foreignness and using a foreign language, it is inevitable that human beings experience both diversity and ambiguity.

What could foreign language education do in order to develop learners' abilities to act in multicultural situations? The answers that we discovered in our teaching experiment emphasise the significance of authenticity. We emphasised the use of authentic study materials and personal experiences of using the foreign language in many ways in the school, and especially during the site visit to the foreign culture. Mutual contact between students of different cultures proved to be useful, and reciprocal site visits offered authentic interaction situations and learning opportunities. The experiment also emphasised the use of modern technology to facilitate intercultural encounters. The ongoing development in information networks is bound to increase opportunities and open up new possibilities for such encounters in the future.

In order to promote the goals of intercultural learning in foreign language education, teachers need more opportunity to develop their own intercultural action competence. Changes in attitudes are necessary in the light of the rapid changes taking place in the world. Modern teacher education appears to be responding to these demands through increasingly open dialogue, integration of school subjects, open learning environments, and flexible curricula that allow some freedom of choice. The international networking of student teachers and increasing study opportunities in foreign countries also support the goals of intercultural learning in schools. Teachers are also increasingly in a position to take advantage of modern technology in using foreign languages and nonverbal forms of cultural communication. Along with toleration of diversity and ambiguity, there is emerging a view of learning and teaching as a holistic process of promoting the growth of the whole person. It is such developments in teacher education that will help to change school practices in the desired direction. As long as teachers see foreign language teaching as a predominantly cognitive event, their pupils can hardly experience it as anything else. Both pre-service and in-service teacher education will therefore have an essential role in moving school culture towards the goal of experiential foreign language education and intercultural learning.

3.6   REFERENCES

Alix Ch and Kodron Ch (1989) Schüleraustausch als Teil interkulturellen themenzentrierten Zusammenarbeitens. In Müller B-D (ed.) *Anders lernen im Fremdsprachenunterricht.* Berlin: Langenscheidt, pp 175–92

Althaus H-J and Mog P (1992) Deutsch-amerikanische Beziehungen und Wahrnehmungsmuster. In Mog P and Althaus H-J (eds) *Die Deutschen in ihrer Welt.* Berlin: Langenscheidt, pp 17–42

Altrichter H, Posch P and Somekh B (1993) *Teachers investigate their work: an introduction to the methods of action research.* London: Routledge

Austin J (1962) *How to do with words.* Oxford: Clarendon Press

Bauch K-R, Christ H and Krumm H-J (1994) *Interkulturelles Lernen in der Fremdsprache. Arbeitspapier der 14. Frühjahrskonferenz zur Erforschung des Fremdsprachenunterrichts.* Tübingen: Gunter Narr

Bredella L (1992) Towards a pedagogy of intercultural understanding. In Hornung A *et al.* (eds) *American Studies* **37**: 559–94

Bredella L (1993) Ist das Verstehen fremder Kulturen wünschenswert? In Bredella L and Christ H (eds) *Gießener Diskurse. Zugänge zum Fremden. Band 10.* Verlag der Feber'schen Universtitätsbuchhandlung, Gießen, pp 11–36

Byram M (1989) *Cultural studies in foreign language education.* Clevedon: Multilingual Matters

Byram M (1993) Language and culture learning: the need for integration. In Byram M (ed.) *Germany. Its representation in textbooks for teaching German in Great Britain.* Frankfurt: Diesterweg, pp 13–18

Byram M (ed.) (1997) *Face to face, learning language and culture through visits and exchanges.* London: CILT

Byram M, Morgan C (1994) *Teaching-and-learning language-and-culture.* Clevedon: Multilingual Matters

Byram M and Zarate G (eds) (1997) *The sociocultural and intercultural dimension of language learning and teaching.* Strasbourg: Council of Europe

Byram M and Zarate G (1998) *Jugend, Vielfalt und Fremde. Anregungen für den Umgang mit kulturellen Unterschieden.* Wien, Graz: BM/UK. (Young People Facing Difference: Some proposals for teachers. Council of Europe 1995)

Christ H (1991) *Fremdsprachenunterricht für das Jahr 2000.* Tübingen: Narr

Christ H (1993) Schüleraustausch zwischen Verstehen und Mißverstehen. In Bredella L and Christ H (eds) *Gießener Diskurse. Zugänge zum Fremden. Band 10.* Gießen: Verlag der Feber'schen Universtitätsbuchhandlung, pp 181–202

Doyé P (1993) Neuere Konzepte der Fremdsprachenerziehung und ihre Bedeutung für die Schulbuchkritik. In Byram, M (ed.) *Germany. Its representation in textbooks for teaching German in Great Britain.* Frankfurt: Diesterweg, pp 19–30

Eco U (1976) *A theory of semiotics.* Bloomington, IN: Indiana University Press

Edelhoff Ch and Liebau E (eds) (1988) *Über die Grenze. Praktisches Lernen im fremdsprachlichen Unterricht.* Weinheim und Basel: Beltz

Engelmann B (1991) *Du deutsch? Geschichte der Ausländer in Deutschland.* Göttingen: Steidl

Gardner H (1983) *Frames of mind.* New York: Basic Books

Gardner H (1993) *Multiple intelligences: the theory in practice.* New York: Basic Books

Goleman D (1995) *Emotional intelligence.* New York: Bantam Books

Grothuesmann H and Sauer H (1991) Völkerbilder in fremdsprachenunterrichtlichen Lehrwerken. Ein Literaturbericht. *Zeitschrift für Fremdsprachenforschung* 2: 66–92

Haarmann H (1993) *Die Sprachenwelt Europas.* München: Fink

Habermas J (1971) Vorbereitende Bemerkungen zu einer Theorie der kommunikativen Kompetenz. In Habermas J and Luhmann N (eds) *Theorie der Gesellschaft oder Sozialtechnologie – was leistet die Systemforschung?* Frankfurt: Suhrkamp, pp 101–41

de Haen I (1994) Was tun, wenn der Täter sympatisch ist? In Winkler B (ed.) *Was heißt denn hier fremd?* München: Humboldt, pp 77–84

Hymes D (1972) On communicative competence. In Pride J and Holmes J (eds) *Sociolinguistics.* Harmondsworth, UK: Penguin Books, pp 269–93

Kaikkonen P (1990) Interkulturelle Kultur- und Landeskunde und interkultureller Fremdsprachenunterricht. *Neusprachliche Mitteilungen* 4: 230–6

Kaikkonen P (1991) Erlebte Kultur- und Landeskunde, ein Weg zur Aktivierung und Intensivierung des Kulturbewußtseins der Fremdsprachenlernenden – eine Untersuchung mit LehrerstudentInnen. *Acta Universitatis Tamperensis* ser A, vol 325. Tampere: Universität Tampere

Kaikkonen P (1993) Fremdsprachenerlernen – ein individueller, kulturbezogener Prozeß – einige Beobachtungen im Rahmen eines erlebte Kultur- und Landeskunde betonenden Unterrichtsversuches. *Unterrichtswissenschaft* 1: 2–20

Kaikkonen P (1993 and 1995) *Culture and foreign language learning* 1 and 2. Reports from the Department of Teacher Education in Tampere University. A16/1993 and A1/1995. Tampere: University of Tampere (in Finnish)

Kaikkonen P (1994) Kultur und Fremdsprachenunterricht – einige Aspekte zur Entwicklung des Kulturbildes der Fremdsprachenlernenden und zur Gestaltung des schulischen Fremdsprachenunterrichts. In Neuner G (ed.) *Fremde Welt und eigene Wahrnehmung.* Kassel: Universität Kassel, pp 54–70

Kaikkonen P (1995) Entwicklung des Kulturbildes der Fremdsprachenlernenden. In Bredella L (ed.) *Verstehen und Verständigung durch Sprachenlernen?* Beiträge zur Fremdsprachenforschung. Bochum: Verlag Brockmeyer, pp 159–67

Kaikkonen P (1996) Erziehung zur Interkulturalität durch einen interkulturelles Lernen betonenden Fremdsprachenunterricht. *Unser Weg* 51(2): 73–7

Kaikkonen P (1997a) Fremdverstehen durch schulischen Fremdsprachenunterricht. *Info DaF* 24(1): 78–86

Kaikkonen P (1997b) Learning a culture and a foreign language at school – aspects of intercultural learning. *Language Learning Journal* 15: 47–51.

Kaikkonen P and Kohonen V (eds) (1997) *The living curriculum 1.* An action research project between the University of Tampere and six Finnish schools on the development of teacher professionalism and site-based curricula. Reports from the Department of Teacher Education in Tampere University A9. Tampere: University of Tampere (in Finnish)

Keller G (1983) Grundlegung einer neuen Kulturkunde als Orientierungsrahmen für Lehrerausbildung und Unterrichtspraxis. *Neusprachliche Mitteilungen* 4: 200–9

Kohonen V and Kaikkonen P (1996) Exploring new ways of inservice teacher education: an action research project. *European Journal of Intercultural Studies* 7(3): 42–59

Kramsch C (1993) *Context and culture in language teaching.* Hong Kong: Oxford University Press

Levinson S (1990) Interactional biases in human thinking. *Working Paper No.3. Project Group Cognitive Anthropology.* Berlin: Max-Planck-Gesellschaft

Loenhoff J (1992) *Interkulturelle Verständigung. Zum Problem grenzüberschreitender Kommunikation.* Opladen: Leske+Budrich

Luce L and Smith E (eds) (1987) *Towards internationalism. Readings in cross-cultural communication.* Cambridge, MA: Newbury House Publishers

Lustig M and Koester J (1993) *Intercultural competence. Interpersonal communication across cultures.* New York: HarperCollinsCollegePublishers

Mönninghoff J (1992) *Das Bewußtsein des Lehrers.* Berlin: Luchterhand

Nestvogel R (1991) Sozialisation und Sozialisationsforschung in interkultureller Perspektive. In Nestvogel R (ed.) *Interkulturelles Lernen oder verdeckte Dominanz?* Frankfurt: Verlag für Interkulturelle Kommunikation, pp 85–112

Neuner G and Hunfeld H (1993) *Methoden des fremdsprachlichen Deutschunterrichts.* Berlin: Langenscheidt

Nicklas H (1991) Kulturkonflikt und interkulturelles Lernen. In Thomas A (ed.) *Kulturstandards in der internationalen Begegnung.* Saarbrücken: Verlag Breitenbach Publishers, pp 125–40

Nieke W (1993) Wie ist Interkulturelle Erziehung möglich? In Kalb P *et al.* (eds) *Leben und Lernen in der multikulturellen Gesellschaft.* Weinheim und Basel: Beltz, pp 110–52

Nieke W (1995) *Interkulturelle Erziehung und Bildung. Wertorientierungen im Alltag.* Opladen: Leske+Budrich

Paige R M (1994) On the nature of intercultural experiences and intercultural education. In Paige R M (ed.) *Education for the intercultural experience.* Yarmouth, ME: Intercultural Press, pp 1–19

Pelz M (1989) Durchführung von Begegnungen zwischen deutschen und französischen Grundschulkindern. In Pelz M (ed.) *Lerne die Sprache des Nachbarn. Grenzüberschreitende Spracharbeit zwischen Deutschland und Frankreich. Schule und Forschung.* Frankfurt: Diesterweg, pp 77–88

Reisch B (1991) Kulturstandards lernen und vermitteln. In Thomas A (ed.) *Kulturstandards in der internationalen Begegnung.* Saarbrücken: Verlag Breitenbach Publishers, pp 71–101

Robinson G (1988) *Crosscultural understanding.* London: Prentice Hall

Roth W (1989) Vorerfahrungen und Stereotypien: Ihre Veränderbarkeit durch zweisprachige Kontakte? In Pelz M (ed.) *Lerne die Sprache des Nachbarn. Grenzüberschreitende Spracharbeit zwischen Deutschland und Frankreich. Schule und Forschung.* Frankfurt: Diesterweg, pp 134–49

Röttger E (1996) Überlegungen zum Begriff des interkulturellen Lernens in der Fremdsprache. *Zeitschrift für Fremdsprachenforschung* **7**(2): 155–70

Schmitt G (1989) Interkulturelle Wahrnehmung als Voraussetzung für grenzüberschreitende Begegnung. In Pelz M (ed.) *Lerne die Sprache des Nachbarn, Grenzüberschreitende Spracharbeit zwischen Deutschland und Frankreich*. Schule und Forschung. Frankfurt: Diesterweg, pp 150–69

Schwerdtfeger I (1993) Begegnung mit dem Fremden im Fremdsprachenunterricht. Erleichterungen und/oder Hindernisse? In Bredella L and Christ H (eds) *Gießener Diskurse. Zugänge zum Fremden. Band 10*. Gießen: Verlag der Feber'schen Universitätsbuchhandlung, pp 162–80

Scollon R and Scollon S W (1995) *Intercultural communication*. Cambridge, MA and Oxford: Blackwell

Searle J (1969) *Speech acts*. Cambridge: Cambridge University Press

Seeley H N (1984) *Teaching culture. Strategies for intercultural communication*. Lincolnwood, IL: National Textbook Company

Seeley H N and Wasilewski J H (1996) *Between cultures. Developing self-identity in a world of diversity*. Lincolnwood, IL: NTC Publishing Group

Segall M *et al.* (1990) *Human behavior in global perspective. An introduction to cross-cultural psychology*. New York: Pergamon Press

Sendzig J and Rahlwes S (1988) Lernort Frankreich: Schüleraustausch als praktisches Lernen. In Edelhoff Ch and Liebau E (eds) *Über die Grenze, Praktisches Lernen im fremdsprachlichen Unterricht*. Weinheim und Basel: Beltz, pp 79–109

Shweder R and LeVine R (eds) (1984) *Culture theory. Essays on mind, self and emotion*. New York: Cambridge University Press

Sternecker P (1992) *Kulturelle Identität und interkulturelles Lernen*. Opladen: Leske+ Budrich

Taylor D (1984) Race, prejudge, discrimination, and racism. In Kahn A *et al.* (eds) *Social psychology*. Dubuque, IA: Wm. C. Brown

Valdes J (ed.) (1986) *Culture bound. Bridging the cultural gap in language teaching*. New York: Cambridge University Press

Wahrlich H (1991) Wortlose Sprache – Verständnis und Mißverständnis im Kulturkontakt. In Thomas A (ed.) *Kulturstandards in der internationalen Begegnung*. Saarbrücken: Verlag Breitenbach Publishers, pp 12–31

Weaver G R (ed.) (1994) *Culture, Communication and Conflict: Readings in Intercultural Relations*. Needham Heights, MA: Simon and Schuster Education Group

Young R (1996) *Intercultural Communication. Pragmatics, Genealogy, Deconstruction*. Clevedon: Multilingual Matters

Belles-lettres sources

Blixen K (1985) *Samlede Essays*. Kopenhagen: Gyldendal (own translation)

Böll H (1967) *Irish Journal*. Evanston, IL: Northwestern University Press

Brecht B (1961) *Threepenny Novel*. Harmondsworth: Penguin Books

Enzensberger H-M (1992) *Die Große Wanderung*. Frankfurt am Main: Suhrkamp (own translation)

Hesse H (1965) *Steppenwolf*. Harmondsworth: Penguin Books in association with Martin Secker and Warburg

Høeg P (1993) *Miss Smilla's Feeling for Snow*. London: Flamingo

Tucholsky K (1929) *Deutschland, Deutschland über alles*. Reinbek bei Hamburg: Rowohlt (own translation)

Chapter 4

Autobiographical knowledge in foreign language education and teacher development

Riitta Jaatinen

4.1 AUTOBIOGRAPHICAL EXPERIENTIAL KNOWLEDGE IN FOREIGN LANGUAGE TEACHING AND LEARNING

4.1.1 Concepts

The language teacher's work has become more and more demanding in today's multi-dimensional, ambiguous and constantly changing world. In addition to the knowledge of a foreign language the teacher should have such basic skills and qualities in command as a flexible and large selection of different learning and teaching methods, ability to encounter and collaborate with individuals, different groups of people and communities, research and study skills that guarantee his or her life-long learning, and responsibility and willingness to develop awareness of all human life and the world. As far as the demands for developing *a foreign language learning environment* are concerned, considering the environment just as a means of acquiring linguistic knowledge and developing communication skills is not enough in today's world. Broader goals are set: the foreign language learning environment should provide a valuable resource for the whole human growth including a possibility to broaden one's views and conceptions through understanding different patterns of thought, cultures and societies with their different systems and traditions. The understanding of the uniqueness, individual differences and nature of human learning is called for when creating rich and effective language learning environments.

In order to respond to the challenges formulated above, educational institutions need strong and sensitive teachers who have courage and will to develop themselves, their art of teaching and various learning environments collaboratively with their students. Teaching-in-the-world calls for the integration of the knowledge of the subject (e.g. language and culture) with the knowledge of the human being in his or her life situation, in the context of a certain place and time. The following concepts *'life-world', 'experiential learning', 'teaching', 'knowledge' and 'autobiographical knowledge'* form the core conceptual framework for discussing experiential, autobiographical, knowledge-based foreign language education.

Life-world: The term life-world refers to our experiential, inner world. Our life-world is organised and built up in an individual and unique way during our personal history. It includes all the meaningful elements of our human life such as language, social institutions, other people, nature and culture. As *a subjective context* it is constantly changing: we select and interpret information, we accept, reject and change it in that subjective context which consequently changes. The starting-point in the change is always the process of interpreting and giving subjective meanings to things and objects that reach our consciousness. It sets the limits and offers possibilities for our actions and thinking.

Since we have built up our life-world during all our lifetime, it at least partly consists of such meaning-structures that are so familiar and self-evident to us that we may not notice and even less question them. Learning, however, often presupposes exploring and altering some of these self-evidences and peeling away the layers of meaning that have been structured in our consciousness. It involves understanding existing meaning-structures or reinterpreting them, and then composing and building up new ones.

Experiential learning: Experiential learning in this chapter means *exploring and studying in the world* oneself, the environment and the world immersed in the world; it means exploring the world and its phenomena such as they are, as honestly as we can, and paying attention to all its various meaning-structures that are stored in our life-world and embodied in our feelings, language, thoughts and actions. The nature of learning as human action is experiential and situated; learning means creating new meaning-structures, which are context-bound and cannot be fully understood without the context, without a concrete and particular (pedagogical) situation. When learning experientially we create new meanings in our immediate reality, in our existing meaning-structures, in our personal life-world. In this sense all meaningful learning is experiential learning.

The person's immediate reality is always unique, because it is the result of his or her development, personal history and individual experience. Therefore, each person's learning processes and meaning-structures are also unique, different from anyone else's. Each student's best modes or strategies of learning can be discovered and attained in a community of inquiry where the student has personal space, time and opportunities for self-encountering and encountering the others, learning to understand his or her life-world and learning from others. The importance of such a community of inquiry can be seen in the following extract in which a student of social pedagogy writes about her learning process and the experiences of her learning environment. The extract is part of her English essay.

> I have been studying to be a social pedagogue [child welfare worker] for two years now and a lot has happened.
>   The most significant thing that I have learnt or, actually I am still learning it, is to do things with different kinds of people. I have always been interested in

people and now I am getting where I want: to work with people. I have worked
with babies, children, teens, adults, and elderly people, and persons with or
without a disability. I know that I haven't seen everything, and I don't even
want to, because it would be so scary and I don't think that it is even possible.
I know I don't have to worry about finding all the answers because there are as
many answers as people.

Our little 'community' in Puutarhakatu [Garden Street] is a wonderful place
to learn about people. First, you have a great chance to 'study' your teachers
and classmates. Then within various projects you get to know new people,
maybe your employer in the future. Of course, we study many theories, too, and
it is important to understand what you are reading and why.

I think that the most important thing is to learn to understand yourself: to
know why you react the way you do in certain situations and still, be what you
really are. And to learn those things you need to put yourself into test. In fact,
that is easy to do. Just go out and talk to people and watch them. Then just
notice what kind of feelings and thoughts are coming up in you. Remember,
those are just your feelings and thoughts. That is interesting.   (Tiina)

Creating and maintaining such a community of inquiry is a constant challenge
for both the teacher and students. Such a community provides a safe environment for the students to explore and discover their personal meanings and
meaning-structures. It also provides a place where the students can explore
themselves and their community collaboratively.

Teaching: If learning is understood as an exploring, inquiring process
initiated by a person's lived experience and resulting in a change in the
learner's unique life-world, the teaching is *more 'being' than 'doing'* (Pinar *et al.*
1995). In ideal circumstances teaching means *being in a dialogue*: teaching as
a dialogue is encountering the learner, listening to and respecting him or
her as a whole human being, sharing experiences with the learner and helping him or her to expand his or her experiential reality (Lehtovaara J 1994
and in this volume). The learner's meaning creating relation to his or her
inner and outer reality is thus the basis of all meaningful learning. Giving
space and time to the learners encourages them to challenge and explore
themselves and their environment. This is of utmost importance especially
in language learning. The 'use' of the learner's lived experience in teaching
situations is a sign of *respect for him or her as a whole person with his or her personal
history*; it is accepting the learner as the Other, as an independent human
being, who has the full right and responsibility to build up his or her life-
world and to find his or her own modes and strategies in learning.

Knowledge: If pedagogical situations are built on the learners' lived experience the things being discussed remain with the learners, in their reality.
They are not taken away and put into an abstract and unknown, non-
personal and non-contextual reality. The 'new', learnt knowledge, the changed
or completely new meaning-structures become part of the learner's reality,
his or her life-world. Therefore, there is no knowledge without the knower.
Knowledge, also *the knowledge of a foreign language, is personal and always
contextualised*, part of quite specific relationships, cultures, and situations.
The knowledge can also be *tacit* (Polanyi 1962). The tacit knowledge is

non-verbal, intuitive and formless. Tacit knowing means becoming aware of
and realising unities and integrated wholes from numerous cues or observations. Such tacit, integrative, mental action is involved especially when a
person is forming a conception of him/herself. Although his observations
are diverse, numerous and changing, the person understands himself as one
unity. However, he/she is not able to fully verbalise that understanding
(Lehtovaara M 1994). According to Lyons (1990) teacher knowledge can be
understood as relational, or *nested knowing*: the knowledge is not limited to
what one person knows, but is the intersection where the knowing of the two
or more persons-in-relation overlap. The conception of knowing as nested
derives from an ethic of care and being-in-relation with students. Caring in a
teacher's knowledge is a way of *knowing in the relation* and a way of *knowing
with the body and mind* (Webb and Blond 1995).

Autobiographical knowledge:
Autobiography may be described as a life-story of just one individual who is
the central character of the life drama which unfolds. It presupposes that the
person has developed an identity, an individuality, and a consciousness in order
to organise his or her own private history from the perspective of the present.
As an idiosyncratic rendering of lived experience, it is personal both in its
selection of events and in its expression of style. As such, the search for unity
and coherence (order), characteristic of traditional forms of educational enquiry,
gives way to disunity and incoherence (chaos) in life.   (Solas 1992: 212)

Autobiographical knowledge is *experiential and subjective knowledge of ourselves*.
We have 'collected' that knowledge in the course of our life history and it is
narrated by ourselves (Bertaux 1981). It is individual, lived and experienced,
often incoherent, imperfect and fragmentary. It is not a direct reflection of
what has happened or how things have been in our past, but it is a narrated
description of the past events told or written retrospectively via memory. The
term 'life-story' refers to the narrative, experience reconstructing aspect of
that knowledge. According to Huotelin (1992: 4) 'a life-story consists of events
which the individual feels are significant, that come first to mind as worth
telling and that in the interview situation are chosen as the content of the
narrative. In most cases the meaningful core of the story is preserved despite
the fact that the narration is affected by many factors. Life-stories are inaccur-
ate with respect to details but they are truthful.'

By creating the *personal frame of reference* our autobiographical knowledge
steers and guides our interpretation of reality, including our own experience. Although experience itself is always unique and different, the way of
interpreting the experience has more stability in the course of our life.
When growing older and as a result of formal teaching we often learn various given models of how to 'see' the reality. We are taught to see ourselves
and the world in certain ways, through the eyes of the others, not ours.
As a consequence we may lose the connection to our inner world, to our
genuine experience. That may mean alienation from our real experience.
To prevent that we should learn the process of peeling away the layers of

meaning that different learned interpretations bring to our description of the world.

Peeling away the layers of meaning and becoming more extensively and more profoundly conscious of our experience requires autobiographical inquiry. The experiences, whether they are or are not interpreted and understood, whether they are verbalised or non-verbalised, all have some effect on our life and learning. It is difficult to find any other way of describing our lived experiences than constituting ourselves autobiographically. Therefore, becoming familiar with our autobiography is both a 'window' to our past and also a 'gate' to our future. *By becoming acquainted with our lived, experiential past it is possible for us to gain the understanding of our inner world, listen to our own voice and find a key to development and change.*

4.1.2   Goals of teaching and learning a foreign language

Half of my lifetime I have spent at school. Surely, I have learnt something, too. But to mention some significant learning experiences it's not so easy at all. Why? Maybe because not very often anything significant has happened. The daily routine has been more or less boring. We can divide learning in different categories. Basically there are theoretical and practical parts of learning. We could talk about process, informative, functional, etc. learning, but we don't have to go into all that now.

I remember when I enjoyed studying history at home. I made up my own method because I tried to remember so many years and important events as possible. It was quite hard work for a young woman, but still rewarding. I wrote down the main points of the material. I wrote them down on different pages, a kind of the basic structure, then I formed a queue of them chronologically. I spread those papers on the floor so that I could see the whole thing at once, at a glance. Practically, I used my optical memory and it worked really well. During that year I got maximum points of my history tests, all of them. Once, I got an opportunity to read my answers to the whole class. – That learning was really a significant experience.   (Hannele)

In the above passage *Hannele*, a student of social pedagogy, describes in her English essay one of the most significant learning experiences in her life: *That was not so much learning the subject (in this case history) but learning to learn, finding her own personal method, creating something new in her life.* After that encouraging experience and quite obviously after the reflection on that experience, she had a new view of learning: she had realised that she shouldn't follow in the footsteps of other people, but had to find her own path to go. The discovery of her personal learning methods, of which the above-mentioned is just one example, and her personal and creative choices had made *Hannele* a very self-confident, independent and autonomous student.

Very often we (teachers) think we know how learning, especially language learning, happens or should happen. We have ready-made models and methods for producing maximum learning results. And as often we forget the fact that every individual is a unique learner with his or her own learning strategies and in charge of his or her own learning. Luckily, at least some students more or less accidentally develop their own way, although others may never have enough space to find it. Developing our professional skills *consciously to explore the new ways of learning with our students* could be part of the life-long teacher's professional growth. In the language class that exploring process, if it is part of our daily action at school, is based on *a broader conception of language learning*; such learning goes beyond learning just a linguistic system (Kaikkonen, Kohonen, Lehtovaara, in this volume).

The development of the knowledge of a foreign language is part of the learner's education process, a human being's growth into society and the world as a thinking, feeling and willing individual, as a person who is able to make autonomous choices. According to Wilenius (1994) the most important goal of all education in the post-modern world is a person who is aware of his or her responsibility as a human being and who is able to make independent choices and produce something new in human life and culture. The school-life as an educational environment should promote both teachers' and students' ability to create constantly new things in their life. The school, and *also the language class, is students' and teacher's functional environment, a state of being in the world, a place where many important aspects of life can be and sometimes are learnt, such as choosing and setting personal goals, choosing and practising personal learning modes, assessing oneself and others, sharing ideas and opinions* and so on. The learning environment in school could be understood as what Bauman (1992) calls a 'habitat', a functional environment which provides resources for action and the space where orientation to actions takes place, where the meaningful aspects of the action are being outlined and where also freedom and dependency take their form and are perceived. In the 'habitat' different goals and modes of action, more or less attractive, are available. From the individuals' point of view the important thing is the process of making the choices through which they are able to constitute themselves and live their lives. The character of that process is gradual and always unaccomplished. Therefore, Bauman (1992) calls that process of growth a 'self-assembly'.

The awareness of the responsibility as a human being, the ability to create something new and make constant choices may seem distant and abstract goals for language learning at first. That is because as language teachers we usually concentrate our thoughts on students' specific language skills and their development. We are not so conscious of the development of other aspects of human growth, for example in addition to those already mentioned such further dimensions of education as truthfulness, aesthetic quality and the ethical view of life. According to Wilenius (1982) these aspects of growth develop, when a human being him/herself values, assesses and develops his or her inner and outward action in the direction of certain specific ideals. The development, partly, takes place through thinking. Thinking, on the other hand, needs the language. Consequently, the first and the most important goal for language teaching is *understanding the importance of the knowledge of the language (native and foreign) as a valuable resource and as an integral part of human growth.* Language teaching needs to create *an effective learning environment that provides students with consciously structured opportunities to develop all aspects of their growth* (Kohonen 1992).

Language teaching comprehended as part of the learner's whole educational process, as an important part of his or her growth, is not a one-way process of conveying meanings: it is communication between the teacher and the learner, between a learner and other learners, where a true dialogue (encountering the Other) is possible. The language, native and foreign, is always learnt through endlessly varied, manifold and multilevel, verbal and non-verbal human cooperation, through the dialogue. Sometimes just a few foreign words may open up an important connection between two people. One student wrote about the significance of learning a foreign language in her English essay:

> Every time when I learn a new word of a new foreign language means a lot to me. I think it's very important to have the skill to speak with foreign people. Knowing just a few words of somebody's mother tongue can help you to break the ice between two people who don't know each other. Knowing just those few words is important.   (Anette)

The second goal of language teaching is *to understand the essence and importance of a language in the human action, to understand it as one part of the human dialogue, as a bridge that leads us to each other and at its best improves each other's quality of life.* Understanding language as a bridge that leads us to each other contains the idea that we cannot totally reach another person, his or her inner world. This observation is of utmost importance in all human work and in education especially. According to Turunen (1990) that inner world as a target of teaching has a special quality: neither can it be mastered nor comprehended in explicit terms or using simple logic. To learn at least something of another human being we must try again and again to understand his or her inner world when encountering him or her. Therefore, in language learning, the learning of encountering Otherness is essential and of great value. Of the language skills listening, and the experience of being valuable as the result of being heard, can start a positive development in a human being. Listening and being heard have some healing powers over us. They are a way towards a true dialogue.

A person can have a special power or talent of encountering the Other, but also the learning environment can and must promote this 'skill' of exploring oneself and the Other as a human being. When teaching a foreign language we can help our students to learn to understand each other, to encounter each other in the deep sense of the word; to study the 'skills' of understanding, listening, and expressing. Then a foreign language and the theoretical knowledge of that language (semantic, syntactic, etc.) work as a channel, through which it is possible to find the common language of all people, the dialogue and the language of human understanding.

The third goal of foreign language teaching is *to understand the importance of the language as an expressing and interpreting element in culture and society and to learn the language as well as possible through them.* A culture- and society-orientated language learning environment contains the process of broadening one's views through understanding different patterns of thought, systems, traditions, etc. that are hidden in the concepts, which process promotes us to gain increasing knowledge and understanding of all human life and the world (Kaikkonen 1994 and in this volume). In the changing world language learning should be seen as a lifelong process. This concerns both the knowledge of our mother tongue and also that of a foreign language or languages. When learning a foreign language we should learn to educate ourselves as language learners who see language learning as a natural way of being in the world and who are constantly willing to increase our knowledge of it.

4.1.3 Nature of the process of teaching and learning a foreign language

The process of teaching a foreign language can be planned experientially using the participants' autobiographical knowledge as a foundation. Then the curriculum becomes what Pinar and Grumet (1976) and Pinar *et al.* (1995) call '*currere*' (which is the Latin infinitive and means 'to run'). '*Currere* refers to an existential experience of institutional structures. The method of *currere* is a strategy devised to disclose experience, so that we may see more of it and see more clearly. With such seeing can come deepened understanding of the running, and with this, can come deepened agency' (Pinar and Grumet 1976: vii). In such experiential process teaching and learning situations (materials contents, modes and methods) are planned through *negotiating and inquiring dialogue*, where the experiences of the participants are of central importance. Then learning becomes the responsible action that is shared by all participants (Kohonen in this volume). Everyone's voice is heard. At the same time the inquiring process is being learnt, which according to Rauhala (1978) is the most important and central aspect in all human work, and also the ability to truly communicate using a foreign language. The teaching and learning situations (the curriculum) represent the conceptions and comprehended meanings of the teacher and the learners, their negotiated solutions and decisions, and the practices based on this kind of work.

The teacher–student relationship in experience-based learning is similar to *the researcher–subject relationship* presented by Gitlin and Russell (1994). According to them, in the dialogical process

- participants negotiate meanings at the level of question posing, data collection and data analysis
- both are 'the changers and the changed' trying to reach a mutual understanding
- both participants examine the topic at hand as well as reveal contradictions and constraints within the educative process itself
- the intent is not to discover the truth, but scrutinise normative 'truths' embedded in a specific historical and cultural context
- taken-for-granted notions can be challenged as educators work to better understand schooling   (Gitlin and Russell 1994)

The inquiring process described above is always unfinished. Therefore also *the curriculum*, if understood this way, is never finished, but must be seen as *a constantly changing system*, which is also different for different groups (different learners). *The core of the curriculum is the learning environment where the aims and meanings of teaching and learning are constantly being questioned and clarified.* It is not a list of skills or modes of behaviour to be learnt or mastered. When listening to each other and participating in the dialogue it is possible to discover and understand values and meanings that are hidden in the everyday life in school, and also create new ones, which can be a beginning of change. The curriculum can be as Doll (1993: 151) says 'a fascinating, imaginative realm wherein no one owns the truth and everyone has the right to be understood'.

In the inquiring process, where the maximum use of experiential knowledge is the main resource of the work, *the language learning situations* can be realised in many ways: they can be conversations, presentations, essay writing, lectures, projects, individual, pair or group work, etc. The modes of teaching as such are not of great importance. The most essential point is the world-inquiring dialogue (Scudder and Mickunas 1985) that can be realised through various modes of learning. The aim is to create *a 'true connection' of the learners with the content to be learnt, with the world and with each other by using a foreign language.* Then *authentic communication* takes place: when questions are asked and various thoughts and ideas are expressed the question which language is being used disappears and the content of the discourse becomes crucial. The true and authentic contact with something or someone leaves us something lasting, an experience. The above-described foreign language teaching is based on student experience and it is also teaching that produces student and teacher experience. The language substance that is learnt through such contacts and content is learnt at the deep level of our consciousness and thus we can also remember it longer.

4.1.4   Autobiographical content in teaching and learning a foreign language

> The language is a system that relates what is being talked about (content) and the means used to talk about it (expression). Linguistic content is inseparable from linguistic expression. But in research and in classroom practice, this relationship is frequently ignored. In subject matter learning we overlook the role of the language as a medium of learning. In language learning we overlook the fact that content is being communicated.   (Mohan 1986: 1)

The language should not be seen just as the means of self-expression or communication: the content (of texts, writings and conversations, etc.) in language learning needs more attention than it has been given this far. The cultural and especially personal meanings conveyed by the language and in the language should be taken into consideration more fully. In experiential language learning the learners' autobiographical knowledge serves as a source of self-knowledge, for example by providing topics for the learner and the teacher from inside themselves. *In language learning situations the learners' (and teacher's) autobiographical knowledge is not only a source of insight and imagination but also that of discovery.* It is a valuable and inevitable part of the holistic language learning. A student does not use the language in a vacuum, but brings his or her personal history with him or her into the classroom. A language student's own voice can be found in every piece of his or her writing. Many important aspects, ideas and attitudes of a young person's self and personality are exposed in essays and writings, talks and presentations. Therefore, *learning a foreign language, if given the opportunity to narrate and explore oneself and one's life, can become an essential and important part of growing as a human being: becoming a subject of one's own life.*

In the following two extracts the students of health care and nursing write about important changes in their thinking. The extracts have been written in the English class and their contents discussed afterwards in oral language work.

Violence inside the family

It's a beautiful, peaceful Saturday evening. I'm sitting in the living-room with my mother and we are watching *Chicago Hope*. It's a tradition. Dad hasn't come home yet, but he certainly will. That is a tradition, too. My thoughts return to the childhood again. Our life was so different from what it is now.

I can still remember some lovely weekends when we were all together, the whole family. We used to go to the picnic or to the amusement park or we just were staying at home, played some games or went to fish. It was just great. We all loved and enjoyed those moments together. But hasn't someone said 'You never know what you have got until it's gone'?

Everything started to go wrong after Dad was fired. At the beginning Dad really tried to do something during the days. He tried voluntary work. He tried to fix cars. He tried to be a perfect husband, a perfect dad. None of those made him totally happy. He became frustrated. Dad started to buy some 'sauna beers' for himself, and before we even noticed, Dad was taking 'just a few beers' every evening.

Then one evening he didn't come home with his 'few beers'. The hours went on and on until finally, the door was opened, and there was Dad. He was so drunk that he hardly could stand with his own feet. He had been in a bar with his friends. Well, Mom went to help Dad to get his shoes and jacket off, when it happened. Mom had no chance of saying a thing, when the first punch came and then another one and another one etc. Finally, Mom was on her knees on the floor crying, begging and praying Dad to stop. It seemed as if Dad had become deaf. He started kicking at Mom and at the same time he was beating her over and over again. I went to help my Mom out of there. When Dad noticed me, he slapped me at my face. When I was screaming, Dad seemed to get his brain in control. He just stood there and kept saying over and over again: 'What have I done, what have I done?' He was very upset and very, very sorry about what had happened.

My thoughts stop suddenly when the door is opened. There he is again. As drunk as a duck. His eyes find me in the armchair. He smiles at me as a cruel clown and he comes and sits next to Mom. Dad asks Mom to give him a bottle of gin from the cupboard. Mom says that she thinks he has already drunk enough and it's better for all of us, if we just go to our beds. That is too much to Dad. There it goes again, the same old story. I try to get into my own room so that Dad wouldn't see that I'm going. Otherwise I'll get my part of what he wants to give with his hands and legs.

Well, on Monday morning Mom is going to see the doctor, again. She'll tell the doctor how she fell down the stairs because of the cat that ran to her feet when she was going downstairs. I don't know, if the doctor believes her, but one thing is sure: She can't go to work, if her face is all over black and blue and full of bruises.

If I can get upstairs without Dad seeing me, I'm going to go into my room and lock the door. I'd like to call the police, but that would only mean a very fast dying to me after Dad got out of the jail.

Now I'm only sitting here in the dark hoping that I'd still see tomorrow and get through this nightmare. In one way or another. And I think that I really mean another way . . .   (Marianne)

Marianne wrote about her family and the domestic violence in it. We had read a psychological text on domestic violence and battered women and watched a film dealing with the same subject in the English class. Violence is a topic that interests the students partly because they see violent acts in the streets and partly because they know they will face abused people at their future work as practical nurses. I often ask the students to write about their thoughts or experiences of violence, because the writings are a good starting-point for the discussions about the topic. When writing about the physical and verbal abuse in her family history *Marianne* compared the past situation with the present one. This painful situation had lasted long and seemed to be an endless struggle in the family. She had been questioning why her parents let it continue. When writing her description of those painful and frightening experiences, she was rewriting her personal history, and when writing it she realised one important thing: she came to the conclusion that it is she who has to do something to change the situation, no one else in the family is capable of doing it. It is important to know that although the students were asked to write about the problem of violence the final choice of the intimate topic was hers and no one told her or suggested that she reflect on or analyse the description.

Another example of the use of the authentic and autobiographical content in the language class is the following: the practical nurse students had been practising in an old people's home for a few weeks. Because in Finnish society most elderly people live on their own and not with their children, young students often have very little experience of the elderly and their ways of life. It is not uncommon that they have negative conceptions concerning old age, and that is why some students say that they would not like to work in the future with old people. *Elina* was one of them. After the practical training placement in an old people's home she wanted to write in her English essay about her experiences there. Writing about and discussing that experience made her reflect on what had happened: her attitude to old people and their life in the institution had changed for the better during the placement. She realised that she had started to see the institutional life in a different way and she might even work in an old people's home in the future. This kind of reflective process is, of course, part of the practical nurse students' normal supervision process after and during the placement and usually it takes place in small groups as part of the students' vocational studies. This time, however, it became part of their English studies, their authentic language use. This is *Elina's* description of the changed experience:

Looking after old people

Taking care of old people is hard work. I have worked in Koukkuniemi old people's home, so I know what I'm talking about. There are many demented people in the old people's home and most patients have mobility problems, so you have to help them in almost every daily action: move them out of their bed to a wheelchair, bathroom, help them to get dressed, undressed, give medicines and so on. Some patients' faculties had got so bad that they couldn't see very well and most of them couldn't hear what I was saying. I had to shout into their ears. I listened to their stories, I read newspapers, and went out with them.

Dementia is a serious illness, but still, it made me smile, when one kind old lady told me the same story all over again. The demented people could never remember where their room or bedroom was. For an old person's family the dementia must be much harder to deal with than for the patient. For example, when the family comes to see their grandmother, she doesn't recognise her own daughter or some other close relatives of hers. Well, anyway that didn't happen very often.

Earlier I thought that it is not good for old people to move to an old people's home, but I noticed that actually the patients were enjoying living there, in the safe atmosphere with many old friends, as old as them, and with caring nurses. Every patient had their own room, so if they wanted some privacy, they got it. In the day room the patients can watch television or just talk to other old people. They always talked about their memories: good old times.

It was an interesting experience to work in an old people's home.   (Elina)

Experiential language learning is exploring and studying oneself, the environment and the world without removing oneself from the world. Language is an integral and important part of that world. Although the human experience is more closely connected to a person's mother tongue because of the basic and first connection of language and thought, also in foreign language learning the experience is an inseparable part of the process. It means exploring the world and its phenomena (including oneself, one's personal history) such as they are, as honestly as a human being can, and with the attention to all its various meaning-structures that one can attain. *In the exploring process, where students are thinking of their personal histories, their autobiographical experiences, and either talk or write about them, they at the same time rewrite their personal histories by analysing and trying to understand what has happened;* they create new meanings in their immediate reality, in their existing meaning-structures, in their personal life situations. They change. *The change, the growth, is not based on a vacuum but on building upon, extending and reconstructing the past experience.* As Kagan *et al.* (1993: 517) say 'Intentions, feelings, thoughts and acts are self-authoring constructs that are always in the process of becoming.'

Human development is the process of becoming. Personal growth takes place through experiencing, thinking, acting, talking and writing – through dialogue. Understanding language teaching as a passage or a channel of a personal growth for our students cannot be overemphasised. *In the foreign language class students can be encouraged to write and describe the situations and everyday action where they have experienced something meaningful concerning the topic to be discussed.* Using the phenomenological terminology they are asked to describe something of their life-world, their autobiographical experiences, but *no pressures should be put on them to analyse the experiences, to draw conclusions, or even to fully understand them* (Becker 1992; Giorgi 1988; Perttula 1998). While writing or talking about his or her life-world or personal history a person rewrites and revises it; he or she clarifies his or her perception of him/herself, his or her identity and constructs his or her self. For that process each person needs his or her own space, pace and time. Van Manen (1984: 7) has stated,

> ... the experience must be recalled in such a way that the essential aspects, the meaning-structure of this experience as lived through, are brought back, as it were, and in such a way that we recognise this description as a possible human experience, which means as a possible interpretation of that experience.

We as teachers could just respect the students' own voice, their subjectivity by letting them 'speak' for themselves and feel being heard. *Authentic communication means being in a dialogue with one another.* It is enough to let the student describe his or her experience of the phenomenon as accurately as possible. The teacher's and other students' role in such pedagogical situations is not that of an analyser, assessor or corrector. It is the role of a listener and someone who is sharing those experiences. Kelchtermans and Vandenberghe (1994: 57) state that by respecting a person's own voice 'we also avoid too cognitivistic, rationalistic an approach, which would make us lose out of sight the emotional, irrational and unconscious elements in a person's [in the original text: a teacher's] thinking and acting.'

Writing helps the students to turn the experience (at least part of it) into meaningful themes and topics that they can discuss and think about (Kagan *et al.* 1993). The students should have their own pace, their freedom to investigate their experience, also emotional and irrational, to develop their identity, their individuality and consciousness – that is, to learn about themselves. Writing becomes as van Manen (1989: 238) says 'a kind of self-making or forming. To write is to measure the depth of things, as well to come to a sense of one's own depth.' *When writing about autobiographical experiences, the language is not artificially separated from the person and his or her life-world; it becomes a natural part and medium of growing up.* The foreign words and expressions that are connected to our inner self, our feelings and emotions are best remembered and recalled from our memory later on. Therefore, *experience utilising foreign language teaching not only provides opportunities for a person's growth but also promotes more permanent language learning results.* Writing is inquiring, it is research. Autobiographical writing is something that exercises our ability to see and understand ourselves. The importance of the use of autobiographical knowledge when learning writing in a foreign language can be seen as a growth-supporting element in the holistic language education.

The meaning-constructing process in language learning, although highly personal and individual, of its nature needs social contacts to the outer world. Reading a text, a piece of literature for example, written in a foreign language is a typical case of a very personal meaning-giving process: each of us interprets and understands the text in a different way according to our experiential, autobiographical background and also the level of the language skills. At the same time reading is social and at its best it encourages interpretation, interaction and participation. It is a dialogue of the reader and the text or the author of the text. *When reading about their own experiences the students are in the dialogue with themselves. When sharing their experiences with each other they learn authentic communication in a foreign language.* According to Pinar *et al.* (1995: 437) 'understood phenomenologically, reading is an embodied being-in-the-world, with others'. Reading autobiographical writings is a form of 'embodied' action, it is a meaningful mode of being in the world.

4.1.5 Description of some guiding principles and activities in a language course for specific purposes

The language education to be described in this chapter was carried out at the Tampere Institute of Social Work with a group of practical nurse students. The students of 16–19 years of age studied English for social and health care purposes for one year with the autobiographical experiential knowledge being an integral part of the content and orientation in their language studies. The first principle in the language education was to understand *the holistic conception of man* and to try to live through that principle in practice. The holistic conception of man in the current course was understood as consisting of three dimensions in a human being: bodily being (existence as organic processes), consciousness (existence as experiencing) and situationality (existence in relation to the world) (Rauhala 1981, Lehtovaara, in this volume). The situational dimension of the holistic conception of man includes the idea of *man as a historic being.* A person carries his or her past, present and future with him or her. He or she is not a static figure, but in the process of becoming. *The life situation where a person lives today is affected by the past and the perspectives of the future.* Being in the world is being in relation with what has been and what one can expect or is looking forward to being. This principle was lived through in the course in many ways: not only in the structure and the choice of topics in the curriculum but above all in the learning modes and methods.

Inquiring into oneself, society and the future work (as a qualified practical nurse), and encountering others were the central aspects of orientation when planning the course together in collaboration with the students. The questions as a starting-point for planning the language course were as follows:

(1) Which groups of people and what kind of people does a practical nurse meet and help in his or her work?
(2) What aspects of life and lifestyle are central in the life of those groups?
(3) In which circumstances do you think you would meet those groups in society? And within what kind of problems do you think they would need your help?
(4) Which institutions or places provide help for those groups of people? And where would you like to work in the future?

The purpose of these questions was both to elicit information on the practical nurse's job in order to provide the possibilities for the students to get the professional knowledge of the language during the course and to create the situation where the inquiring and the dialogical process could take place. The students had a better knowledge of their future work, I as their teacher had the better knowledge of the English language. This situation turned out to be a good start for a negotiating situation where real, authentic communication could happen. After negotiating the questions we got the following *contents* to be dealt with in our course:

Groups of people	Life, lifestyle	Health and social problems	Institutions, Placements
1. Children	Needs Activities Hobbies, Interests	Abuse Child battery	Day care centre Helpline for children
2. Young people	Home and friends Relationships Education Food, keeping fit	Running away Intoxicant abuse Exclusion Eating disorders	Safe house Detoxification clinic
3. Adults	Living in a family Living alone Housing, housework	Domestic violence Poverty, exclusion Homelessness	Shelter Home help office
4. The elderly	Needs Activities Life-history Death	Loneliness Weakening health	Old people's home Hospice
5. Persons who are ill or disabled	Good life Body and mind Health care and nursing	Illnesses Disabilities	Hospital Health care centre Residential home
6. Finns and Foreigners	Finnish lifestyle The country and society Social security and services	Racism	Refugee centre Social welfare office

The work of a practical nurse is caring work. It is encountering clients and helping them often in very distressful situations. According to Webb and Blond (1995) the relationship between caring and knowing in caring situations is complex. The level of subjectivity and knowing which involves both bodies and minds is difficult to define and verbalise. The caring today involves a constant reflective process, where the client and the worker have an equal position and a purpose of the process is the client empowerment. In such situations it is important to understand knowing as relational, embodied and dynamic. When considering the use of the language in caring situations the art of listening and encountering as well as the choice of words and expressions are of utmost importance. The words may have as well healing as destructive power. Therefore, also a foreign language should be learned as *a dialogue* where encountering skills are practised and in maximal use. This presupposes *communication where personal meanings are consciously looked for, recognised and created.*

The meanings of the words and expressions in the language are not universal in the sense that everyone understands them in the same way, but they are at least to some extent personal and also changing (Kaikkonen, in this volume). In the language class we tried not only to find our own personal meanings for the professional vocabulary of a practical nurse, but also to find words and ways of expressing things and referring to people in the language that would work as *changing, constructive and healing elements in culture and society.* An example of this kind of procedure is the choice of various terms concerning disability: our view in caring work for people with a disability was to see the person first, not his or her disability. In learning the use of English we tried to show this by consciously using 'words with dignity':

Instead of . . .	We learned to use . . .
Disabled, handicapped	Person(s) with a disability
Crippled by, suffering from	Person who has . . . or, Person with . . .
Lame	Person who is mobility impaired
Bound, dependent on a wheelchair	Person who uses a wheelchair
Deaf, deaf mute, hearing impaired	Person who is deaf, hard of hearing
Mentally retarded	Person with a developmental disability
Spastic (as a noun)	Person with cerebral palsy
Physically challenged	Person with a physical disability
Mental patient, mentally ill	Person with a mental illness
Learning disabled	Person with a learning disability
Visually impaired	Persons who are visually impaired

The change of the viewpoint from seeing a disability to seeing a whole person is extremely important and necessary in modern holistic care and nursing. (Active Living Alliance.) The concepts of a language may show the way to or sometimes be ahead of the development, and thus function as a changing element in society.

The sentence 'Beginning is the most important part of the work' by Plato formed an important guiding principle: in order to connect the content of the topic with ourselves and our personal history we (the teacher and the students) tried every time to begin dealing with the topic from our own experience as the following examples show.

1. Children
Sharing the experience

'A photo of my childhood'
Bring a photo of your childhood (incl. yourself) with you. Choose the photo that helps you to recall a special and important memory from your personal history. Write (or tell the others): What things, objects etc. are there in the picture? When, where and in what circumstances was it taken? What kind of a memory or memories are awoken by the picture? What is your relationship with that picture? What does it tell you about yourself, your childhood? Share as much as you feel you can of the experiences with your partner or with your group.

2. Young people
Sharing the experience

'A mind map of my relationships'
Draw a mind map of your close and distant friends and relatives. Try to characterise your relationship with each person by writing down at least one sentence. Share as much as you feel you can of the experiences with your partner or with your group.

'Watch what you eat'
Write down what you eat during four days of the week and describe your typical daily diet. What does it look like? Is it healthy, unhealthy, tasty, balanced, etc.? Share as much as you feel you can of the experiences with your partner or with your group.

'Keep fit'
Describe your physical appearance. Make a list of all the possible ways to keep fit in different times of the year. Underline the ways you use or have used in your lifetime. Share as much as you feel you can of the experiences with your partner or with your group.

'Drugs and drinking'
Describe the drinking habits of your childhood family. Report one event when you have seen someone drinking too much or when someone has been intoxicated by drugs. When a young person like yourself is offered drugs, what kind of reasons could there be for and against taking them? Share as much as you feel you can of the experiences with your partner or with your group.

3. Adults
Sharing the experience

'The life-cycle of my family'
Draw a life-cycle of your family from the year when you were born to this year. Mark all the years when you think something important (pleasant or unpleasant) happened in your family. Choose the points and events that you want to tell the other classmates. Share as much as you feel you can of the experiences with your partner or with your group.

'The two homes'

Write (or tell) about an ideal home where you would like to live. Describe the rooms, furniture and decorations and also the surroundings of your home. Who would live there? What would their lifestyle be like? How close is this imagined lifestyle to that which you have at the moment? Share as much as you feel you can of the experiences with your partner or with your group.

'Pictures tell us more than words'

Look at the pictures of homeless people from different parts of the world. Choose one picture and try to imagine what his or her typical day could be. How does it differ from your typical day?

'Fear for violence'

Tell the others about the following: What are the places, streets, parks, etc. in your life where you feel you are not safe? What are the dangers in these places? How does fear restrict your life? How do you protect yourself, if you have to go or be in these dangerous places? Share as much as you feel you can of the experiences with your partner or with your group.

4. **The elderly**

Sharing the experience

'Get to know elderly people'

Write about your experiences during the practical training placement in an old people's home. Talk with an elderly person you know well and who wants to share his or her life-story with other people. Make notes and prepare to tell the class mates about his or her everyday life, activities, health, housing, friends and relatives, career . . . Share as much as you feel you can of the experiences with your partner or with your group.

'Imagine yourself as an elderly person with an alternative lifestyle'

Make a list of all the possible alternative lifestyles you can imagine. Choose one of them. Imagine that you are an elderly person and have had that alternative lifestyle. Write an essay on your life as an elderly person. Share as much as you feel you can of the experiences with your partner or with your group.

5. **Persons who are ill or disabled**

Sharing the experience

'Share an experience of being sick'

Have you ever been treated in hospital? When? Where? What for? Your experiences there? If someone gets ill in your family, what do you do? How do you act? Have you helped any person who is ill in your family or neighbourhood? When? Where? In what way?

'Identify yourself with a person with a disability'

Do you know any person with a disability? What is his or her disability or handicap? Try to identify yourself with this person and tell about his or her everyday life as if you were him or her. Begin with 'When I wake up in the morning . . .' and so on. Then compare your daily routine with that of the person with a disability. Finally, describe what kind of a relationship you have to this person. Share as much as you feel you can of the experiences with your partner or with your group.

6. The Finns and Foreigners
Sharing the experience

'What does our country mean to us?'
Listen to some pieces of music by Finnish composers such as Sibelius, Merikanto, Leskinen, Kuoppamäki, Kärki, Mononen, etc. While listening write down as many images of our country as you can.

'Media make meanings'
Follow the news on foreign people in our country in a daily newspaper during one week. Choose a couple of news items that you find most interesting from your point of view. Prepare to explain briefly, what information, attitudes and opinions of foreign people they contain. Why did you choose them?

'Getting to know a foreigner, a refugee, an asylum seeker . . .'
Arrange an interview with a foreign person you know and who wants to share his or her experiences with you. Make notes and prepare to tell the classmates about his or her everyday life and activities in his or her own country and his or her ideas and opinions of that country. Or ask him or her to visit our English class and tell us about his life and culture.

To study and learn the encountering skills does not mean just studying and learning expressing oneself and listening to others. The effective expressing and listening succeed only in *the climate of psychological safety and trust* (Rogers 1969). To be able to communicate something from one's inner self, one's personal history presupposes other people's acceptance. To gain such a trustful and safe climate in a group may sometimes be very difficult. The students should be helped to make a personal choice of what and how much of themselves they want to share with others. We had always the same groups, so called 'home groups', where the students worked whenever the autobiographical knowledge was used in discussions. Also pair work was used and then always the same two people (often close friends) worked together. Thus also the choice of with whom the students worked was theirs.

We tried as much as possible to discuss our own experiences (of which we had nearly always written at first) and then simulate the situations at the students' future work where they might need the foreign language skills. The target was *'real', authentic (written and oral) communication*. The following list collected by Burnard and Chapman (1990) from literature on teaching methods in nurse education gave us an idea of the rich selection of different oral activities and turned out to be very useful for our experiential language learning course. The list included:

- Role play
- Pairs activities
- Co-counselling exercises
- Psychodrama
- Relaxation exercises
- Structured group activities
- Role rehearsal
- Encounter group activities
- Social skills training (Green A J 1995)

As far as the reading and listening practice during the course is concerned our purpose was to rely on *authentic materials*, such as articles from newspapers and magazines, brochures, TV news items, current affairs programmes, pieces of literature and lyrics, etc. The selection of materials was done on the basis of the topics in the units planned together with the students. In individual work the students had a lot of possibilities to choose materials according to their interests and the level of their language. *The most valuable authentic material, however, was the material produced by the students themselves, their autobiographical and experiential pieces of work:* essays, reports, presentations, interviews, discussions, chatting, etc. These materials, often in the form of a narrative, formed the core of the course: *our opportunity to inquire into ourselves, our thinking, making choices and encountering.*

It was clear from the start of the course that the students were experts on knowing what they want to learn and what they have to learn of the English language in order to help foreign clients in practical nurse's work, plus what the best and most convenient way was for them to learn these things. In collaboration we chose the topics for autobiographical experiential content, the informative content that was relevant and of current interest for the students' future work, the vocabulary and grammar needed to communicate effectively in the chosen situations, and the inquiring, encountering learning modes and methods needed at work. As a teacher taking the attitude of a recipient and a negotiator, not a 'teacher' or a controller in the classroom, gave me an opportunity and challenge to live through and participate together with the students in exploring the dilemma of freedom and dependency, choice and responsibility – in other words the core of the educational and growth process – in language learning situations.

4.2 THE KNOWLEDGE OF LEARNERS, THE KNOWLEDGE OF LEARNING

4.2.1 The importance of sharing experiences in learning

The goal of all education and for all participating in it can be: to become whole persons, human beings, who trust their own experience so much that through and with that experience they are able to be themselves in the world (Varto and Veenkivi 1993). In learning situations arranged to match this goal both the teacher and the learner work as co-researchers trying to explore the conditions and ways in which each participant's life-world, the world as it reveals itself in one's experience, his meanings, beliefs and conceptions, is constituted, developed and altered. When becoming familiar with such an exploring process and realising the uniqueness of each other's life-world, we become conscious of learning as an individual and unique process that concerns the person as a whole. *No two human beings learn in exactly similar ways.*

Understanding and assessing personal action through co-reflecting autobiographical knowledge increases teachers' and learners' knowledge of themselves and builds the foundation on which to found their own, personal solutions and to develop better educational practice. The prerequisite for such successful dialogue as an educational practice is the ability to listen to and 'hear' each other's experience. Knowledge gained through listening to and hearing one another increases our possibilities to understand each other's ways of acting and working in everyday life in school. Striving towards a better understanding of each other's cultural backgrounds and the rest of this human and historical world, our life-world, makes such a dialogic starting point possible in education. We should reach it, if we want to support and guide the learner's personal, holistic growth.

The person's ability to be in a dialogic relationship with reality, the ability to create new meanings in and into his or her life-world, to constitute his or her own life and consciousness, is realised when he or she is given space for personal, subjective, and autonomous action, the core of which is the inquiry into his or her experiential, autobiographical selfhood. When the person learns to understand the conditions under which and the ways how his or her meaning-structures are changing, his or her ability to control and direct his or her life and action, including learning, will be better. This dialogic relationship with reality (Varto and Veenkivi 1993) – learner autonomy – can be seen as the basic and central goal of education.

4.2.2 Significant learning experiences

No two people experience the same classroom situation in the same way. A person's experience is always unique. The significance of a particular event, act or happening for a person varies from individual to individual. Therefore, in teaching situations it is impossible to 'offer' or 'provide' such experiences that could guarantee everyone's learning. Instead, students need time, space and perhaps some assistance to find their own ways and best strategies of learning. Merriam and Clark (1993) studied the underlying structure of the significance of life-experience learning in adult learners: why do we learn from certain life experiences and not from others? Why do some of the experiences from which we learn have a greater impact on us than others? What makes learning significant? The findings of their study suggested that for the learning to be significant:

(1) it must personally affect the learner, either by resulting in an expansion of skills, sense of self, or life perspective, or precipitating a transformation and
(2) it must be subjectively valued by the learner (Merriam and Clark 1993: 129)

The above conceptions of learning experiences get support from the following descriptions of significant learning experiences written by the students of social pedagogy at the beginning of their English course.

> When I began to think about the topic *Significant learning experiences*, the first event that crossed my mind happened in my second year in the comprehensive school. I went to a small school of about 300 pupils. We had a garden in the

school yard that the pupils had to take care of with the teachers. One day the teacher took us outside and showed us how to cross an apple tree and a currant bush. Although I cannot recall, if it succeeded or not, even today I remember how the crossing happened. I think the reason it stayed in my memory was that we actually *did* the crossing, not only read it in the biology book . . .

Another time I was very impressed and learnt a lot once in a commercial college. A former intoxicant abuser came to tell us about drugs and his life. He told us about incidents in his life, what drugs had brought into his life. I was very shocked to wake up to the reality and the situation in Finland. Afterwards I asked the man what I could do to help youngsters who are using drugs. Well, one thing led to another, and I found YAD (Youth Against Drugs *Association*). I have now been actively involved with YAD almost for three years, and I have been a member of the board for four months now. What was so special about that man? At least he was very honest and serious. He truly believed in his matter.

(Sini-Marja)

For *Sini-Marja* learning by *doing it herself* is important. She has found out that *the person's own experience* is important and convincing in learning and teaching situations. The experiential content dealt with in a teaching situation is a sign of the reliability and seriousness of the communicator.

In my school years I have always liked to make and listen to presentations. I think it is a good way to learn things, when you have to search for information, write it down and then give a presentation to other people. It is also very interesting to listen to other people's presentations.

The most significant learning experience for me has been my practical training placement in Birmingham in England. I was there three months working in a children's nursery. I worked with two- and three-year-old children. Most children and staff were black, which was quite an experience for me. It was interesting and different. The children were really wonderful and cute and the staff really caring and friendly, too. I took part in everything that one can do in a nursery. The staff and the leader of the nursery counted on me, so I had quite a freedom to do anything that I wanted with the children. That was really great and I learned a lot about the work in the nursery and about the people from different cultures. (Krista)

Krista has discovered that *self-compiled presentations* are excellent in learning. Searching for information and presenting what one has found out and listening to other students' presentations help her to learn new things. She has also learnt that the teacher's or supervisor's *trust* and the *freedom* given by them in learning situations are important.

I think that the most significant learning experience for me was the moment when I learnt to read. That moment was as a door opened to a new, interesting world. That significant experience happened in my first autumn at school. Of course, after that there have been so many other significant learning experiences, too.

Every time when I learn a new word of a new foreign language means a lot to me. I think it's very important to have the skill to speak with foreign people. Knowing just a few words of somebody's mother tongue can help you to break the ice between two people who don't know each other. Knowing those few words is important . . .

The most significant learning experiences I have got from project work. It is learning by doing, really. I have taken part in many projects, for example family, ship, open kindergarten and Vyborg project. Those projects have taught me many new things of social work and people. In Vyborg, for example, there can happen almost anything and you still have to do things to the end. That is very useful to learn. You can also find out that although people and countries are different, the problems are the same in all over the world.   (Anette)

For *Anette* learning to *read* was a great experience, because it opened a new world. Every new word learnt of *a foreign language* is significant, because it gives a chance to make contact with foreign people. She has also had significant experiences of *learning by doing* in various projects.

I was on the secondary level of the comprehensive school and maths was difficult to me. I didn't understand that subject at all, at least I felt that way. The teacher gave me private lessons, which was good, but still, it was so hard to learn maths. Then came a New Year's Eve and I promised myself to study maths harder in the future. So I did. It was hard for me but I studied and studied. When I got my certificate in spring my maths grade was 9 (before it had been 6) [scale 4–10]. I was proud of myself and so was my teacher. She gave me a scholarship. So, I learnt that nothing is impossible, if you really try hard and believe in yourself. Nowadays when I feel that I am not able to do a duty or task I remember my maths achievement. That gives me strength to go on and helps me reach the aim.   (Teija)

Teija has learnt that there is nothing in learning that is impossible; if she tries hard to learn something, she will learn it. *The person's own will, conquering oneself,* is important when learning something difficult.

I have always been fond of children. Even as a child it was quite obvious to me that I would like to work with children. At first I wanted to become a childminder, because I was looked after in family day care when I was under five years old. Before starting the primary school I spent at the kindergarten for about two years. Still I wanted to be a childminder.

As time went on I grew up and started the secondary level of the comprehensive school. There we had a few new subjects such as home economics, for example. At home I had made it easily. I didn't have to clean my room or prepare meals. So, when the home economics started at school, I realised something important. A childminder's occupation is hard work. You have to take care of the children and at the same time prepare meals. Your home should be quite clean, too, so that the environment is safe and healthy for the growing children. The childminder is always present at the workplace. During our home economics lessons I realised all that.

Since those lessons I started to think other occupations in which I could work with children. At that time I didn't know about all the different occupations or professions that there are in kindergartens. Our student counsellor told me about a children's day care nurse's and a kindergarten teacher's jobs. I wanted to study more. So now I am qualifying as a social pedagogue.

(Minna)

Minna's occupational choices were changed, when by *doing things herself* in the home economics class, *observing the work* and *drawing personal conclusions* from it she had realised how demanding and hard it was.

In sections 4.1.1 and 4.1.2 above you can find two more descriptions of the best learning experiences. *Tiina's* experience (4.1.1) concerns *learning in a community* and *Hannele* (4.1.2) tells about the way of *developing her own method of learning* to remember important years and historical events.

The students' writings above bring out a variety of conceptions of situations where a human being learns effectively. Those conceptions have been discussed in many theoretical books and articles and in that sense they are not new or original. But for the teacher who has received such knowledge of her students' learning at the beginning of the course the conceptions are 'new' and they are of a special value: they have been discovered by the students themselves. They are personal and unique. And they inform of the best and most significant learning experiences in each student's personal history. *Exploring this type of experiential knowledge increases the teacher's sensitivity to understanding the various ways and strategies the students have in learning and how they feel and experience things.* Sharing the students' earlier experiences in learning in general, and learning a foreign language in particular, helps to develop a thoughtful and appropriate practice. The students' experiences are the 'new' knowledge that a teacher cannot study at the university or in teacher education, but it is the knowledge that a teacher has to gain and study again and again in every classroom with each group and each student. Such *autobiographical experiential knowledge of learning functions as the basis for developing authentic methodology for each group and for facilitating each individual's unique learning process.*

4.3 AUTOBIOGRAPHICAL EXPERIENTIAL KNOWLEDGE IN TEACHER EDUCATION AND TEACHER DEVELOPMENT

4.3.1 Autobiographical knowledge in teacher education and teacher development

> . . . much educational research is involved only in a process of amputating the private from the public. An account of a long journey such as learning and teaching cannot be observed merely once or twice in the course of the voyage.
>
> (Solas 1992: 212)

To experience continuity in our lives and careers we need the knowledge of who we are, where we have been and where we are going to. *Our autobiographical consciousness constitutes the core of our self-identity.* As a subjective and dynamic conception of ourselves in the world it both restricts and gives opportunities in life. Ignoring this historical aspect of a person in any education is ignoring a person's identity and right to define him/herself as a changing, developing human being. Just as there is a history of language, a history of meanings and a history of changing professional thought, there is also a history of each individual student or teacher. The historical autobiographical insight into our development in life and becoming aware of the changes in it enables us to become more independent and self-aware learners and educators, persons who are consciously orientated to the future, while acting here and now.

The teacher's autobiographical knowledge is a person-specific, unique meaning-structure. It consists of the teacher's conception of man, beliefs, interpretations of his or her action, relationships, possibilities, what he or she is or is not allowed to do, and so on. Typically such thoughts and conceptions of the teacher's life and career are made explicit in his or her life-story by means of narration. The meaning-giving process where the significant past experiences are written or told contains personal interpretations of experiences, which are selected by the person's memory and directed and controlled by many internal and external factors. *The teacher's autobiographical knowledge understood as a subjective interpretation of his or her life offers a valuable starting-point in teacher education and development.*

According to Knowles and Holt-Reynolds (1994: 9–10), autobiographical knowledge has an enormous influence on teachers and their work:

> Our personal histories influence the ways in which we interact and work, the ways in which we view teaching and teachers, the ways we develop the course work and pedagogics, the ways in which we interact with our students, and the manner we research our practice and the practice of others.

The importance of autobiographical knowledge or personal history explains why teachers' actions differ so much despite the fact that they may follow the common curriculum, have the same syllabuses, use the same textbooks and teaching methods, and have studied the same educational theories. According to van Manen (1991), pedagogical understanding and pedagogical acting go hand in hand: a talented teacher, who is more than an instructor, knows what is pedagogically the 'good' or 'appropriate' thing to say or do. He or she possesses *a sense of tact*, a certain thoughtfulness or active mindfulness, which means some kind of intuitive readiness to make 'good' or 'appropriate' choices, judgements and decisions within rapidly flowing pedagogical situations and fluctuating circumstances of school life. *Concerning the whole person, not the head and mind only, such educational knowledge has been learned through lived experience during the teacher's personal history and it forms an integral part of his or her life-world.* Van Manen's conception of the talented teacher's qualities involves the idea of a broader view of learning 'teaching methods' or 'classroom practice'. To become a good teacher is a process concerning the whole human development including the teacher's past, present and future.

In order to overcome the rather solitary nature of educational work teachers are nowadays encouraged to *inquire into and change their practice by reviewing, criticising and reflecting it.* Experiences, everyday actions and conventions are made explicit by writing them down in a journal in the form of a narrative, which is afterwards shared with others by describing the experiences orally and discussing them in groups. Sharing such experiential and rather personal material in pre-service and in-service teacher education offers both the supervisor and the person supervised an opportunity to understand better her/himself, his or her conceptions and emotions and especially the choices and didactic decisions concerning the work and action. In this way our personal history, our experiential background works as a medium for growth and as a medium for altering and developing our practice.

There are some undeniable advantages to be gained by the use of autobiographical experiential knowledge. Firstly, the autobiographical knowledge combined with educational theories provides teachers with an experiential base in their education and development. The most important goal for acquiring and sharing autobiographical knowledge in teacher education is to try collaboratively to *become aware of the individual modes of interpreting experiences of reality, to uncover personal, often implicit, pedagogical theories and to discover each participant's own, personal methodology in teaching.* With the autobiographical knowledge it is possible to strive to reach the person's subjective reality and his or her assumptions and beliefs of reality. When we report and describe our experiences and events in our life we at the same time interpret what has happened to us, what we have experienced (Benyon 1985). *The interpretation of pedagogical situations is a central element in the teacher's work* because it sets the ground for pedagogical actions. Our personal way to interpret what we have faced and experienced directs our course of life and consequently our professional growth as a teacher. It also controls our ways to meet and treat the others in education. By inquiring into the autobiography it is possible for a teacher to find the connection of his or her experience, its interpretation, and current teaching action. As a consequence, *the teacher can discover and constitute his or her subjective educational theory and develop the professional self.* These things in turn lead to a better control of the work (Butt and Raymond 1992; Clandinin and Conelly 1987; Goodson 1992; Knowles 1993; Schubert 1992).

The second advantage of using teacher autobiographies concerns the context. *By utilising the autobiographical knowledge we are able to explore our individual life as part of a wider context, the social and economic system and the time in which we are living* (Benyon 1985). We get information about society, culture and era, as they are seen and experienced by an individual in his or her life-world. From the point of view of a teacher the autobiographical knowledge of his or her growth environment and school is of great importance. Each of us has his or her own conceptions of what it means to bring up children, educate people and to work as a teacher. Those conceptions we have gained through our experiences as a growing child at home and as a learner in school. Knowles (1994: 57) sees the powerful influence of personal histories centring

... on prospective teachers' memories of education-related events and contexts. These memories about teaching and teachers are also often enshrouded in circumstances associated with critical incidents and reveal not only their selective nature but their fading and distortion with time. Moreover, such memories represent views of teachers' actions made without regard for the thinking behind the particular actions.

The conceptions based on personal memories are an important part of the basis of the teacher's understanding; he or she 'sees and knows' the teacher's profession and pedagogical work in a certain light, such as he or she has experienced them in his or her personal history. There is hardly a better way to start developing as a teacher than 'lift these conceptions and meanings onto the table', discuss and investigate them in their historical context – time, institution, educational thought, circumstances, society, etc. – in which the meanings have become part of the teacher's life-world. The historical and societal perspective gives teachers a new point of view from which to explore their own and their former teachers' patterns of thought and their interpretations of the educational experiences. By placing the experiences in a certain specific time, society and culture with its values and beliefs, it is easier for the teacher to understand his or her autobiographical conscious-ness and start developing educational work in the current reality. At the same time the teacher gets a wider view to the cultural factors that control the learning process and the meanings that are created in different growth environments. This wider view may help the teacher to understand better his or her different students who come from different cultures and socio–economic backgrounds, and who consequently may have very different ways of learning.

The third *use of the autobiographical knowledge in teacher education and develop-ment is its assessing or evaluating function.* Autobiographical knowledge reveals, on the one hand, the complexity and intricacy of a person's life-world and experience and, on the other hand, a person's, perhaps, very defective or imperfect conceptions of a certain phenomenon (Benyon 1985). Typical problems are, for instance: a teacher has learnt to see learners' (or his or her own) developmental potential as limited or the teacher's role as part of a very restricting hierarchical system. Therefore, he or she expects orders from the administrative officials and keeps the learners under his or her strict control. *Such patterns of thought cannot be changed unless they are exposed and re-evaluated.* One reason why educational systems and school cultures change and progress so slowly may be the fact that we all 'know' them through our own experience. We have all gone to school, been part of the system, part of that familiar culture. The things that are familiar and self-evident we don't question so easily. Self-evident and familiar phenomena are for example the classroom system, the teacher's evaluation and assessment, timetables, con-ceptions of teachers' and students' roles in school, and so on. Becoming familiar with the past and present school culture with the help of the auto-biographical knowledge, the teacher can get rid of such old conceptions that limit his or her work and action. Such knowledge may also open up new and even radical ways to conceptualise and develop school life, educational envir-onments and the teacher's educational modes and methods. A permanent and sustainable way to a new teachership leads through becoming aware of the past, exploring and peeling off one's existing meanings, assessing them critically and, if needed, changing and modifying one's conceptions and practice.

Which meanings are to be investigated or dealt with? According to Knowles (1993) when dealing with a teacher's autobiographical knowledge we can inquire into his or her inner dialogue concerning school and teaching, and his or her beliefs of these phenomena. The student teachers who have not much teaching experience seek the grounds for their solutions in the classroom from their earlier experiences as pupils or students. They have their own inner dialogue on how they (or some imagined learner, their own classmate, for example) would have reacted or experienced that particular practice. The professional teachers' grounds for their decisions are found in what Clandinin (1985) calls 'personal practical knowledge': the combination of theory and practical knowledge born of lived experience, the knowledge which is imbued with all the experiences that make up a person's being. The inner dialogue based on such knowledge consists of the arguments concerning the theory and practice that are considered meaningful and 'right' when working with learners in various groups and courses in school. The arguments as *linguistic* statements are easily identifiable to be used in a collaborative inquiry.

Experiential, autobiographical knowledge is stored in our memory also in a *non-linguistic* form: as feelings or physical sensations. Such experiences, too, can be the basis for accepting or rejecting a certain practice in teaching and learning situations. Dealing with the joys and happiness of teacher autobiography as a positive vehicle to learning and fears and anxiety as obstacles or a negative vehicle to learning, for example, should be part of teacher education and development. Although people cannot totally verbalise their feelings or physical sensations, it does not mean that they cannot be dealt with. *Observing teaching situations and different feelings and sensations coming to expression in them, recognising and re-experiencing both positive and frightening events and then investigating them should be part of regular supervision work in teacher education and development.*

The introduction of the concept of '*metaphor*' as part of teacher education research has been useful as it gives one way of reaching also the non-linguistic knowledge in our consciousness. An example of a typical metaphor concerning the teacher could be 'Teacher is a boss'. It is a figurative way of describing a teacher by referring to a boss who has the qualities that we think the teacher should or should not have. According to Cole (1990: 5–6) metaphors are

> . . . linguistic expressions of tacit levels of thought, fictional constructs of the actual. Deriving from the Greek 'to carry across', metaphors provide a way of carrying ideas and understandings from one context to another so that both the ideas and the new context become transformed in the process.

By reflecting experience and representing elements of personal histories metaphors allow access to individuals' thoughts. They are vehicles of thinking over our experiences, they organise our thoughts about subject matters, activities or theories coherently and in a compact way. By using a symbol system they also allow us to convey experiences that cannot be literally described (Knowles 1994). Metaphors create very colourful and persisting images, for example, of teacher's roles, hardworking students, slow learners, the school as an institution, discipline and so on. And, as Pavio (1979: 152) says, 'perhaps through imagery, a metaphor provides a vivid and, therefore, memorable and emotion-arousing representation of a perceived experience'. As part of teachers' implicit educational theories the metaphors may have a long-lasting effect on their work. Therefore, *the teachers should be encouraged and helped to identify and analyse their metaphors concerning school life, learners and teacher's profession.*

The experiential knowledge, whether it is in the form of arguments, feel-ings, physical sensations or metaphors, is 'lived' knowledge, and as such more permanent in the memory than the information acquired by studying books or by listening to lectures. Growing and developing as a teacher pre-supposes the process where the distorting and limiting meanings constructed in our personal histories become conscious in our minds, where they are dissolved, and new meanings are constructed on that ground. The process most naturally takes place in a group or with a supervisor. *When reflecting on autobiographical knowledge with other people we often have to share very intimate knowledge.* Tigerstedt (1990) states that while writing or reporting his or her autobiography (even on his own) a person evaluates his or her piece of work in interaction with the imagined reader. The reader or the listener always has some influence on the quality and contents of what has been written or reported. Therefore, the role and art of the supervisor must also be under inquiry in these situations. The supervisor must respect the supervised per-son's story and give space for his or her intimacy and growth. The meanings that have been recognised as significant (by the supervised person) form the basis and starting point of the dialogue between the supervisor and the person supervised.

The goal of the collaborative inquiry is to make the invisible meanings visible. In this kind of research process that takes place between two (or more) people the primary aim is to make the supervised person's art of living better. Therefore, one must take care of the fact that the supervised person's experienced meanings can remain unique (Lehtovaara M 1992). Because of the personal and intimate nature of autobiographical knowledge it is obvious that dealing with it and discussing it must take place in a secure relation-ship, in a relaxed atmosphere. Reporting and discussing must be voluntary. *The reporting person has the right to choose the distance and the degree of openness to the person with whom he or she shares his or her autobiographic knowledge.* There should be several pieces of written narratives on lived experiences and many encounters, since the meanings that are considered to be most important for the supervisor and the person supervised should become better and better understood, more and more specified during the dialogue. The task of the educator is, as Bullough (1994: 108) says '. . . to help them to develop the kind of understanding of self as teacher that will enable them to establish a role in a school and within the community of educators that is education-ally defensible and personally satisfying, congruent with a desired teaching self'.

4.3.2   Autobiographical knowledge – reminisced experience

When studying their own autobiographies the teachers are at the same time both researchers and the subjects that are being researched. The autobiographical method, the hermeneutic understanding of life, makes it possible for the researcher to study individual experience and for the one that is being researched it offers the means to reach understanding of him/herself as a more integrated person. In the autobiographic research process a person telling him/herself about his or her experiences gets two kinds of information: first, he or she remembers and collects documents on historically true events and episodes. Secondly, he or she reports his or her subjective truth, personal meanings. His or her memory interprets the events of the past, arranges, classifies and selects them; it reconstructs the past (Saarenheimo 1991).

According to Peskin and Livson (1981) and Saarenheimo (1992) the past experiences narrated today are not the objective truth of what has happened or how the things were then; they are the narrator's present, subjective, interpreted conception of what has happened or how things have been. *When inquiring into lived experience we have to find out, as much as it is possible, how the experiential knowledge that we can remember at that moment corresponds to what we have really lived.* The experience, when it is recalled and narrated, doesn't manifest itself as it was at that time, but it is influenced by the present moment, the narrator's self and situation in life: the past and the present (often also the future), the earlier experience and the present one are mixed (Castelnuovo-Tedesco 1978). *Reminiscing about, recalling and interpreting autobiographical knowledge is an interaction between our past, present and future.* When a person is reminiscing about his or her past experiences, his or her memory selects and emphasises some events, and evaluates everything that has happened. Therefore, the told or written autobiography is not a collection of the events that happened in a person's life, but, instead, it is a restructured picture of oneself (Titon 1980). A teacher can simply ask him/herself the question 'What can I recollect about my teaching last week, yesterday, this morning?' He or she will immediately notice how selective his or her memory is. When we write down in our journal about our past experiences, we may tell more about what we are now, how we experience the events, problems, etc., now, than how the things were when they happened. The recalled and narrated experiences are interpreted again, and the interpretation is a little different every time it is narrated again. Although the original experience stays the same, the writer's interpretation and narrative of it changes in the course of the lived weeks, months or years.

According to d'Epinay (1995) a person's narrative of his or her experiences, his or her life is always the narrator's view, where part of it may be even imagined. The imagined part, however, has borrowed elements of the narrator's 'real' world and life. It is part of his or her life-world and therefore, the 'story' told is not of less value. *The teacher's description of his or her experience, when containing imagined material, may give some kind of an idea of what he or she would like to be like as a teacher or what he or she would have wanted, hoped or feared to happen.* These things, too, are part of the person's self. When using autobiographical knowledge in teachers' supervision situations one problem to be investigated is how far the teachers are able to recognise the structure and motives of their own stories, what in them is something that has really happened and what has been restructured in their minds.

The teacher's description of his or her experience (a problem situation in the classroom and how it was solved, for example) may be tinged with a kind of wishful thinking, an illusion of how he or she would have wanted the things to be or happen or how he or she had feared them to be or happen. Experiencing people, things and events rises from the totality of the human being, his or her way of experiencing people, things and events in general, the way of experiencing being the result of an individual autobiographical development process. Therefore, in supervision encounters with teachers *it is as important to pay attention to a narrator's way of interpreting his or her experiences as to the experiences themselves.* If the teacher is not able to make a difference between the truth and the imagined in a certain classroom situation, he or she may start reflecting and reaching a solution of something that has never really happened except in his or her mind. To be able to understand one's way of experiencing people, things and events and one's action as thoroughly as possible, one has to return to the roots of one's own experience by exploring one's autobiography, by peeling away meaning-structures and trying to reach the essential. Such research helps us to understand our personal way of experiencing the world, creating and interpreting meanings, making choices, constructing and reconstructing our memory. The research literature concerning the use of experiential autobiographical knowledge emphasises the fact that we have to be aware of the mechanism through which our memory is constructed, because that knowledge helps us to consider the experiential material critically. In other words, *to be able to develop as teachers we must become acquainted with the structure of our own identity and consciousness with its conception formation in order to fully understand our experiential narratives* (Graham 1991; Saarenheimo 1991; 1992; Wallace 1992).

In order to understand what we have experienced and in order to be able to interpret it properly, we have to study our own present meaning-structures and changes in them. As far as the research of experience is concerned, according to Reason and Rowan (1981), the researcher must possess a very high level of self-awareness. It is hardly possible to do valid research on one's self without another person or a community. Resorting to other people's collaborative assistance is thought to be the best way of improving the process of inquiring into and expanding our self-consciousness in an educational and supervisory situation (Butt and Raymond 1992). In such a collaborative process, an inquiry into a person's meaning-structures and the construction and changing of them is not enough. Such process should also contain the inquiry into the inquiring process including all participating individuals with their autobiographies, since the knowledge of a human being is created in a cultural and social context (Aldridge 1993; Stanley 1995).

Recalling past memories, reminiscing about experiences means evaluation of life and interpretation of various meanings in the life-world. In such a process of interpreting his or her meanings the teacher has to *try to approach the inner logic of his or her experiential world and examine the individual meaning-structures as an integral part of the whole. Reminiscing about, evaluating and reinterpreting one's life including one's career is one way to constitute oneself when trying to reach a better personal integration in life.* Our memories, because they are not static or clearly defined, offer us *a constant opportunity of being and becoming reinterpreted and reunderstood* by showing us what we have been like and how we have developed. They help us to see ourselves anew in a constantly changing time and environment. This process develops us as teachers and promotes our ability to maintain the identity and dignity in today's changing and ambiguous reality.

4.4   REFERENCES

Active Living Alliance for Canadians with a disability. E-mail: disability.alliance@rtm.activeliving.ca

Aldridge J (1993) The textual disembodiment of knowledge in research account writing. *Sociology* **27**(1): 53–66

Bauman Z (1992) *Intimations of postmodernity.* London: Routledge

Becker C (1992) *Living and relating: an introduction to phenomenology.* Newbury Park, CA: Sage

Benyon J (1985) Institutional change and career histories in a comprehensive school. In Ball S J and Goodson I F (eds) *Teachers' lives and careers.* London: The Falmer Press, pp 158–79

Bertaux D (1981) Introduction. In Bertaux D (ed.) *Biography and society. The life history approach in the social sciences.* London: Sage, pp 5–15

Bullough R V Jr (1994) Personal history and teaching metaphors: a self study of teaching as conversation. *Teacher Education Quarterly* **21**(1): 107–20

Burnard P and Chapman C (1990) *Nurse education: the way forward.* London: Scutari Press

Butt R and Raymond D (1992) Studying the nature and development of teachers' knowledge using collaborative autobiography. *International Journal of Educational Research* **13**(4): 402–49

Castelnuovo-Tedesco P (1978) The mind as a stage. Some comments on reminiscence and internal objects. *International Journal of Psychoanalysis* **59**: 19–25

Clandinin J (1985) Personal practical knowledge: a study of teachers' classroom images. *Curriculum Inquiry* **15**(4): 361–85

Clandinin J and Conelly M (1987) Teachers' personal practical knowledge: what counts as 'personal' is studies of the personal. *Journal of Curriculum Studies* **19**(6): 487–500

Cole A L (1990) Teachers' experienced knowledge: a continuing study. Paper presented at the Annual Meeting of the American Educational Research Association, Boston, MA

d'Epinay C L (1995) What story? In Haavio-Mannila E, Hoikkala T, Peltonen E ja Vilkko A (eds) *Just tell the truth. The autobiographical nature of the biographical research.* Helsinki: Gaudeamus, pp 45–51 (in Finnish)

Doll W Jr (1993) *A post-modern perspective on curriculum.* New York: Teachers College Press

Gitlin A and Russell R (1994) Roby's story: out of silence. *Teacher Education Quarterly* **21**(1): 121–44

Giorgi A (1988) Sketch of a psychological phenomenological method. In Giorgi A (ed.) *Phenomenology and psychological research.* Pittsburgh, PA: Duquesne University, pp 8–21

Goodson I (1992) Sponsoring the teachers' voice: teachers' lives and teacher development. In Hargreaves A and Fullan M (eds) *Understanding teacher development.* New York: Teachers College Press, pp 110–21

Graham R J (1991) *Reading and writing the self. Autobiography in education and the curriculum.* New York: Teachers College Press

Green A J (1995) Experiential learning – a critical evaluation of an enquiry which used phenomenological method. *Nurse Education Today* **15**: 420–6

Huotelin H (1992) *Methodological choices of the biographical research. The methodological choices of the project 'Searching for the Meaning of Education'.* Research Reports of the Faculty of Education No. 46, University of Joensuu, Joensuu (in Finnish)

Kagan D M, Freeman L E, Horton C E and Rountree B S (1993) Personal perspectives on a school–university partnership. *Teaching and Teacher Education* **9**(5–6): 499–519

Kaikkonen P (1994) *Culture and foreign language learning.* Juva: WSOY (in Finnish)

Kelchtermans G and Vandenberghe R (1994) Teachers' professional development: a biographical perspective. *Journal of Curriculum Studies* **26**(1): 45–62

Knowles J G (1993) Life-history accounts as mirrors: a practical avenue for the conceptualizing of reflection in teacher education. In Calderhead J and Gates P (eds) *Conceptualizing reflection in teacher development.* London: The Falmer Press

Knowles J G (1994) Metaphors as windows on a personal history: a beginning teacher's experience. *Teacher Education Quarterly* **21**(1): 37–66

Knowles J G and Holt-Reynolds D (1994) An introduction. *Teacher Education Quarterly* **21**(1): 5–12

Kohonen V (1992) Experiential language learning: second language learning as cooperative learner education. In Nunan D (ed.) *Collaborative language learning and teaching.* Cambridge: CUP, pp 14–39

Lehtovaara J (1994) On the philosophical foundations of teacher education. In Kaikkonen P and Pihlainen P (eds) *Guidelines for developing subject teacher education and school at the Department of Teacher Education in Tampere.* Reports from the Department of Teacher Education in Tampere University A19. University of Tampere, Tampere, pp 17–37 (in Finnish)

Lehtovaara M (1992) *The subjective world-picture as an aim of the educational research.* Acta Universitatis Tamperensis ser A vol 338. University of Tampere, Tampere (in Finnish)

Lehtovaara M (1994) The knowledge of him/herself in the totality of a person's meaning-structures. In Lehtovaara J and Jaatinen R (eds) *In a dialogue – on the way to a possibility.* Reports from the Department of Teacher Education in Tampere University A21, University of Tampere, Tampere, pp 57–79 (in Finnish)

Lyons N P (1990) Dilemmas of knowing: Ethical and epistemological dimensions of teachers' work and development. *Harvard Educational Review* **60**(2): 159–80

Merriam S B and Clark M C (1993) Learning from life experience: What makes it significant? *International journal of life-long education* **12**(2): 129–38

Mohan B A (1986) *Language and content.* Reading, MA: Addison-Wesley

Pavio A (1979) Psychological process in the comprehension of metaphor. In Ortony A (ed.) *Metaphor and thought*. Cambridge: Cambridge University Press, pp 150–71

Perttula J (1998) *The experienced life-fabrics of young men*. Jyväskylä studies in education, psychology and social research 136. University of Jyväskylä, Jyväskylä

Peskin H and Livson N (1981) Uses of past in adult psychological health. In Eichorn D, Clausen J, Haan N *et al*. (eds) *Present and past in middle life*. New York: Academic Press

Pinar W and Grumet M (1976) *Toward a poor curriculum*. Dubuque, IA: Kendall/Hunt

Pinar W F, Reynolds W M, Slattery P and Taubman P M (1995) *Understanding curriculum. An introduction to the study of historical and contemporary curriculum discourses*. New York: Peter Lang Publishing

Polanyi M (1962) *Personal knowledge: towards a postcritical philosophy*. New York: Harper

Rauhala L (1978) The philosophical conception of man as a foundation of empirical research on human beings and work with human beings. In *The yearbook of nursing* **XV**, pp 270–90 (in Finnish)

Rauhala L (1981) The structure and analysis of the human existence – Martin Heidegger. In *Psychotherapy – theory and practice*. Espoo: Weilin+Göös, pp 52–79 (in Finnish)

Reason P and Rowan J (1981) *Human inquiry – a sourcebook of new paradigm research*. London: Wiley

Rogers C R (1969) *Freedom to learn*. Columbus, OH: Charles E Merrill Publishing Company

Saarenheimo M (1991) Autobiographical memory and biography. *Gerontology* **5**(4): 260–9 (in Finnish)

Saarenheimo M (1992) Reminiscing as a therapy, pastime and way of constituting the self and the world. *Gerontology* **6**(4): 265–75 (in Finnish)

Schubert W (1992) Our journeys into teaching: remembering the past. In Schubert W and Ayers W (eds) *Teacher lore*. New York: Longman, pp 3–10

Scudder J R and Mickunas A (1985) *Meaning, dialogue, and enculturation. Phenomenological philosophy of education*. Current Continental Research 502. Washington DC: Center for Advanced Research in Phenomenology/University Press of America

Solas J (1992) Investigating teacher and student thinking about the process of teaching and learning using autobiography and repertory grid. *Review of Educational Research* **62**(2): 205–25

Stanley L (1995) *The auto/biographical I. The theory and practice of feminist auto/biography*. Manchester: Manchester University Press

Tigerstedt C (1990) The analysis of specific themes in autobiographies. In Mäkelä K (ed.) *The analysis and interpretation of qualitative data*. Helsinki: Gaudeamus, pp 99–113 (in Finnish)

Titon J T (1980) The Life story. *Journal of American Folklore* **93**: 276–92

Turunen K (1990) *Understanding a human being*. Jyväskylä: Gummerus Kirjapaino Oy (in Finnish)

van Manen M (1984) *'Doing' phenomenological research and writing*. Edmonton: The University of Alberta Press

van Manen M (1989) By the light of anecdote. *Phenomenology + Pedagogy* **7**: 232–56

van Manen M (1991) Can teaching be taught? or are real teachers found or made? *Phenomenology + Pedagogy* **9**: 182–99

Varto J and Veenkivi L (1993) *Visible and invisible. Philosophical discussions*. Tisalmi: Oy Yleisradio AB (in Finnish)

Wallace J B (1992) Reconsidering the life review: the social construction of talk about the past. *The Gerontologist* **32**: 120–5

Webb K and Blond J (1995) Teacher knowledge: the relationship between caring and knowing. *Teaching and Teacher Education* **11**(6): 611–25

Wilenius R (1982) *Human being and 'Bildung'*. Jyväskylä: Gummerus (in Finnish)

Wilenius R (1994) How could we insinuate 'Bildung' into universities? *Helsingin Sanomat* Helsinki 2.10.1994 (in Finnish)

Chapter 5

What is it – (FL) teaching?

Jorma Lehtovaara

> What is a good man?
> A teacher of a bad man.
> What is a bad man?
> A good man's charge.
> If the teacher is not respected,
> And the student not cared for,
> Confusion will arise, however clever one is.
> This is the crux of mystery.
>
> Lao Tsu 1997, ch. 27

5.1 APPROACHING THE QUESTIONS OF (FL) TEACHING

Introduction

I have written this chapter as a FL teacher and teacher educator with the practising teacher in mind. I will discuss some issues of (foreign) language teaching which I have come to consider important and in need of professional investigation. While appreciating the value of the technical know-how of teaching, I also wish to emphasise the need and the benefits of a contemplative reflection on the foundational principles of our practices. The main reasons for choosing this approach are: firstly, the lack of a philosophically well-argued analysis of our (FL) practice and, secondly, the personal challenge of committing oneself to such a process of professional growth.

A profound clarification of the foundational principles of our professional life for ourselves helps us and our students experience increased interest and challenge in our daily living as a whole. In addition to teaching, all dimensions of our life – profession and personality, life in school and at home – gradually begin to appear more like aspects of an integrated whole. The core of the question to be reflected on is the basic nature of man, the view of man that guides our actions.

Having a well-argued conception of man as the foundation of our educational decisions can ease much of the uncertainty inherent in all educational situations. It also makes teaching more self-directed and, I believe, more rewarding – we can work out most of the implications of the well-argued underpinnings for our teaching *on our own* or in a *voluntary* collaboration with our colleagues. And, if we so decide, we can endeavour to realise them in practice through an open dialogue with our students. We have examples of how to put ideas like these into practice elsewhere in this book (see especially Jaatinen).

When a teacher has clarified for herself her personal conception of man, she is better equipped to find a satisfactory answer to the basic question: *What does it mean to be a foreign language teacher?* This recurrent question addresses our whole lives, our freedom and our skills (or 'craft') to be and do what we choose – what we are as persons and professionals, that is. When a teacher profoundly understands the nature of her own path of being in the world – what it means to be *the* human being *she* is – she can 'express her own original ideas' and make her contribution to the community (May 1985: 3). Then she also knows how to avoid becoming overwhelmed by all kinds of dehumanising trends that abound in the present-day world, even in her own school. (To avoid making the text unduly clumsy I refer to a teacher with the pronoun she.)

In order to justify my approach to (FL) teaching and learning I will make explicit the view of man underpinning my *current* thinking. I base my arguments on an existential or hermeneutical phenomenological conception of man which provides *a* philosophically well-argued possibility of understanding the basic nature of man. For reasons of space, I can present only a minimum outline of it in this chapter. (For more information, see the references Rauhala 1972–1998; Lehtovaara M 1994; Puhakainen 1995; Pihlanto 1997; Vanharanta *et al.* 1997; Carr *et al.* 1998.) I will focus on discussing the importance of investigating our conceptions of man (Sections 5.3.1 and 5.3.2) and working out some implications for (FL) teaching and learning that emerge from reflecting on my conception of man (Section 5.4).

The reader who is less interested in the details of a philosophical conception of man is still invited to skim the sections 5.3.1 and 5.3.2 because they explain why it is important for every teacher to be well-grounded in the underpinnings of what occupies a great part of her life – her professional life. To begin with, I will discuss briefly a few aspects of the present-day *Zeitgeist* which I think is necessary in order to provide a sufficient background for my arguments.

Preliminary exploration of FL teaching

The assignments in many current FL materials are still rather empty as regards the personal content for the students. Even in communicatively orientated approaches language skills are often practised in contexts that the students cannot naturally and immediately experience as personally meaningful. Only some of the dialogues carried on in formal (foreign) language learning situations are real-life interchanges of ideas between people who are truly personally committed to what they are doing. To convince him- or herself of the weight of my claim the reader would only need to make a rough estimate of the number of words and phrases in his or her (FL) teaching material that human beings need for dealing with their emotional and ethical relationships with reality.

Assignments in which students do not develop, express and exchange truly *personal meanings* are usually justified by saying that they are efficient because they focus the students' attention on the language system. Accepting this also as a pedagogical justification seems to indicate that teaching languages has become a *basically* non-problematic activity in people's minds. It has very often become only a technical problem where language, foreign or otherwise, has been reduced to just another 'instrument' – language is not seen and 'taught' as part of the whole of existing as a human being. (About personal meaning in FL education see the autobiographical approach presented by Jaatinen in this book.)

Even students' motivation to learn a (foreign) language has often become an issue about what technique the teacher should use in order to motivate the students to learn what they are supposed to learn. We seldom ask the basic question: 'What is it to be motivated, to be eager to learn?' Yet it is only through first exploring questions which take us to the roots of the matter that we can gain genuinely and radically new perspectives on reality.

A technical approach to teaching is quite understandable in many cases, of course, considering the circumstances under which many teachers have to teach – over-crowded classrooms, too little time for teaching, inadequate teaching materials and equipment, and so on. In conditions like these, people easily resort to emphasising the method or technique and the subject matter as a system. Through mechanising and formalising their action, depersonalising it, they can keep their task manageable.

Formalising and institutionalising one's work obviously makes it intellectually and emotionally clearer. It decreases its ambiguity and uncertainty through providing safe routines. People generally prefer working on something definite, something they can clearly define and demarcate – something that is easy to describe to others and account for. Taking a technical stance to one's work makes it easier to see oneself, and to be seen by others, as an effective and 'accountable' professional and, thus, to pass the 'quality control' with honour. It is much more difficult to explain and to 'operationalise', to show in any measurable form, what one does and what the results are when one focuses, for example, on enhancing one's students' creativity and *personal life skills*, among which the language skills are of primary importance.

Learning the necessary technical skills of classroom management and teaching language mainly as a system is certainly a demanding task for a teacher. But I would still like to pose the challenging question: is this all there is to FL teaching and learning – just learning or teaching an instrumental skill, how to handle a tool? If we do not stay alert, we may end up understanding and using the human language only as an instrument whose main purposes are to manipulate people and merely express something. Heidegger (1959: 51) presents quite a gloomy picture of what has become of language and man's relation to it:

the language in general is worn out and used up – an indispensable but master-less means of communication that may be used as one pleases, as indifferent as a means of public transport, as a street car which everyone rides in. Everyone speaks and writes away in the language, without hindrance and above all *without danger*. That is certainly true. And only a very few are capable of thinking through the full implications of this misrelation and unrelation of present-day being-there [i.e. man's existence] to language.

How far has this impoverishment of language progressed in the field of education? To what extent is this true of *my* language? How often do I teach (FL) words as if they were unambiguous signs, 'binary digits' used in calcula-tion, instead of teaching them as true symbols of different aspects of human life with multilayered, metaphorical and personal meanings?

My question in the title of this chapter (What is it – (FL) teaching?) suggests that our relation to language and especially to FL teaching and learning is not (or should not be) so self-evident. Could we still find some fresh mystery about FL learning and teaching which would invite us to look at it more closely and in a radically more thoughtful way than we usually do in everyday work?

We can start with reflecting on whether the following claim has any relevance for our personal conception of language: 'Poetry proper is never merely a higher mode (*melos*) of everyday language. It is rather the reverse: everyday language is a forgotten and therefore used-up poem, from which there hardly resounds a call any longer' (Heidegger 1975: 208). Poetry, as it is understood here, does not only refer to what is conventionally called poetry. *True poetry is thoughtful thinking in the verbal or languaged mode.* It may take the form of a poem but it may manifest itself in the prose form as well.

The essence of FL teaching

Bracketing FL in the title and elsewhere in the text is intended to pose questions like 'In what way is the question of the nature of FL teaching and learning a question about language?', 'In what fundamental respects do FL teaching and learning differ from teaching and learning in other spheres of human living?' Such questions need to be taken seriously because it is in and through questions that we choose our perspectives, both with regard to their content and the *language* we formulate them in. These questions lead us to the foundation of FL teaching. *My present view on the basic questions of FL teaching is that they are intrinsically more educational and pedagogical than linguistic by nature.* We therefore need to expand our views on the knowledge base that is necessary in foreign language education.

The picture of man behind the present-day modes of living

With the purpose of sketching the often alarming nature of the landscape where I have been exploring my path towards a better understanding of the essence of FL teaching and learning, I would like to mention briefly a topical problem in the field of education. That is, the increasing number of tired, 'school-weary' and even almost burned-out teachers and other helping professionals. *What is wrong with our present-day modes of living, not only those of teachers and students but of society as a whole?* I cannot go into the details of this issue and its possible causes here. I only suggest we take a good look at one fundamental aspect of this serious problem. What I have in mind is the conception of man underpinning our modes of living. There is a deep incompatibility between *the picture of man* emerging from recent scientific practice and *the picture of man* that most teachers and other human helpers (intuitively) feel they should actualise in their work in real-life educational situations.

In the post-industrial societies, it seems to me, most present-day scientific approaches can be described as rationalistic–technological: they objectify and 'instrumentalise' and thus depersonalise what they deal with. The attitude or stance of technology demands us to see every aspect of reality as an object to be exploited by man according to *his* needs and will. For example, trees in the forest are thus seen and treated as raw material and 'money', not as *essential* living parts of the global ecosystem with an indisputable right to exist as what they inherently are. Taylor (1992: 265) describes in a succinct way what will happen when we take a primarily technological stance to the world:

> [W]hen we turn away from living among things . . . and identify them as context-free objects, susceptible of scientific study; and even more so when we are swept up in the technological way of life and treat them as just standing reserve. If we make these our dominant stance to the world, then we abolish things, in a more fundamental sense than just smashing them to pieces, though that may follow. 'Science's knowledge, which is compelling within its own sphere, the sphere of objects, already had annihilated things as things long before the atom bomb exploded.'

This tendency to operate in the 'sphere of objects' is also reflected in how educational matters are discussed. According to this line of thinking, schools are often seen as production plants, curricula as production plans, students as raw material, products or customers, teachers as production managers or producers of 'educational commodities' and so on. Further, in the interest of measurable efficiency and the accompanying quality control, schools, teachers and students are forced to compete against each other for resources and power. This development results from a one-sided view of man and also maintains this view: people tend to be seen as *nothing but* competitors, either successes or failures, winners or losers.

In this way multidimensional human beings are reduced to cardboard objects and reified, that is, deprived of most of their other human qualities. Any person genuinely interested in helping other human beings surely feels, at least intuitively, that reifying a human being is dehumanising for both parties.

It is common knowledge that science's rationalistic, abstract and mechanical picture or *representation of life* and the real, personally meaningful *lived life* of the unique human being do not match well. The general, abstracted, quantitatively measured and 'value-less' knowledge of science is fundamentally different from the personal, real-life, qualitative and value-laden everyday knowledge that human beings live by and are embedded in. What causes stress here is the mismatch between the immediate reality of the classroom lived by the unique teacher and the abstract and general images of teaching constructed by rationalistic–scientific and abstract idealisations.

When a teacher enters the classroom, she has to encounter immediate, living human beings of flesh and blood while the *Zeitgeist* of scientific education, contrary to its wishes, admonishes her to view them as objects of treatment, as *theoretical* units in 'the sphere of objects' – as abstract representations in the human mind, that is. Understandably, teachers are especially sensitive to stress caused by this kind of ambiguity as they have entered the profession with an assumption that they will work primarily with live unique human beings in real-life contexts.

If we want to develop FL teaching and learning and remedy our 'misrelation to language' seriously, we should give careful thought to *the crucial question*: In what ways and to what extent do I let the one-dimensional picture of man dominate my beliefs about or conception of the nature of man? We cannot ignore this question: *how we understand the human being determines how we act in relation to him or her.* Our view of man does not only determine our ways of relating to other human beings but also governs the way we relate to the rest of reality. As our conception of man is normative, value-laden, it is only in abstract theorising possible to overlook the value aspects of man's being-in-the-world. (I use hyphenated combinations of words to highlight the inseparable interconnectedness of the phenomena they refer to. In this case I wish to emphasise the situational character of man's existence, his embeddedness in his life situation.) In no sphere of practical human existence can we escape the question about values and norms. Says van Manen (1991: 172):

> All education is normative. The question is whether the teacher will or is able to opt for pedagogical as opposed to non-pedagogical norms.

As teachers, to what extent are we able and have got the courage 'to opt for pedagogical as opposed to non-pedagogical norms', that is, the norms of science, technology, free-market economy and so on?

Inspired by the following extract from Heidegger (1975: 186), I would like to suggest the metaphor of a life-path for FL teaching and learning. 'Everything here is *the path of a responding that examines as it listens.* Any path always risks going astray, leading astray. To follow such a path takes practice in going. Practice needs craft. Stay on the path, in genuine need, and learn the craft of thinking, unswerving, yet erring' [emphasis is mine]. To me, the notion 'craft of thinking' aims at showing how a teacher's thinking is in its essence similar to the thinking of a craftsman. Craftsman-like thinking never loses its touch with reality, what is really going on. It never abstracts itself up into a safe theory from the uncertainty and indeterminateness of the lived situation at hand. It is thinking embodied in and manifesting itself in all his behaviour. This metaphor is meant to suggest that although a person works as a FL teacher, her work is only a specific set of life situations that constitutes a certain fragment of her life-path. She walks this stretch of her path being the same person as for the rest of her path – *even as a teacher man is first and foremost a person(ality), not a (role)character.*

An attitude of humility and tactful respect – letting go

I feel that the path as a metaphor of human life highlights the importance of listening to one's personal first-hand experience as well as the possibility and necessity of making personal choices. It reflects an attitude of humility and tactful respect for what reality is in itself. According to Highwater (1981: 74) this is the attitude or stance of the primal mind (of North-American Indians):

> Indians do not address nature as underlings nor do they command. Their participation in the world is *symbiotic* to such an extent that they discover nature within and outside themselves.

This attitude resembles the way of relating to reality which is called by Heidegger (e.g. 1977) *Gelassenheit*, usually translated into English as 'releasement', letting be or go. Letting something be in this sense means that I try to be open to it, to see what it is in itself, as such. I seek to *release* it from the grip of my mental representation, my imagination, let it manifest itself as it is, not as I imagine or want it to be. If we learn to take such an open and holistic attitude to things, human and otherwise, we may learn to enter into an *open dialogue* with other human beings and see the world and the nature of man in a very different light.

This is the kind of attitude through which the authors of this book wish to approach the reader. Therefore, the paths of FL teaching and learning that we explore here are not *The* Paths. The basic idea of this book is to describe some unending paths for teachers who are genuinely interested in the human possibilities offered by FL teaching and learning. Our purpose is to avoid telling, through any kind of restrictive definitions, what our paths are like and where they begin and end. In real life we do not know all aspects of our paths. *The right path for a thoughtful person is a path of his or her personal choice.* Since the destinations and the routes of our paths, if they are truly human paths, unfold and take shape all the time as we move along, there is no need to define and name them in advance in exact terms. I hope we have the courage to let our paths of FL teaching and learning develop as 'the path of a responding that examines as it listens'.

Some of the main problems of teaching today

I will focus on some of the basic problems of being a teacher today and provide a heuristic background for discussing them. Rather than deal with specific issues of FL teaching and learning I will focus on the essence of the pedagogical relationship in more general terms. I will explore the underpinnings of the educational praxis because *I believe that the main prob-lems of any kind of teaching today lie in the difficulty of being fully human in real-life educational situations rather than in teachers' knowledge of their subject matter and in their technical skills in using didactic classroom methods.* This idea is well expressed in Lao Tsu's text in the motto for this chapter. Also the following saying hits the mark: 'What you are speaks so loud that I cannot hear what you are saying.'

What these aphorisms *do not* mean to me is that all the powers to change the situation are in the hands of teachers. Not at all. *The problems of education are problems that the whole society is responsible for.* What these sayings *do mean* to me is this: unless there is a genuinely open dialogue between the teacher and the learner as unique persons, there is little significant learning taking place in the relationship – that is, learning worthy of the designation 'genuine human learning'. One of the basic human factors promoting significant learn-ing is therefore the art or the 'craft' of open dialogue, at least on the part of the teacher. But it should be equally obvious that the teacher's art of open dialogue cannot work wonders in an environment where the rationalistic and technological mindset predominates.

I justify my orientation to education, FL education included, with the following thesis: *If the task of education is to foster human growth so that people learn how to live a good life, the most efficient FL teaching is teaching for learning a good command of the art of open dialogue.* It is obvious now that I cannot see the question concerning teaching and learning the 'language' of open dialogue as a question about language alone. I try to explicate my point of view in the spirit of the *hermeneutical principle of understanding*: human understanding is always someone understanding something in a certain light, from a certain point of view.

Two basic questions concerning a (FL) teacher's self-reflection

The fact that we can see every human being both as a means to an end and as an end in him- or herself poses a perennial question to us: 'What is man (to me)?' Obviously, this is not only an academic question. What is it like to be a human being presents itself as a very concrete recurrent challenge to every reflective professional. This is the problem of man. In order to find a personal solution to this question we as (FL) teachers need to ask ourselves the following two basic questions and also answer them as honestly and as deeply as we in our life situations can. They are: *What does it mean **to me** to be a human being who teaches something (e.g. a foreign language) to somebody?* And *What does it mean to be a human being **whom** I am teaching?* These are questions that ought to be given serious thought every now and then by every teacher who claims to be a professional educator. Pondering over the problem of man in a personal way is, in fact, a never-ending task to be worked on for a whole lifetime.

Obviously, asking these questions means that I also see myself as a true research problem for myself, a personal task to be worked on continuously. If

I want to be(come) a fully human being, how do I and how should I realise myself as a human being? Understandably, being a fully human being is an ideal impossible for any man to reach in full. Although it is unattainable, it still is not an empty or utopian ideal. It can give us the direction in which and an end towards which we ought to strive. It is a challenge that can help us keep a flexible and living touch with life: we can always become more human. To some people this may sound quite demanding while others may find it challenging.

The nature of conventional responses to the problems of (FL) education

Conventional attempts to solve these problems have had at least one thing in common: they have been basically *rationalistic–technological* in nature. They have viewed the problems of being and becoming human as technical and technological *how to* and causal *why* problems: How can we make better use of 'natural resources'? How to educate good citizens, that is, how to make efficient (spare) parts of the machine called society? Why does this method work/not work? Why is this technique more efficient than that one? How to teach grammar more efficiently? How to prepare authentic materials for language teaching? etc.

To answer questions of this kind, it has been necessary to idealise reality and then objectify it, man included, and to divide it up into calculable parts that can be measured, at least in principle, and then statistically correlated with one another. All this is needed in order to make it possible to apply simple causal thinking to all aspects of reality. *Controlling* reality requires this kind of calculative and technological thinking. A good example of this stance is the stern and rigid discipline in school, not so unfamiliar to us old-timers at least. For a teacher favouring a strict discipline it is only rational and self-evident that she alone defines the educational situation – students are in school to be educated and to serve the purposes of the society that provides the education. There is no need to allow them to participate in defining the situation, let the experts do it.

Rationalism, science and technology

As will be evident in my text, *I am not an enemy of either rationalism or technology.* And, for that matter, not of calculative thinking, intellectualised teaching and learning, nor sciences either. *We have use for all of them in appropriate contexts.* My attitude is rather a relative distrust of them. I want to challenge their present predomination over what is legitimate human knowing, and seek to find a proper balance between them. I mean a situation in which it is legitimate and respectful to cultivate first-hand experiencing and contemplative, meditative, poetic, metaphoric (and any other way of thinking that I cannot yet imagine).

Ways of thinking worth a closer look are provided at least by the hermeneutical phenomenological tradition, by the great philosophies of the

East and by the ways the primal mind experiences reality. Highwater (1981) uses the word primal instead of primitive when talking about the culture, art, etc. of aboriginal peoples, for instance Native Americans. As we know, primitive mentality used to be considered, and is still very often considered, to be little more than the pathetic confusions of some dark and remote ancestral childhood. But, if we examine our conception of man thoughtfully enough, we can find a good and logical reason for valuing the primal dimension in ourselves and others. Not for fearing it. I strongly believe that the capacity for experiencing reality in the primal way is a valuable potential we still possess. We can make a good use of this capacity if we only appreciate it enough to take the trouble of reviving it in ourselves.

We might even have to admit that the capacity for experiencing reality *also* in the primal way is a necessary condition for any humanly worthwhile philosophising. It is only *rational* to think so because the capacity for primal experiencing is part of the whole that our rational and sensible faculties constitute, our consciousness. It would be *irrational* to ignore it.

I suggest that we, following Kearney (1986: 75), differentiate between reason in a narrow and a larger sense. Being rational in the narrow sense is to think in terms of 'strictly logical, mathematical and empirico–metric calculation'. *Being rational in the larger sense, again, is using the whole critical and regulative capacity of man, that is, reason, without belittling the power of human intuition, judgement and ethical deliberation.* As I see it, modern science and technology rest heavily on a narrower variety of reason, which I term rationalistic, whereas the more open and dialogical approach to reality builds on the larger variety of reason which is contemplative and sensible by nature. Thus, the latter is also 'rational', but it is not rationalistic.

The importance of what questions for human living

If the main problems of teaching and learning today are not technical *how to* and causal *why* problems, how can we describe and approach them? To better understand the human condition, and teaching as part of it, we can start with asking *what* questions. When we understand clearly and thoroughly what we are dealing with, we already know how we are and should be related to the thing in question. It is revealed in our understanding, in our conception of the thing if we can only let ourselves see it. Seeing it requires the attitude of releasement, letting go, letting it show itself as itself, not demanding it to manifest itself as something I choose to see it as. This way of seeing the world, again, calls for practice and 'practice needs craft'. The point of my argument is this: *When we truly know* **what**, *we also know* **how**.

So, when we know *what we are dealing with*, we know, through adequate practice, *how* to behave appropriately in relation to that (*what*). Yet the *what* questions are not considered interesting in a realm where rationalistic-technological thinking reigns, that is, where everything is viewed as something to be technologically exploited by man to his purposes. This is the kind of realm we now seem to inhabit globally.

More what *questions*

We need a different matrix, a truly 'human substrate', from which appropriate what *questions can emerge*; questions that reach reality behind or under our intellectualising, itemising and hierarchically cataloguing constructs with which we now try to get hold of it. We need questions like: What does it mean to be a human being? What does it mean when we say that being human means being situated or situational, being-in-the-world? What is man's life-in-meaning? (In this case hyphenation is meant to highlight the fact that the central structure of man's existence as a *human* being is his relating to reality through his meaning relationships.) What does it mean to be a teacher or educator? To educate? To be educated? To be the object or subject of education? What is teaching-in-the-world? (See also Jaatinen in this book.) Who defines the educational situation? What does it mean to be truly committed to the purpose of the teacher's profession? What is the content of education? What is FL education? What do we do when we teach a (foreign) language? What do we have schools for? etc. And most importantly, what does all this mean to *me* personally?

These questions may challenge our beliefs of what it means to be human. They can literally change us as persons. Challenging as they are, these are the questions that every professional teacher ought to take a personal stand to. There is no escaping this choice: *some* stand will be taken in any case through the decisions concerning the teaching methods, materials and evaluation practices. The question is: Are these choices our personal and conscious decisions or something that is imposed on us from outside (e.g. by textbook writers)?

5.2 WHAT IS THE CONTEXT OF OUR QUESTIONS ABOUT (FL) TEACHING?

Social construction of our lived world

As FL teachers and learners we live and work in the socially constructed reality of everyday life like other people. This is a common-sense reality where we go about living our everyday lives as best we can. Since we are teachers, however, we influence many people's lives in many significant ways. We therefore have a greater responsibility to ensure that we promote the quality of (human) life. Our influence on other people's lives is based heavily on what we are as persons. What we are and how we act depends to a great extent on how we understand the nature of man (ourselves included), the nature of society, the nature of culture and language, the nature of the work we do, and so on. This is why we need to clarify for ourselves what kind of assumptions and conceptions underlie our lives. Logically, the conception that constitutes the basic frame of reference in and through which we give meanings to everything is our conception of man.

Because much of our common-sense reality is taken as given, we are easily lead to think that the knowledge we acquire by observing our everyday life is valid empirical knowledge about reality *as it inherently is.* Yet what we see is nothing but our personal interpretation because we see it through our primordial understanding, our everyday conceptions, beliefs, conventions, language, etc. If we succeed in looking at it through different conceptions, beliefs, etc., we will see a different 'common-sense reality'. We cannot read reality as if what it is were written on its surface in some unambiguous sign language. We therefore need to examine our conceptions and beliefs and the rest of our primordial understanding. What, then, is the essence of the 'common-sense reality' where we all live today? What is the essence of common sense in the present-day world? These issues directly concern everyone, and especially those whose responsibility it is to promote human growth in themselves and other human beings under everyday circumstances.

The essence of the present-day Zeitgeist – a calculative and technologically orientated mindset

The modern *Zeitgeist,* to put it crudely, seems to be governed by the way of thinking which we necessarily resort to when using money – calculating or 'computing' has started to monopolise all our thinking. Thinking in a calculative way does not mean only calculation that uses numbers. Any thinking is calculative that operates on the premise that there is, at least in principle, an unfailing rational logic knowable to man and, consequently, a correct answer to every problem, be it technical, mathematical, human, etc. Due to its simplicity, measurability and lack of ambiguity calculative thinking seems to have such an enchanting power over man that it is conquering all spheres of human experiencing. In this process, art, education, entertainment and so on have come to be seen as something to be consumed and even relationships between persons may stop being human and personal: they become reified, that is, transformed into impersonal 'business transactions'. Like the economic market, life in general has come to be regarded as similar to nature in that all reality is now considered to be a conglomeration of objects governed by 'natural laws'.

As we know, however, the so-called natural laws are actually only principles *invented* by man to explain natural events and things and to get them under human control. Obviously, in this mindset, the only rational(istic) way for man to act is technological exploitation, to see himself as the subject whose job is to rework reality with his technology. *This stance of technology pervades all aspects of human life.* What else could we expect? It is only 'natural' since the modern picture of the world, modern science and modern society are inextricably interwoven (Töttö 1989: 39, 40).

In post-industrial societies, the calculative way of thinking connected with the attitude of technology is spreading almost unchallenged from science and information technology market to the national level of educational administration, and further to colleges and departments of teacher education and to schools. Administrating on the basis of the reasonably simple rules of calculation is of course an easy way out when dealing with the complex problem of man. When one confines one's view of man to seeing him merely as an object, it is only 'rational' to apply to him the same principles as to any other natural objects. FL teaching methods based on behaviourism are a good example of this.

Objectivation and reification – dehumanisation on the increase

Objectivation is the 'process by which the externalized products of human activity attain the character of objectivity'. Reification is a kind of dehumanising objectivation. It can be described as an 'extreme step in the process of objectivation, whereby the objectivated world loses its comprehensibility as a human enterprise and becomes fixated as a non-human, non-humanizable, inert facticity' (Berger and Luckmann 1987: 78).

Institutions can be conceptualised and dealt with as thing-like entities, but so can also social roles of people. Even unique persons can be 'handled' like that. For instance, treating students or their (FL) skills as measurable 'products' of the educational process is a worrying example of what we can expect to happen when the objectivation process in the field of education is allowed to turn into a process of reification. As to the essence of reification, Berger and Luckmann (1987: 108) point out: 'The paradigmatic formula for this kind of reification is the statement "I have to act this way because of my position" – as husband, father, general, archbishop, chairman of the board, gangster or hangman, as the case may be'. In this process the individual is totally identified 'with his socially assigned typifications. He is apprehended as *nothing but that type*'.

Especially interesting for us as (language) teachers is the role that language plays in this process. When people express their beliefs and conceptions of any aspect of their reality, they simultaneously strengthen their sense of this reality. If a person 'languages' the specification of a role often enough, it is quite likely that he or she starts to believe it. But there is also an opportunity in this 'crisis' – when we verbalise our beliefs and conceptions of reality (and listen to our colleagues' reflections), we may become aware that there is something worth questioning in our assumptions. We may then begin to reflect upon the matter. Reflecting on our conceptions of various aspects of reality, our ways of acting on them and our ways of languaging them is now becoming an increasingly important part of teacher development programmes. It would be wise to devote a good portion of the time reserved in the curriculum for teacher reflection to the analysis of the reification process: thoughtful thinking 'serves as a standing corrective to the reifying propensities of theoretical thought in general' (Berger and Luckmann 1987: 108).

Intercultural learning as an opportunity for de-reifying dialogue

Of course, seeing man as a 'mathematical and empirico–metric' problem makes him certainly a more easily manageable issue. I do not think, however, that administrators or other authorities resort to this kind of reification intentionally; it is extremely difficult to detect the essence and the effects on man of calculative thinking and the attitude of technology accompanying it. And it is even more difficult to make them visible. This is typical of any social construction of reality: 'The world of everyday life is not only taken for granted as reality by the ordinary members of society in the subjectively meaningful conduct of their lives. It is a world that originates in their thoughts and actions, and is maintained as real by these' (Berger and Luckmann 1987: 33).

To simplify complex matters a little, when people have started (today mostly prompted by monetary sanctions) to act (work, study, practise art, spend spare time, etc.) according to the principles laid down by technical–rationalistically and calculatively thinking 'authorities', *they very often start experiencing themselves as working efficiently only when treated in this way.* We have students who believe that they can learn only when somebody teaches them – they have become 'teacher-bound' learners. But we also seem to have teachers who believe that they work efficiently only because they are continuously supervised and evaluated by administrators. It seems, thus, that calculative thinking is an important skill to learn, both for administrators and for those administrated.

If we do not want to have calculative thinking as our *only* mode of thinking in a very near future, we must act now. If we do not see what is happening, maybe even in our own FL classes, and act accordingly, we necessarily contribute to the expansion of the calculative and technological mindset through 'maintaining it as real by our thoughts and actions'. If other kinds of thinking are not considered important, their development is not fostered.

To my mind, situations where old certainties become ambiguous or break down are very promising situations for man to become aware of the nature of the reification process and to find ways of de-reifying social structures. Foreign language learning as intercultural learning is a good example of such situations. If the de-reifying process takes place within an atmosphere of *unthreateningly* ambiguous and indeterminate dialogue, the learners can feel that they are only invited, not coerced, to approach various aspects of reality in a new light.

Another way of viewing the problem of man

What can we as (FL) teachers do? *What can I as an individual person do?* Once we start asking these important questions, I believe, we make room for hope – we can do our share in keeping up the multidimensionality and diversity of human life and experiencing. These qualities of human life *can* present themselves naturally and explicitly in FL teaching and learning. This means that we can make an impact as the teaching profession.

Actually, the essence of FL teaching and learning carried out in the spirit of open dialogue means searching for another, a more multidimensional way of seeing the problem of man. Of course it is not so easy to step out of one's familiar and safe ways of seeing and doing things, especially if they are well established in the profession and the community at large. Kaikkonen (in this volume) refers to this phenomenon with his phrase 'grow out of the shell of their mother tongue and their own culture'. I believe that the hardest thing for us to do is to muster up enough courage to allow ourselves to *really* believe that we can find our best ways of doing things *on our own* (with a little help from our friends!).

It may provoke some anxiety when we realise that this is actually what we need to do in the end: no other human being can know what is truly best for another person. The responsibility in taking this step is not small and it may cause some difficulty for persons who have internalised the message that is continuously sent to us teachers: your job is conscientiously to implement scientifically collected and tested knowledge and curricula. *Do we have to accept this reified role? How can we justify our answer?* We first have to make clear for ourselves what kinds of phenomena we deal with in (FL) teaching and learning.

The basic question: How do we see the nature of man?

We can start discussing this question by exploring, for ourselves and even on our own, the now prevalent view of what good science is. Judging by what the world is like today, we have every reason to ask whether the way of present-day science is after all the only legitimate and the most adequate way of gathering knowledge for the purposes of education and other helping activities. The attitude we take towards science and technology depends, of course, on our conception of man – our basic perspective on what the world is. 'What is man?' is obviously a philosophical question. The philosophy we need here is, however, rigorous thinking or reasoning that does not detach itself from the person's lived experience. It is basically common-sense reasoning that is possible for every normal person who is willing to use his or her human capacity for thoughtful thinking. We need not be academic philosophers to do that. However, thinking only in terms of technology-minded calculation is not enough.

The assistance for thoughtful reflection offered in this book is not in the form of another 'scientifically tested method' or 'tool' that teachers can just pick up and feel safe using after reading the instructions for use. What is offered here is a more rewarding as well as challenging approach: it entails a more open imagination, a deeper understanding of the nature of man and a 'craft of teaching' that is more flexible, more sensitive to and more consonant with what is going on in the actual life situation. I outline the basic concepts briefly in the following section.

5.3   A PHILOSOPHICALLY WELL-GROUNDED CONCEPTION OF MAN AS A NECESSARY BASIS FOR (FL) EDUCATION

5.3.1   The underpinnings of a (FL) teacher's beliefs and actions

The importance of investigating one's conception of man

When discussing the nature of man, the most important thing is not whether the conception of man we have chosen is the right and true one. The most important thing is what is taken up for discussion when we explore different conceptions of man and how we relate to others, on the basis of our conceptions. This entails a challenging personal question: How well are these conceptions in accordance with the ways in which I approach the world in my concrete life situations? *Do I live up to my professed conception of man?*

To deserve the qualification 'scientific' in the sense of rigorous and trustworthy, any science must necessarily rest on an explicit and adequate philosophy of science which grounds its research practices and explanations (see, e.g., Rauhala 1981). It is only together with a well-argued philosophy of science that empirical research can constitute a sufficient account for the domain of reality it claims to investigate. In its essence, this requirement also applies to education and other human helping activities that are claimed to be well-grounded and competent. They too need an adequate 'philosophy of praxis' to make understandable and justify their practices and explanations. Without appropriately investigating what we deal with, we cannot even be sure if we are dealing with the aspect of reality we think we are dealing with (see Rauhala, e.g. 1972; 1981). *FL teaching makes no exception: it too needs a full philosophical analysis and explication of its underpinnings.* This does not mean that there should be only One 'philosophy of praxis' for FL teaching. But this *does mean* that there should be a great deal of serious philosophical, that is, truly thoughtful reasoning about the conception of man on which the praxis of FL teaching and learning is grounded.

The need for such thinking is all the more urgent in the present-day postmodern world whose predominant features are uncertainty, ambiguity and indeterminateness. Because of its one-dimensionality and rationalistic pretensions to determinateness and certainty, the now omnipresent technological mindset actually only underscores the need for open thinking. An attitude or perspective does not merely express our preconceptions and prejudices (how we see and value different aspects of the world). It also organises our knowledge and emotions and thereby directs our actions. An attitude can be seen as a call for activity of a certain kind. Since it is always possible for us to re-examine our attitudes, they are our choices and *we are responsible for them.*

All the manifestations of the culture we are born into and live in transmit certain attitudes from generation to generation. It is language, in and through its metaphors and structures, that the major part of our culture is embedded in. As language teachers we therefore have a special responsibility for developing a clear awareness of the perspectives on reality which language suggests to us. We are responsible not only for our own awareness of them but very much for that of our students' too. From what perspective do I view my teaching and learning? From what perspective do my students learn to view reality? These are first and foremost questions of my personal view of the nature of man. Actually, in order really to understand another person it is much more important and, thus, more interesting to find out the *position* where he or she views the world than it is to hear what he or she says about the world. Things look so very different when we look at them from different perspectives.

A philosophical conception of man as the basic perspective on any human activity

A conception of man is curious in the sense that we always have one. Whether a teacher is aware of it or not, she necessarily entertains a conception of man. For instance, her lesson plans and methods already presuppose something of the 'object' of her work, the human being whom she intends to help to learn a foreign language. Her methods presuppose many things, such as: the person is capable of dealing with symbols, the human language is a means of communication, it is good for the student to be treated in this way, the student can be compelled to learn in this way against his or her will, I cannot define the teaching situation without consulting my students, and so on. *The teacher's conception of man is thus inherent and embedded in her practices.* This means that every teacher necessarily makes an *ontological decision*, that is, becomes committed to a decision concerning her preconception of the basic nature of man. The decision determining how the phenomenon in question is allowed to reveal itself is always and necessarily taken – it is built in our methods and practices.

What our ontological decision is, then, has a crucial effect on the way we approach the problems we face. Feyerabend (1979: 126) provides us with a very down-to-earth example: 'The scientific physician ... views the patient through the spectacles of some abstract theory; depending on the theory the patient becomes a sewer system, or a molecular aggregate, or a sack of humours.' It is not possible for us to separate a method of teaching from the conception of man it is based on. When we adopt the former, we adopt the latter – *our methods are our philosophy of praxis.* Even though we always have an implicit conception of man, we seldom take the trouble to make it explicit, clarify it through rigorous reflection – that is, philosophical reasoning in the sense used in this chapter.

Believing that we could understand life in all its diversity in the now dominant rationalistic–technological orientation is like thinking that we could see with only one eye all the differences in depth and other aspects of the world in as rich a variation as we can see them with two healthy eyes. *To be fully human is to be open to exploring different views of reality,* open to an adventure or a mystery that is human life. To succeed in this, we need at least 'two eyes', that is, two different conceptions of man. Diversity is as natural in this matter as it is in all life. 'What sets worlds in motion is the interplay of differences, their attractions and repulsions. Life is plurality, death is uniformity' (Octavio Paz; quoted in Highwater 1981: vi).

The teacher and the emergent human–scientific approach – some questions

Traditional scientific approaches do not help much in restricting to proper contexts the attitude of exploitation embodied in the ever-expanding technologisation. We need a rigorous *human–scientific* approach that takes man seriously for what he truly is, not just for what he has been constructed as by the rationalistic human mind. We need genuine contemplative thinking based on a lived and personally experienced open dialogue – not thinking that is distanced from man's lived experience. The *seemingly* detached, disinterested, perspectiveless thinking of science and technology will not do.

Before starting to reflect on any action (e.g. FL teaching), the first question the teacher should ask herself is 'In what way must *I think* to be thoughtful enough?' After getting a satisfactory answer to this question she can proceed to other questions, such as: What is it – being human? What is the meaning of that for *me*? How am *I* to be a fully human being? How does man realise himself as a learner, as a teacher, as a parent, as a child, etc.? What about *me*? How can *I* approach a person's way of being-in-the-world so that I let it be what he or she experiences it to be? How can *I* approach a person's being-in-the-world so that it may remain a whole which it inherently is? To what extent can and dare another person manifest him- or herself as he or she inherently is in *my* presence? And so on.

As is evident in these questions that are very likely to be posed in this emergent humanistic–scientific approach, the question that is more often seemingly the most urgent one, 'What should I do?', is to be asked only *after* the more foundational questions. The primary questions are ontological, epistemological and ethical in nature and they need to be asked and answered at suitable intervals before starting to act and, whenever the flow of life allows, during the process.

While engaged in the action itself, a person who fully actualises him- or herself becomes part of the stream of life: he or she does not conquer, force, coerce, subjugate it to his or her use or deprive it of its intrinsic value. He or she forms part of it remaining still true to his or her own modality. This is like shooting the rapids in a kayak: a competent rapids shooter knows how best to merge with the stream, 'to become the stream'. He or she is a person who accepts and takes the rapids for what they are in themselves, lets them be and respects them but yet alertly observes and follows their changes, doing what he or she must do in the quickly changing situations to keep up the good relationship with the stream. To me, the *essence* of the skills, the 'craftsmanship', needed by a competent rapids shooter is the same as that needed by a competent (FL) teacher.

5.3.2 A conception of man – the outcome of an ontological and an epistemological analysis of man

All aspects of being human are in need of continual rigorous discussion

My point of departure is the claim that *we lack ontological and epistemological analyses of what (FL) teaching and learning is.* If we want to proceed in a rigorous manner, we have to start with the question *What is man?* As this question may tempt us to consider man in too thing-like a manner, it might be better to ask: 'What is it – being man?' 'How does man manifest himself as man?' 'How is man realised?' 'How does man exist?' An adequate answer to these questions demands a genuinely thoughtful and experiential analysis. It may be a philosophically well-argued conception of man or it may be a more down-to-earth but well-grounded common-sense view of the nature of man.

Our conceptions of (FL) teaching and learning and, consequently, our practical activity *can be adequate,* in terms of rigorous and systematic human–scientific thinking, *only when they are based on a conception of man analysed in a philosophically adequate manner.* The process necessarily involves facing uncertainties. Yet a teacher who is also a researcher needs to be able to tolerate the ambiguity and uneasiness of being thoughtful.

Searching for an adequate conception of man does not mean that we should seek to replace the now predominant One way of approaching the problem of man with some other One way of viewing man. Working out a different philosophically well-grounded picture of man and comparing it with the dominant picture of man can have a heuristic effect on our thinking. By 'juxtaposing' the different assumptions and practices based on them we can uncover new perspectives which can suggest new ideas for discussion. This analysis can help us make visible at least some of our unreflected ways of being in the world and release us from the constraints of narrow theories and other current intellectualisations. It sensitises us to the immediate reality, especially to the other living human beings in our immediate presence. I think this kind of hermeneutics is a good way to resist unduly intellectualised, dogmatic and covertly biased, that is subjective, approaches to the nature of man. Perhaps we can gain a wider recognition for the idea that 'Nothing is more subjective than objectivity blind to its subjectivity' (Laing 1983: 17).

We must therefore be careful not to choose a narrow conception of man or one that is a closed system. The existential phenomenological way of thinking I introduce here is open by definition. The holistic conception of man emerging from it invites me to 'step outside the house' of the system of my beliefs about the nature of man; remaining inside the house and just opening more windows is not enough to open up a truly new perspective on reality (see Heidegger 1969).

5.4 IMPLICATIONS FOR (FL) EDUCATION EMERGING FROM A HOLISTIC CONCEPTION OF MAN

5.4.1 Education – practising of good living

The following definition of pedagogy by van Manen (1991: 18) catches something of the very essence of education: 'Pedagogy refers *only* to those types of actions and interactions intentionally (though not always deliberately or consciously) engaged in by an adult and a child, *directed* toward the child's *positive* being and becoming' (see also Värri 1997). According to this description the pedagogical or educational relationship always promotes the good of the people involved in it. *Actions and interactions that are harmful to human beings do not deserve to be termed education. They are mal-education.* Education means accompanying a person in the spirit of open, tactful dialogue on that stretch of his or her life journey which we are destined to travel together.

It is quite common nowadays to depict education and pedagogy as basically moral and thus normative activities in which educators and parents orientate themselves to the good (whatever this good may mean in particular circumstances) (van Manen 1991: 220). Even though we cannot say exactly what the good is that we are searching for, we can know and demonstrate enough of it to arrange life in our educational relationships so that we may term it 'practising of good living' (*eupraxis* – Max van Manen's (1991: 221) term). When we succeed in this, life in school becomes a real life for all participants, living here and now, not just waiting for real life to start some time in the future.

In FL education and pedagogy based on a holistic conception of man normativeness means that we need to be constantly concerned both with '*the linguistic norm*' and '*the norm of the good life*' and also be ready consistently to question our norms. When investigating the quality of our teaching in the spirit of open dialogue, we will most certainly confront the following question: 'How does the child, the student, the other person, experience this particular situation, relationship, or event?' (see van Manen 1991). This is a crucial question, although it may seem to be a self-evident starting point of all teaching. But is it so self-evident after all? Dare we ask ourselves, e.g., the following questions: *How often do I plan the activities of* **our** *lesson in genuine collaboration with my students? How often do I let the learners do their things, things that are genuinely their own? In what ways do I accomplish this? How often do I violate this principle on truly good grounds? How often do I interfere with their learning process in the well-intentioned illusion of helping them?*

Evidently, every teacher has to answer these questions for herself but this does not mean she has to process them alone. In schools and other educational institutions where the culture is favourable for open learning teachers examine these questions in collaboration with their colleagues and their students. The life situation of a student is a very essential part of the whole that he or she is. When we define and arrange or order a person's life situation for him or her, we do not only organise his or her external environment but *we interfere with his or her existence in a very significant and concrete way.* We define how and where he or she can manifest him- or herself as a human being. *We order his or her existence* – nothing less.

The ordering may take very concrete forms. I can only give a few examples here: the amount of light and the temperature in the room, the seating plan, the number of students, the rules and values of the society, school and group, equipment available, learning materials, assignments, the 'atmosphere', ourselves as persons, our ways of asking questions, the language we use, the quality of our interference in what the students do, etc.

When there are twenty to thirty-five students in the class, it demands a great deal of strength from the teacher to let the following question come into her conscious awareness: 'How does every one of my students experience this particular situation?' How can she ever know what her students are as unique persons? I would like to quote here Werner Heisenberg, the winner of the 1932 Nobel Prize for physics (Postman and Weingartner 1983: 82): 'We have to remember that what we observe is not nature itself, but nature exposed to our methods of questioning.' When we change some words in the text to fit the context of our discussion here, Heisenberg's sentence might read as follows: We have to remember that *what we observe is not our students as they are in themselves, but students exposed to our methods of questioning and other means of arranging their life situations* in school or other educational environments.

Can it be possible for a teacher who is forced to work under the present-day constraints of time and resources to have the courage and strength to openly reflect on the question of personalising her teaching? It is high time for us to realise and take seriously the hugeness of the challenge that teachers with classes of dozens of students accept when they try to apply 'the norm of good living' to their interaction with their students in such circumstances.

5.4.2 Learning

Learning – the essence of being human

Learning for a human being is a never-ending process of actualising his or her possibilities to be more fully human. It entails developing his or her modes of existence towards an integrated whole that corresponds with the person's 'place' in reality. Learning is seen here as an innate manner of being and becoming a more fully human being. *Learning is the most natural process in man: being human is learning!*

To claim that to be human means to be a life-long learner inevitably raises the question about motivation. If be(com)ing human is learning, man must be intrinsically motivated to learn things that are important in his life. (A brief look at a normal human baby suffices to prove that!) Therefore, when a person has to be motivated by an external agent to learn something, he or she does not simply see it as meaningful for his or her life. The learning situation does not belong to his or her life *as he or she would define it.*

In such cases, what is the essence of the process of the teacher using some motivation techniques to coax the person into doing something that others have defined for and on behalf of him or her? Why does the innate process of learning not run its course? Is it because the learner experiences the teacher's activation and motivation more like indoctrinating, persuading or decoying? Seen from the perspective of the holistic conception of man, *man's learning is not a process that needs to be specifically initiated by an agent (internal or external to him)* except in cases where the development of the person as a human being has been disturbed somehow. Normally learning ends only when the person dies.

What can we do to arrange life in our own school in such a way that it can be felt to be part of 'my life' by every student, teacher and other member of the school personnel alike? My personal answer to this question is currently that we, all the members of our school community, need to begin through as open a dialogue as we can to discuss and then define together what a good life situation would be for us all to thrive as truly human persons. After having *co-created* such a definition of our life situation, we would start to *co-research* what we can do in order to reconstruct all the possible objectivating and reifying institutionalised routines and practices which have prevailed in our school. This is what school where people learn to live as fully human beings means to me at the moment – *a living community of continuously learning educational co-researchers seeking to practise good living through collaborating in and through open dialogue.*

Human learning – personal learning

If we consider the phenomenon of learning in the light of the analysis discussed in this chapter, it is somewhat tautological to term learning 'experiential' because learning is seen here as a special case of experiencing. All humanly significant learning is to a very large extent formation, development and reorganisation of meaning relationships between man and his world, that is, experiencing. As a *psychological* term, however, experiential learning very well highlights the importance of learning in a personally meaningful and holistic way, as a whole person, not just merely intellectually or emotionally or bodily. It refers to personal learning, living one's learning personally, as one's own, not just acquiring vicarious experiences through memorising other people's experiences as 'narratives' or 'texts'. As we know, the 'vicarious experiences provided by these texts tend to go to our heads, so to speak' (van Manen 1991: 10).

The term experiential learning also helps us keep in mind the role language plays in experiencing. The world is given to us mainly in and through experiencing that is embedded in language, not only in abstract language and idealised concepts but also in 'poetic' and metaphoric language, personal language. We should, however, analyse the philosophical foundations of our thinking about experiential learning and enrich the language we use to talk about it. To begin with, I suggest that we could make a clearer distinction between *genuinely human learning* and *the acquisition of information* (see, for example, Rogers 1969; 1980, and Kohonen in this book). Perhaps we could reserve the term 'learning' for referring to the phenomenon we now call 'experiential learning' and start referring to the process of acquiring information with the more apt term 'acquisition of information'.

Genuinely human learning is learning-in-the-world

There is always an undecidability, ambiguity, uncertainty and indeterminateness about being human. As a bodily, situational and experiencing being, man is always man-in-the-world and his action cannot be studied adequately if it is separated from his life situation. Thus, *a learner is always a learner-in-the-world* and learning is a specific way of being-in-the-world.

Obviously, situationality applies not only to learning but also to the existential constitution of human experiencing or consciousness in general. Consequently, *we must approach and investigate man as an integrated being*, that is, as a unique person who is embedded in culture, language, society, history and the physical world. When we as FL teachers approach the issue of man as a language learner in the holistic way, we are practising the very essence of intercultural teaching and learning (see Kaikkonen in this book).

Genuinely human learning is constructive development and reorganisation of one's relationships with the world

When man learns, the way he experiences the world (himself included) is modified. Since the human being is a whole, learning is always a holistic process: it involves all man's basic modes of existence. New meaning relationships with the world develop and his existent meanings undergo changes. But so do also his bodily being and his life situation: they too are at least somewhat modified. *Genuinely human learning is refinement and enrichment of a person's relationships with the world through their constructive development and reorganisation.* For example, when a person learns that he or she need not be afraid of pronouncing a foreign word incorrectly in the class, he or she cancels the meaning 'frightening' (at least for the moment) and substitutes for it, e.g., 'bearable', begins to feel better at home in the situation and starts to participate more actively in the activities. Although man can consciously reorganise his relationships with the world to a great extent, *all significant meaning relationships are not conscious to the degree of being verbalisable and yet they may be very important for the person's decisions concerning his or her life.*

Although every learning event is unique, we also have 'objectively' the same or almost similar situational components in common with other people, that is, we share many things that determine and direct our experiencing and learning. One of the most important components (if not the most important one) in a student's life situation at school is his or her teacher. Consequently, the quality of the development and reorganisation of the student's meaning relations is significantly affected by what the teacher says and does and, first of all, by what the teacher *is*.

5.4.3 Language

The hermeneutic phenomenological perspective suggests that language is something much more profound than just an instrument for thinking, self-expression, communication and conservation of knowledge. It is 'a mirror of mind in a deep and significant sense' (Chomsky 1976: 4). According to Heidegger (1977: 40–1):

> Language first gives to every purposeful deliberation its ways and byways. Without language, there would be lacking to every doing every dimension in which it could bestir itself and be effective. In view of this, language is never primarily the expression of thinking, feeling and willing. Language is the primal dimension within which man's essence is first able to correspond at all to Being and its claim and, in corresponding, to belong to Being. *The primal corresponding*, expressly carried out, *is thinking*.

While thinking is man's ownmost manner of being man, the primal dimension of a *thoughtful* being is language. 'All ways of thinking, more or less perceptibly, lead through language in a manner that is extraordinary' (Heidegger 1977: 3). To help us resist the temptation of separating thinking and language from the rest of man's existence, I would like to quote the Japanese poet Sosho (in Claxton 1981: 126). He expresses very succinctly and beautifully the idea how, when ideal, man's modes of existence fuse with each other into a harmonious whole to form a unity with the world:

> A man with no form, no shadow
> Turns into a rice pounder
> When he pounds rice.

To me, the expression 'Man with no form, no shadow' refers to a person who has not defined him- or herself neither to him- or herself nor to others, neither in thoughts nor actions, to be anything *specifically* determined and known beforehand. In his or her mind, there is no confusion of what his or her self is and what it is not – he or she knows his or her outlines so well that he or she need not be afraid of losing temporarily his or her identity while merging into what he or she is experiencing and doing. That is like a person who knows the 'craft of carrying on an open dialogue' with the world. The person pounding rice in this manner yields him- or herself so totally that he or she and the rice pounder have become a smoothly functioning unity. There is no separation between thinking, language, culture, instrument, object and so on while this process is taking place. Understood in this way, language, thinking and culture are inseparable aspects of one process.

Only a few languages have words and phrases for expressing this aspect of human existence. Lee (1976: 11) gives an example of how the quality of the interrelatedness of the aspects of man's being-in-the-world can be expressed in the human language. She gives a description of a male Wintu Indian telling her that his son is ill. Using a special suffix added to the verb he said:

'I am ill my son.' The *I* in the expression must not be understood as pre-supposing 'a separate, bounded self acting upon another separate, bounded self . . . but rather: . . . I am ill in respect to my child.' The same quality of relatedness is expressed in another of her examples: '. . . not: John *and* Mary have arrived but: John Mary they have arrived. This may imply that the coming of John and the coming of Mary are not separate, to be joined by an *and*; yet John and Mary were clearly differentiated.'

Although reflecting thinking more or less fixed in words is the *primarily human* way of forming meaning relationship, we should not forget that it is only one aspect of man's modes of existence. Emphasising and cultivating only one part of an integrated whole always has an unbalancing effect: for instance, exclusive cultivation of man's intellectual faculties impoverishes other human capacities. The predominant habit of seeing man in a frag-mented, non-holistic way is a 'visual illusion' which seems almost as if built in the nature of man's existence. In everyday life man always acts under con-crete conditions of reality. Although what he sees is determined by the com-ponents of his life situation as a whole, he sees things from a perspective.

To put it in another way, how he views and understands the world, depends on his primordial understanding. His seeing and understanding are always perspectival. When he views one aspect of a thing, the other aspects of it are concealed – man cannot see all aspects of a phenomenon at the same time. It is only in a thoughtful, or philosophical reasoning that man can view any aspect of reality holistically. But even then he cannot be totally free of per-spectives. His perspective is now only somewhat broader and more abstract.

Even the human language itself contributes to man's tendency to experi-ence reality as fragmented. When man learned how to verbalise his observa-tions of reality, his language helped him to divide reality into ever more minute fragments and then 'freeze' them into nouns and preserve them as objects in his mental representations. And now that science and technology have chopped the world up into self-evident 'facts', we seem to forget *that theories are languages – languages that give birth to the facts*. What we take for facts are man-made, imagined constructs (Latin *factum*; *facta*). As Claxton (1981: 2) puts it: 'The world is not perforated, like a toilet roll, so that all you have to do is tug gently and it will fall apart into ready-made "concepts". The divisions are attributed to it, for the purpose of talking about it and predicting it.'

The nature of a language and the ways of existence of people who speak it as a native language are inseparable. *Man is literally embedded in his language and his language is embodied in him.* This is the grounding for seeing the essence of (foreign) language teaching as education for intercultural aware-ness and understanding or multiculturality. Language is not only inseparable from the 'spirit' of the group of people who speak it: *Language is an essential and concrete component of an individual's life situation – every human being is born into a language.* In the same manner as we live our experiences *we live our language.* Stereotypes offer good examples of this: e.g. teachers are women, firemen are men, foxes are sly, people of different nationalities are such and such, etc. (see Kaikkonen in this book).

Or, if we look at the matter from another perspective: *language is an essential dimension of man's primordial understanding. It is a foundational existential structure in which man experiences the world and himself.* This is why human meanings are not only linguistic units – they are basically multidimensional meaningful relationships between the world and man as a whole.

As is evident from this discussion, we are not master creators of our language – we are born into it. 'We do not and cannot miraculously create meaning out of ourselves. We inherit meaning from others who have thought, spoken or written before us.' And further, 'I derive my meaning through my relationship with the other (be it the individual, communal or ontological other)' (Kearney 1986: 128). Consequently, we have to listen to what language has to say. '*Language speaks*' (Heidegger 1975: 190). And what does language speak? According to Kearney (1986: 128) 'we are always obliged to listen to (*hören*) what has already been spoken, in other times and places, before we can in turn speak for ourselves in the here and now'.

When we listen attentively to what language has to say, we can also hear the call of things. We can hear how they ask to be taken as meaning something and to be allowed to show themselves as what they are in themselves, not only as objects constructed by man through his capacity for conceptual representation. For Heidegger 'the proper function of words is not to stand for, to signify. Rather, words point to something beyond themselves. They are translucent bearers of meaning. To name a thing is to summon it, to call it toward one' (Heidegger 1977: xix).

I think we can refer to a word whose meaning is learned experientially as the *track of a thing* like we refer to the tracks of an animal (in the snow or sand, for instance). Those of our words that are 'tracks' of our personal, lived experiences we can call *personal words*. They are words that are as if cut out of the very essence of the person who uses them – they are his or her 'verbal fingerprints' or voice-prints. Words like these – apt and adequate words, that is – are required for thoughtful reflection as well as for character and personality development. And it is only words of this kind that can truly help another person in his or her attempts to grow as a human being – they are words needed for creating open dialogue.

It is obvious, then, that (foreign) language learning can be greatly enhanced by teaching students to become sensitive to and aware of this basic nature of words. I think spending some time discussing and practising the denotation and connotations of words, even studying quite a lot of the etymology of words and phrases with the aim at a good command of paraphrasing, could be a way of doing this. To convince ourselves of the need of such practice, we can check how often we accept the use of an only very roughly synonymous word or expression instead of requiring of ourselves and our students that the word should really name the thing we mean in a way that 'calls it towards us'.

It is easy to see that 'the proper function of words' cannot be learnt by repeating word lists. It seems that vocabulary and the rest of language is best learned 'by participation in the activities that constitute it' (Feyerabend 1979: 86). Lee (1976: 53) offers a good example of language teaching as the fostering of learning how holistically to verbalise one's experiencing, one's being-in-the-world. She tells about an Oglala Sioux mother 'who would take her baby out and attract his attention to different animals and birds long before he talked; and only after he had learned to notice them unlabeled, did she name them for him'. I believe we have here the essence of a 'method' that helps the language learner learn to discover words and other linguistic means that match his or her own unique way of being-in-the-world. It enables the person to learn a language that epitomises his or her very existence instead of a language that is merely a 'worn out and used up' means fit only for impersonal and calculative purposes.

An active use of the language for developing and expressing *personal* meanings in open dialogue might be the basic pedagogical 'menu' of the (foreign) language class. Reading authentic literature written in vivid and varied language is also helpful, if not necessary, for practising towards these ends. This means *reading for personal meanings*. It may include thoughtful reflection on what is read but it does not require carrying out a literary analysis on it.

5.5 LANGUAGE LEARNING AS LEARNING THE ART OF *OPEN* DIALOGUE

5.5.1 The essence of the art of *open* dialogue

Open dialogue can be seen as man's basic modality of being in the world when he actualises himself as a *fully human* being in the sense given to this notion here. Obviously, like 'fully open', 'fully human' is an ideal unattainable in the real life of any concrete person. It is not, however, an empty ideal for at least two reasons: first, we can never know what man is like when he is fully human and, second, it gives an ethical norm for us to fulfil in our lives. Of course there are bound to be situations where we have to compromise – we do not live a socially unrestricted life.

The need to compromise is especially true of teachers as professionals who work within constraints superimposed on them by the school as an institution. If the teacher is fully aware of its philosophical underpinnings and consciously chooses to strive towards the end of open dialogue, she knows when it is appropriate to compromise. It is also easier for her to see the good aspects of herself, her students and the circumstances. When the teacher has an open dialogical orientation to reality, her students feel that they can approach her whenever they need, want and are ready for it.

The notion of *open* dialogue is not a synonym for free conversation or exchange of ideas. Through qualifying dialogue with *open* I want to suggest that the quality of the dialogue discussed here is very different from ordinary conversation and especially the technical type of dialogue used as a method of practising, e.g., FL speaking. Open dialogue means going deeply into exploring phenomena of life together through joint efforts supporting and encouraging one another. It also means basing the exploration on personally lived experience and autonomous perception of reality.

Persons encountering each other and the world in open dialogue are not arrogant and self-sufficient egos or subjects who take themselves to be the sole originators of their ideas and actions. They act on the understanding that human beings and the world co-constitute each other – open dialogue rather happens than is rationalistically produced by independent and totally separate human agents. For a person who masters the art of open dialogue, thinking is first and foremost contemplative, poetical, metaphorical and it has a strong intuitive bent. Because it has become only natural on our technological 'highway' of living not to experience things as things but only as objects of our consciousness, phenomenology urges us 'back to the things themselves' (German: *zu den Sachen selbst*).

A *path* most likely to take us towards things themselves is releasement (German: *Gelassenheit*), that is, letting them be what they in themselves are, or waiting in which 'we leave open what we are waiting for' (Heidegger 1969: 68). Choosing this path means approaching things at first in a non-judgemental openness, giving up the attempt to be good, creative, spontaneous, to do the right thing and so on (see section 5.5.2). However, *when needed, the way of approaching things can also be technical–rationalistic, atomistic and calculative.*

In an open dialogue between man and another being, the other, a whole new world comes into being. In such a relationship both or even a small group of persons experience themselves in a sense *immersed in the same life world*. But it is not of course exactly the same to each of them since they all view it from their own unique points of view or worlds. *It is a world between them* (see Varto 1994). All that 'is essential does not take place in each of the participants or in a neutral world which includes the two and all other things; but *it takes place between them in the most precise sense, as it were a dimension which is accessible only to them both*' (Buber 1985: 205. My emphasis). I see the 'between' here as an interface connecting the participants: it is the 'common ground' of their life situations.

Even though the partners in dialogue enter a common world, their personal worlds do not lose their uniqueness and contours – their boundaries become only more open, more permeable for the time being (see Sosho's poem in section 5.4.3). Although the worlds of single human beings can become quite similar, total homogenisation of the lived worlds of different human beings is not possible. The uniqueness of the whole that is composed of the unique consciousness, body and situationality of every person guarantees that.

It seems that man can only obtain and retain his optimum differentiatedness, that is, his optimum identity or personal authenticity in an open dialogue. In effect, the development of a truly personal identity necessarily requires *two preconditions to be fulfilled: truly personal experiencing and exposure to human relationships where open dialogue prevails*. It is open dialogue that provides man with a life situation where reality can reveal itself as what it inherently is. In such a relationship man listens to reality, observes, explores and wonders at it being fully present in the situation. This also means letting intuition or tacit knowledge have its course, thus providing room for our unconscious attitudes, roles, beliefs, fictions and so on to change in order to conform better to reality.

When a person has achieved such a relationship with reality, his or her learning may reach the optimum as regards the *human* quality of it – it can be genuinely human learning. This applies to the learning of thinking, (foreign) languages, culture and so on.

The essence of an open dialogue is an interested, respectful and thoughtful listening to the other as such. The emphasis is more on listening and really hearing the other, *letting the other be heard,* than it is on talking to one another by turns. Actually, this is the essence of any good conversation both 'in real life' and in all educational situations, especially when teaching languages: *unconditional, prizing, genuine and vivid presence of a person to another person and to the world.* This is something very concrete and something that every normal person can do, at least after some practice, if he or she is only determined enough to do so.

It is in situations like these that a person has the opportunity to check his or her experience against reality. This means that in any learning situation we need to check what we say and how we act in an essentially similar way as we do when we try to get from place A to an unknown place B with the help of a map. We must check what we see on the map against what we see in the actual landscape. In this case reality 'tells' immediately what the 'truth' is. In most educational situations, however, it is the teacher, the textbook or the key to the answers that tells what the 'truth' is. In educational situations like these, students easily learn to live by the 'truth' provided by some external authority. Consequently, they learn to neglect and even distrust the evidence given by their own immediate experiencing. They learn to be 'teacher-bound' learners – in order to learn they always need somebody to teach them. Testing one's judgements mostly against an authority does not promote growth towards authenticity and self-directedness. It is likely to kill personal judgement and could be termed indoctrination or some other kind of mal-education.

Keeping up an open dialogue cannot ever be just a routine or a general-purpose method that we can learn and then practise automatically whenever and wherever we want. As we, the other people and the situations change all the time, we have to learn to initiate and maintain open dialogue anew again and again. The motive for doing so comes quite naturally, however: once man experiences open dialogue, it arouses in him a longing for an opportunity to live it again.

As a partner in open dialogue man can also become truly aware of the innate ethical quality of his existence. Only open dialogue can provide man with open possibilities to choose from. Without this freedom of choice, both psychological and political, there cannot be any true ethics in man's existence (see Varto 1993: 170). Man does not, however, even begin to realise *what is possible for him, ethical or otherwise, if open dialogue has not become a personal, lived experience, that is, a vivid meaning relationship for him.* Merely thinking on a conceptualised level is not enough.

An open dialogue is at its best when it is the most difficult: in a close relationship between two human beings. According to Buber (1985: 205) this relationship is necessary for man to be(come) human: it is only in a human relationship where man encounters man as man that it is possible for man to learn to know another person as a human being. Open dialogue is man's mode of being in the world when *he relates to reality as a whole person experiencing it, acting in it and on it in a way that allows it to reveal itself as what it inherently is.*

5.5.2 Learning and practising the art of open dialogue

Even though the basic modality of man's existence is dialogue, man does not automatically grow to be capable of creating a relationship of open dialogue and being a participant in one. That is, *man does not automatically learn the art of open dialogue.* A small child is certainly by its nature quite open to reality but to sustain that openness and to develop it to the level where we can call it the art of open dialogue requires a lot of practice with the help of at least one person who masters the art of open dialogue in most of his or her encounters with the learner. In the sense given to it here, the notion of mastering some skill, art (see, for example, Fromm (1984)) or craft (see section 5.1) of doing something, does not, however, imply a complete mastery (if there ever can be anything like it): it only expresses that somebody is *proficient enough* in doing something, e.g. speaking a foreign language. As it is with all human learning, to learn something is not first learning something, then stopping to learn and starting to master the doing of that something. *Learning to do something is doing it not well enough yet.*

Learning the art of open dialogue is *not likely to be a sudden once-for-all event.* Although the idea of the basic quality of open dialogue may appear as a sudden insight or illumination, learning to put it into practice in different concrete encounters demands help and support from other people.

Some conditions favourable for all genuinely human learning

The truly experiential way of learning the art of open dialogue, or any other art (e.g. language skills) for that matter, is practising that art in real-life situations. (FL) classrooms *can* provide an optimal environment for learning the art of open dialogue. To do this classrooms need to be made into places where people can honestly feel they are allowed to live a real life, a life they have participated in defining.

There are some conditions that foster the learning and practising of open dialogue. For reasons of space, I can only discuss the most important of them briefly in this chapter. I would like to invite the reader to explore the pedagogical possibilities of these principles in the context of his or her own work, possibly together with a good colleague or a friend.

Personal help from another human being

To learn what an open dialogue is one has to *live* open dialogue. To be able to do this one needs personal help from somebody who is competent in the art of open dialogue. Open dialogue is thus both the goal and the 'method' of learning the art of open dialogue.

Open *possibilities and enough space*

Open possibilities and space both politically and in terms of psychological atmosphere are necessary. The student must have an opportunity to participate in defining the educational situation to the extent that he or she can honestly feel that it is also part of his or her life. Too much of too detailed planning easily makes teaching inflexible and abolishes uncertainty and ambivalence which are (when they are not too threatening) necessary for the unfolding of open dialogue and the development of genuine ethics. Without the attitude of releasement, which means congruence, unconditional positive regard and empathic understanding on the part of the teacher, there is little chance for psychological freedom and openness (see Rogers, e.g. 1969 and 1980).

Genuineness, acceptance and empathic understanding

Being *genuine* is 'putting up no professional front or personal façade' (Rogers 1969: 223; 1980: 115).This means that for instance a teacher does not pretend to know all the answers, nor does she have to hide behind various techniques and methods and use them as defence mechanisms to protect herself from life. She can be *real*, really present as what she intrinsically is. She is *congruent*: what she expresses corresponds to what she is experiencing at the moment. Congruence means accepting one's feeling as one's own without projecting it on others. 'Thus, congruence is the basis for living together in a climate of realness' (Rogers 1980: 160). *Congruence or realness seems to be the most important aspect of an open human relationship.*

Accepting the other person presupposes congruence: openness to experiencing, courage to marvel at life, letting the other be what he, she or it is as such. Acceptance like this does not make conditions: If you do this and that, I will accept you (Rogers 1980: 116). Acceptance and *prizing* are non-possessive and unconditional in quality, *unconditional positive regard.*

Listening prizingly and attentively is as if surrendering oneself to resonating along with what the other person is expressing in words but also on a deeper and more holistic level. It is letting the other and his or her ideas and feelings be what they in themselves are, without forcing them to present themselves as what the other participant wants to have them. Open and accepting listening *is non-judgemental* – whether the speaker's opinion or answer is right or wrong or whether his or her thinking is coherent or non-coherent is not evaluated. And if the listener does not understand what the speaker tries to express, he or she does not pretend otherwise. Pretending to understand leads both the listener and the speaker astray and erodes the basis for the attitudes of realness and genuineness.

Empathic understanding presupposes genuineness, acceptance and unconditional positive regard (Rogers 1980: 160–1). Empathy or empathic understanding requires courage to try to view the world as it shows itself to the other person. Taking this point of view demands integrity of one's subjective world picture or, to use the more common expression, psychological maturity: it may happen that my own world begins to look somehow distorted when I see it from another perspective.

We can say that empathy emerges from realising that *we can never fully understand a human being, not even ourselves.* If helping other people is based on a patronising understanding, it is necessarily based on criteria taken from outside the person to be helped and is, therefore, manipulative in nature. That means it is based on the attitude of technology and calculative thinking. But empathic understanding is not evaluative, diagnostic or judgmental.

An empathic helper is 'a confident companion to the person in his or her inner world' (Rogers 1980: 142). In my frame of reference the dialogists can never enter each others' worlds in the sense that they could experience things and events exactly the same. It is only the 'common ground' *between* their worlds in which they can be 'confident companions' to each other.

It seems that empathy can be learnt in an open dialogue with a person who is empathic, capable of the empathic attitude. Learning this attitude does not seem to require academic intelligence or a diagnostic ability (Rogers 1980: 150). Empathy means to me approaching other human beings in the attitude of open dialogue. Even in a case where I have to use some technique or technology on him or her, the quality of my basic mode of approaching him or her and my primary concern is openness to the whole person he or she is *for him- or herself.*

Patience and endurance – ample time, no haste

To be comfortable with the uneasiness and discomfort of being thoughtful requires patience and endurance. All significant changes in man's meaning-structures – beliefs, attitudes, subjective picture of the world, etc. – take time. It may take quite a long time, a lot of effort and ample support to learn how to learn in a genuinely human way if one has grown to be adult under circumstances where genuineness, unconditional positive regard and empathic understanding have been rare. Especially time to dwell on one's experiences is necessary for genuine contemplative thinking to develop. Haste easily prevents the other person from experiencing the attitude of acceptance. Especially in teaching situations, haste makes both the teacher and the students focus their attention on the student's performance. This easily leads the student to believe that he or she is accepted only in respect to his or her achievements. Consequently, he or she may begin to accept him- or herself only in that respect, too.

Haste is a 'good' excuse for abstraction and generalisation which often mean providing the students with vicarious experiences and dealing only superficially with the subject matter at hand. Haste is often thought to justify the neglect of the more difficult and time-consuming personal experiential reflection and learning in open dialogue.

Avoidance of interfering with the Other's life

To be successful in our effort to establish a relationship of open dialogue we need to avoid *continuous* talking, explaining, giving advice, and asking questions, especially in an interfering manner. It means teaching the essence of that which is following 'the path of a responding that examines as it listens'.

Self-evaluation

Genuinely human learning is based primarily on self-evaluation – dependence on external evaluation is only of secondary importance. This is the foundation of self-directedness, both teacher's and student's. Some thoughtful reflection is necessary for self-evaluation, of course. But it is also important to remember that paying too much attention to one's own experiencing and actions may lead to breaking up the unity and, so, to one's action becoming more difficult. For instance, the surest way of making spontaneity disappear from thinking, feeling and action, is to try really hard to be spontaneous. And, moreover, there is always the danger of separating the reflection from living experience through conceptualising and verbalising it in a technical way.

Subordination of the attitude of technology to the open attitude

In order to develop towards the goal of a fully human being man must subordinate the attitude of technology to the open attitude, that is, to the attitude of *Gelassenheit* or letting be, letting reality manifest itself as what it is in itself. Truly ethical reflection is possible only in open dialogue. The open attitude can emerge under the conditions of genuineness, unconditional positive regard and empathic understanding.

A society that values open dialogue

It is obvious that if the society does not value and foster open dialogue, people mastering the art of open dialogue will be few. Developing open dialogue in education is therefore also a matter of the values and constraints in society at large, and thus a political question.

5.6 CONCLUSION

In the light of the conception of man I have chosen as the basis of my approach to the question about (FL) education, the quality of man's basic relationship with reality seems to be open dialogue. Open dialogue is constructive multidimensional human co-existence in the spirit of tactful consideration for diversity.

In open dialogue we do not need continually to test ourselves and our ways of living or others and their ways of living. There is no need for us to keep accounting to ourselves for ourselves, justifying ourselves or excusing ourselves to ourselves (see Lee 1976). We can be free from the fear of difference and diversity, 'heterophobia' (Bauman 1997).

My basic tenet is that man can realise himself as a fully human person and become an ethical subject only in this kind of relationship. Therefore open dialogue must always be the essence of the attitude through which man *first* approaches reality. Consequently, the appropriateness of other attitudes is to be judged on the basis of the criteria emerging from the attitude of open dialogue. Being able to carry on open dialogue means mastering *the art of open dialogue.* This art or 'craft' is the basis of all educational work – practising this art is what true education is all about.

Through learning to argue the underpinnings of her work well, a (FL) teacher can develop her 'craft of teaching' autonomously to a great extent. The capacity to think thoughtfully gives her courage and enhances her 'craft' of *actualising herself primarily as a human person* while teaching a foreign language. In so doing she can also venture to travel off the beaten path when she judges it fitting. She is confident that she can find out where her life-path goes although others and even she herself cannot always see any path at all where she is going. She can develop 'the confidence to be appropriate', to become a researcher on her own teaching (Clark 1998: 76).

Even though thoughtful reflection can be of great heuristic value for a teacher seeking to improve her practice, it is *ultimately* only in and through concrete, real-life open dialogue between teacher and student, and the pedagogical action based on it, that their lives in the educational situation change. Developing the quality of life in school requires *living* the open dialogue in our concrete life situations. This is possible only in an educational community that values dialogical culture and seeks to live up to its standards. Mere theoretical discussion and looking after other people's morality does not foster openness in human relationships.

In an existential or hermeneutical phenomenological orientation, teaching a (foreign) language to a person is not just teaching it as a system of elements, a set of habits common to a community of speakers, or as a body of one-dimensional sign-like words used by a group of people. It is more like fostering the development of the student's personal art of living in and through open dialogue that aims at organising and reorganising the participants' meaning relationships in a more genuinely human way into their respective subjective pictures of the world. Listening to 'what language has to say' plays a crucial role in this process. To implement all this presupposes 'a real revolution in the prevailing relation to language' (Heidegger 1959: 53). This means, to my mind, that *the basic goal of FL teaching (at least as part of general education) is to help the FL learner learn how to live in an open dialogue with reality as a fully human being who speaks the target language as his or her foreign or second language – not as if it were his or her native language.*

When (foreign) language education advances towards this goal, it makes its full contribution to 'creating a moral society', a society where there is more space for genuinely human learning. Zygmunt Bauman (1997) aptly describes the essence of such society:

> Everyone that values man's capacity to distinguish right from wrong and good from evil should rejoice at the diversity and polyphony of mankind. Diversity and polyphony do not guarantee that society will be moral but the absence of them would destroy right at the beginning the chance of creating a moral society.

5.7 REFERENCES

Bauman Z (1997) The chances of morality in times of uncertainty. Lecture given in Tampere, Finland, 25 May 1997. My lecture notes

Berger P and Luckmann T (1987) *The social construction of reality. A treatise in the sociology of knowledge.* Harmondsworth: Penguin Books

Buber M (1985) *Between man and man.* New York: Macmillan

Carr A and Pihlanto P (1998) From *Homo Mechanicus* to the holistic individual: a new phoenix for the field of organization behavior? In Rahim M A, Golembiewski R T and Lundberg C C (eds) *Current Topics in Management.* Vol 3. London: Jai Press

Chomsky N (1976) *Reflections on language.* Glasgow: Fontana/Collins

Claxton G (1981) *Wholly human. Western and Eastern visions of the self and its perfection.* London: Routledge & Kegan Paul

Feyerabend P (1979) Dialogue on method. In Radnitzky G and Andersson G (eds) *The structure and development of science.* Boston: Reidel, pp 63–132

Fromm E (1984) *The Art of loving.* London: Unwin

Heidegger M (1959) *An introduction to metaphysics.* New Haven, CT: Yale University Press

Heidegger M (1969) *Discourse on thinking.* New York: Harper & Row

Heidegger M (1975) *Poetry, language, thought.* New York: Harper & Row

Heidegger M (1977) *The question concerning technology and other essays.* New York: Harper and Row

Heidegger M (1990) *Being and time.* Southampton: Basil Blackwell

Highwater J (1981) *The primal mind. Vision and Reality in Indian America.* New York: Harper & Row

Kearney R (1986) *Dialogues with contemporary Continental thinkers. The phenomenological heritage.* Manchester: Manchester University Press

Laing R (1983) *The Voice of Experience. Experience, Science and Psychiatry.* Harmondsworth: Penguin Books

Lao Tsu (1997) *Tao Te Ching.* Translated by Gia-fu Feng and Jane English. New York: Vintage Books

Lee D (1976) *Valuing the Self. What we can learn from other cultures.* Englewood Cliffs, NJ: Prentice Hall

Lehtovaara M (1994) *The subjective world-picture as an aim of educational research.* Publications of the Department of Education, ser. A. 53. Tampere: University of Tampere (in Finnish, English summary)

May R (1985) *The Courage to Create.* New York: Bantam Books

Pihlanto P (1997) *The Holistic Concept of Man and Perspectives on Accounting Research.* Turku: Publications of the Turku School of Economics and Business Administration. Series A-11

Postman N and Weingartner C (1983) *Teaching as a Subversive Activity.* Harmondsworth: Penguin Books

Puhakainen J (1995) *Towards coaching a human being: implications of a holistic conception of man.* Tampere: University of Tampere (in Finnish, English summary)

Rauhala L (1969) Intentionality and the problem of the unconscious. *Turun yliopiston julkaisuja, Annales Universitatis Turkuensis.* Sarja – Ser. B osa – Tom. 110, Turku

Rauhala L (1970) Man – the philosophical conception and empirical study. *The Journal of Analytical Psychology* 15(2): 148–54

Rauhala L (1972a) The hermeneutic metascience of psychoanalysis. *Man and World* 5(3): 273–97

Rauhala L (1972b) The myth of mental illness. *Psychiatria Fennica 107–16*

Rauhala L (1973) The regulative situational circuit in psychic disturbance and psychotherapy. *Annales Universitatis Turkuensis* Series B, Tom. 126 *Studia philosophica in honorem Sven Krohn,* Turku: pp 157–76

Rauhala L (1976) Analytical psychology and metascience. *The Journal of Analytical Psychology* 21(1): 50–63

Rauhala L (1981) The problem of meaning in psychology and psychiatry. Turku: *Annales Universitatis Turkuensis* Ser B Tom. 155. *Turun yliopisto*

Rauhala L (1983) *The philosophical conception of man as a foundation of work with human beings.* Jyväskylä Gaudeamus (in Finnish)

Rauhala L (1998) *The uniqueness of man.* Helsinki: Yliopistopaino (in Finnish)

Rogers C (1969) *Freedom to learn.* Columbus, OH: Charles E. Merrill

Rogers C (1980) *A way of being.* Boston, MA: Houghton Mifflin

Taylor C (1992) Heidegger, language and ecology. In Dreyfus H L and Hall H (eds) *Heidegger: a critical reader.* Padstow: Basil Blackwell, pp 247–69

Töttö P (1989) *Sociology as a theory of modern society.* Research Institute for Social Sciences, Sarja A 58. Tampere: University of Tampere (in Finnish)

Vanharanta H, Pihlanto P and Chang A M (1997) Decision support for strategic management in a hyperknowledge environment and the holistic concept of man. In Sprague R H Jr (ed.) *Proceedings of the Thirtieth Hawaii International Conference on System Sciences* Vol V. Los Alamitos, CA: IEEE Computer Society Press

van Manen M (1991) *The tact of teaching. The meaning of pedagogical thoughtfulness.* New York: State University of New York Press

Varto J (1993) From here to somewhere else. Paths from Heidegger. *Philosophical investigations* Vol XL. Tampere: University of Tampere (in Finnish)

Varto J (1994) A philosophical conception of man and otherness. In Lehtovaara J and Jaatinen R (eds) *In a dialogue – on the way to a possibility.* Reports from the Department of Teacher Education in Tampere University A 21. Tampere: University of Tampere, pp 83–113 (in Finnish)

Värri V-M (1997) *Good education – education for good living* (*Hyvä kasvatus – kasvatus hyvään*). Tampere: Tampere University Press (in Finnish)

Index

DATE DUE

SEP 1 0 1991			
MAR 3 1 1992			
APR 1 4 1992			
AUG 2 2 1992			
MAR 2 0 1994			
UG 1 8 1997			
NOV 0 5 1997			